?ACKPACKS, BOOTS
AND BAGUETTES

ｎport·nt ritual, which often signalled the end of our
ｎg da·, was the award of *le con du jour*, the twit of the day.
G   ｎ ou· ·elatively disorganised approach to the business of
tra·e'ling ·s well as our idiosyncrasies, very few days went by
w·hout c·· ·r other of us – or possibly both – committing an
outrageo· · *jaux pas* or making some potentially catastrophic
b· ·der w·th map or compass. The good thing about the process
w·· ·s.o·ped any rancour building up over the long term; on
th·· ·p·rive side, if there hadn't been a reckoning for three days,
·   quite possible for old wounds to be reopened. On this
ｏ· ·ｒ, there was no dou·· about the identity of today's *con*: I
ｒ· ·.·d ｒyself, seconde· ·y Simon, for getting in the car that
··· ·.agged down, an· taking the only free seat, leaving him
o·· ·-ｒouthed and frozen by the roadside in shock at my
iｒ ·ｎsｉderate effrontery.

Also by Simon Calder

No Frills – The Truth Behind the Low-cost Revolution in the Skies

BACKPACKS, BOOTS AND BAGUETTES

Walking in the Pyrenees

by Simon Calder and
Mick Webb

First published in 2004 by
Virgin Books Ltd
Thames Wharf Studios
Rainville Road
London W6 9HA

Typeset by Phoenix Photosetting, Chatham, Kent
Printed and bound in Great Britain by
CPI Antony Rowe, Chippenham, Wiltshire

ISBN 978 0 7535 0902 9

SK 6607

CONTENTS

AUTHOR BIOGRAPHIES –
by each other

MICK WEBB has spent years working, living and travelling in Spanish- and French-speaking countries – ideal preparation for the Pyrenees, unlike his susceptibility to altitude sickness. He began his career as a radio producer for BBC Education specialising in language teaching. He has since made hundreds of programmes for Radio 3, Radio 4 and BBC television, before moving into the online world. Some of them have been quite good, such as a ground-breaking series on Latin America during the conflicts of the 1980s. He lives in south London with his lovely partner Steph, their two surprisingly well-adjusted sons, Alec and Silas, and a bad ankle.

SIMON CALDER may well have frisked you, and indeed me, during his time as a security official at Gatwick airport. He later resurfaced as a Radio Car driver for the BBC, which is where we first met in 1991. In another abrupt change of career direction, in 1994 he became Travel Editor of the *Independent*. His chosen slogan is 'the man who pays his way', but a better description is 'scared of heights' or 'cheap and available', which could explain why he is sometimes invited to film for the BBC *Holiday* programme. Were you to meet his delightful wife, Charlotte, and their equally lovely daughters Daisy and Poppy, they would probably ask you where he was.

ACKNOWLEDGEMENTS

The people responsible for facilitating the completion of this book, apart from our respective and understanding partners, are the generous motorists of the Pyrenees, who repeatedly rescued us when public transport, or our legs, let us down. Hospitality and information, in equal measure, were supplied by Guy Sheridan and Georges Véron. In addition, Ann Noon and Edith Meyer-Kapor at Maison de la France in London have answered hundreds of awkward questions with efficiency and grace. For what could be called 'technology solutions', i.e. lending a laptop when Simon's went over one *col* too many, grateful thanks are due to Nicholas Calder-Bundy.

PREFACE

The wall of mountains that divides France from Spain is more than just a majestic range rich in flora, fauna and history – it is also wonderfully accessible, with something to suit most walkers. Even us.

The barrier between the Atlantic and Mediterranean, cutting off Iberia from the rest of Europe, contains terrain as gentle or as challenging as you could wish. You can climb every mountain, or none at all. When Friedrich von Parrot first crossed from the Atlantic to the Mediterranean on the high-level route along the Pyrenees in 1817, he took 53 days. Some people can sprint the distance in barely half the time. But most sensible travellers will want to take time to enjoy the beautiful surroundings, the wildlife and the complex mix of cultures that thrive in the Pyrenees.

The profound attraction of a range of mountains to two overstretched men with families and responsibilities is such that we have made half-a-dozen trips in the past few years. We began and ended by the beach, having wandered on and off a series of waymarked paths. Just as the French invented the concept of road numbering, the nation was the first to come up with a network of long-distance footpaths – of which the finest is the coast-to-coast trans-Pyrenean route known as the GR10. The habit has spread across the border into Spain, and the mountains are now crisscrossed by hundreds of waymarked trails. During the course of researching this book we made up a fair number of new and mostly unsuccessful tracks ourselves.

We are (fortunately) living proof of the fallibility of travel writers, making a constant stream of mistakes and misjudgements as we wandered unsteadily along, across and occasionally away from the Pyrenees.

'You must be fit and have a sense of balance.' So says First

Choice, one of Britain's top three holiday companies, about one of its Pyrenean adventures for 2005. If only we had known that sooner, it could have saved an awful lot of suffering. And an equal amount of entertainment. An expression in Chinese – for which, no doubt, a Basque may claim credit – conveys the feeling of unalloyed joy. It translates as 'I was so happy, I didn't know which way was north'. The research for this book has, from time to time, generated such intense pleasure that at least one of us has become directionally disorientated. We hope that you will feel inspired to take at least a short walk on a long path, and feel equally glad.

Mick Webb and Simon Calder
London
August 2004

1. FIRST STEPS: FROM THE ATLANTIC

Mick Webb

Early on a clear, sunny morning, I left my home in south London carrying a rucksack instead of the usual workbag, thinking about mountains topped with snow and hoping I'd managed not to look too happy during the family farewells. I know that two weeks away in the Pyrenees isn't quite in the Laurie Lee league of walking adventures, but my sense of freedom was at least as strong as his when he set out on foot on his famous journey to Spain. The song of Streatham's last surviving blackbird was the purest music and the air around the A23, voted Britain's most unpleasant road not long before, was almost fresh enough to breathe. The feeling of contentment even survived the confrontation between those two most incompatible elements: the rucksack and the London bus filled with touchy commuters. This was followed by a train ride to Stansted airport, which was a pleasure in its own right, through a landscape softened with fresh pink and white blossom. My fellow passengers were a group of youthful city-breakers, reading out passages from a guide to Croatia in jokey accents; I enjoyed their noisy excitement without any twinges of envy or grumpy irritation.

If pushed, I would have admitted to the presence of two small clouds on the horizon. The first of them really was concerned with clouds: only the day before I'd found out about an unexpectedly late snowfall in the central part of the Pyrenees that had blocked the higher mountain passes and was going to require a substantial rethink of the original plans. And added to that there was the unexplained absence, temporary I hoped, of my travelling companion and fellow author.

A career in travel journalism has given Simon Calder a general contempt for airport preliminaries and a particular antipathy towards that advice to get to the check-in desk at least ninety minutes before takeoff. This cavalier attitude extended to all other kinds of public transport, so that, during the half-dozen journeys we'd made together to the Pyrenees, I'd become resigned to his nonappearances and sudden disappearances and quite adept at explaining to bus drivers and train conductors in French or Spanish that my *ami/amigo* would be along any second now, honest.

At the airport I killed time buying plasters for blisters, with what turned out to be painful prescience, and trying to find the lightest possible toothbrush to avoid adding unnecessary grams to my load. When Simon eventually arrived, it was with his customary opening remark: 'I'm *terribly* sorry, you're not going to believe it but ...' and I can't remember whether it was a computer, key or child-related disaster that was to blame this time. We checked in for the flight to Biarritz with my pack tipping the scales at 17kg, which is quite heavy enough for mountain walking. In contrast, Simon's, which resembled a pillar box in size, shape and colour, came in at 27kg. 'I didn't have time to leave anything out,' he explained, and a few moments later was helping an airport security officer with his enquiries, having triggered a metal-detector alarm with his belt-buckle, and brought the prospect of missing the plane just that bit closer.

The new terminal at Stansted provides a sequence of ups and downs, stairs and escalators, which are ideal preparation for the real subject of this book: walking in Europe's longest and most fascinating chain of mountains. Rather than a where-to-go or a how-to-do-it guide, this is an attempt to capture the special, often extraordinary places, people and moments you experience in the mountains: I remember standing, quite hypnotised, on a high crest watching a valley filling slowly with the whitest of cloud until it actually lapped at my boots like liquid, while across the now obfuscated valley three disembodied mountain peaks floated freely against the background of the deepest blue sky. Of course, you cannot reach these most remote and beautiful places without putting in some effort, which is all part of the fun: there's nothing to match a day's strenuous walking followed by a timely arrival at a two-star hotel where a well-calibrated shower, a large meal and a good supply of wine are waiting. On the other hand, our most memorable experiences have come from stays in the rather less comfortable surroundings of mountain refuges or the brushes with disaster that have accompanied some of our more ambitious walking days. But then walking in the mountains is nothing if not full of ups and downs.

It's open to question whether what we've done counts as mere 'walking' – if it shades over into the more macho activity of trekking or the more gentle one of rambling; it's probably a mixture of the three. But what we haven't got involved with is mountaineering: we've steered resolutely clear of crampons and pitons and pitches and chimneys, not least because one of us – OK, I'm talking about Simon – is prone to the occasional attack of vertigo. And, while we're in confessional mode, I'll admit we've taken more than our fair share of wrong turnings, got completely lost on a number of occasions and had the odd falling out: I mean, how would you react to someone who marched confidently down a steep, dark valley, swearing blind that the compass bearing was south, when actually it was reading north? It's at times like this you're tempted to think that the great English essayist William Hazlitt had a point when he wrote: 'One of the pleasantest things in the World is going [on] a journey; but I like to go by myself.'

Of course, we caught that plane and Simon even had time to write his newspaper column on the laptop that promised to be the last straw in his heavyweight pack. While I was relaxing over a cup of coffee, he was busy doing an interview by mobile phone with a BBC radio station about the wonders of the new giant Airbus A380, before it was time to join the scramble for a place on a much smaller and less well-appointed plane. Our in-flight entertainment was more of an in-flight challenge: to make some drastic alterations to our planned itinerary.

The original idea had been to spend a couple of weeks crisscrossing the frontier between France and Spain and tying together sections of the three major footpaths that traverse the Pyrenees. Unfortunately, there'd been that unseasonably late snowfall, which had effectively closed not only the high passes between France and Spain but also the ones linking the valleys that run at right angles to the central spine. Equally unfortunately, neither of us had done the unfolding-maps-in-confined-spaces training course, so it wasn't until the first officer announced our impending landing at Biarritz that we managed to reach a decision: to limit our ambitions to the two ends of the mountain chain, where the peaks, the passes and the paths are a lot lower. After a few days in the Basque country, we'd try out one of the lesser-known paths – *le sentier des Cathares* – that winds between castles perched on spectacular crags in the foothills of the eastern Pyrenees.

The good news is that there is never any shortage of new routes to try and things to see in the Pyrenees; the downside, on this particular occasion, was that we'd have to get from the Atlantic end of the chain to the Mediterranean one. This would be an adventure in its own right, since the roads and the railways tend to follow the lines of the valleys and run north–south rather than east–west – but more of that later.

Seen from a distance or viewed on a normal small-scale map, the Pyrenees look like a giant rocky barrier, separating France from Spain. Victor Hugo, who was just one of the distinguished writers who was drawn to these mountains during the nineteenth century, called it: 'A rampart . . . which from one sea to the other, bars a continent.' In close-up, though, they're less of a wall, more of a very thick and well-populated hedge, which is home to all manner of spectacular and threatened things.

Some of these are natural: rock formations like the cirques of Lescun or Gavarnie, and endangered animals like the brown bear or the bizarre desman, which looks like the world's most unlikely hybrid: a cross between a mouse and an elephant. Others, such as tiny cathedrals, churches, abbeys, remote villages and even narrow-gauge mountain railways are man-made. Two of Europe's sturdiest minority cultures, the Basques and the Catalans, owe much of their vigour to their relationship with the mountains, while the many Pyrenean valleys also shelter vestiges of other, lesser-known communities, traditions and languages. Aranese, for instance, is an ancient language, a cousin of Catalan and Occitan, which is still spoken by the inhabitants of the Val d'Aran in the very middle of the mountain chain. When we first saw the Aranese word *eth* on a sign and realised that it meant 'the', it was hard not to think it should really be called 'Anagramese'. There are also anomalous political setups: the state of Andorra, which has remained cheekily outside the European Union; the town of Llívia, which is a Spanish enclave completely surrounded by France; not to mention a tiny island that France and Spain run as a time-share.

Another possible way of looking at the Pyrenees occurred to me while I was having a very early breakfast in a particularly sleazy hotel in Tarbes, one of several French towns that inflates its civic pride by calling itself the 'gateway to the Pyrenees'. While waiting for the coffee machine to warm up, and for want of anything better to do, I was peering sleepily at a map of the mountains on the opposite wall. It was a rather faded relief map, one of those where the place in which you actually are has been almost completely erased by people pressing their fingertips against it. Anyway, it dawned on me, as I looked, that the Pyrenees are actually fish-shaped. It's quite appropriate, really, for mountains that connect an ocean with a sea. The thinnest bit, the tail, is slanted up towards the Atlantic while the head end points to the Mediterranean. There's even a distinct gap for the mouth, where the valley of the river Segre meets the valley of the Têt, though I'd better admit that there's a bit of a flaw in this metaphor – the tail doesn't have any fins. The serious point, however, is that the Pyrenees are not a regular strip along the frontier but are heavily weighted towards the Mediterranean end and, by the way, the lion's share of the high peaks are actually to be found on the Spanish side of the border.

Of its many attractions, the single greatest delight of the Pyrenees is that even now, in our well-travelled age, they have not been entirely 'done'. If you have the inclination, you can always find a hidden, unspoiled corner where you can be quite alone, although in late July and August this is becoming a bit more of a challenge. The sheer scale and relative inaccessibility of this wall/hedge/fish have made them a bit of a latecomer to the European list of must-see places. The Pyrenees have also had to live in the shadow of the Alps, the more successful and better-looking older sibling. There's no denying the fact that the Alps are taller, more spectacular to the eye and generally easier to travel through. Unsurprisingly it's the word Alpine that's become synonymous with mountain landscapes, a benchmark of mountain-ness, and the star peaks of the Alps are much better known than their Pyrenean equivalents: Mont Blanc, Matterhorn and Jungfrau would walk into a pub quiz, but the same could hardly be said for Vignemale, Aneto or Canigou.

Although they were never at the forefront of mountain chic, the Pyrenees were not entirely disregarded. It was adventurous scientists who first came to measure and catalogue their charms: 1781 saw the publication in Paris of Bernard de Palassou's 'Essai sur la minéralogie des Monts-Pyrénées', which doesn't at first sight seem like best-seller material but attracted enough interest to warrant a reprint three years later. The first half of the nineteenth century saw the dawn of Pyrenean tourism with the development of spa towns, whose waters attracted fashionable and aristocratic curistes as well as the romantic literati of France and Britain, who found no shortage of inspiration in the spectacular natural surroundings. The mountains also gained a following of aficionados in the shape of passionate and often eccentric mountaineers, the most extreme of whom was Count Henry Russell a.k.a. Comte Henri Russell.

A Franco–Irish aristocrat, brought up in France, Russell

actually rented Mount Vignemale, the highest mountain on the French side of the border, from the French authorities and had caves blasted out of the mountainside where he was able to live and would even entertain his friends to slap-up meals. According to Russell the Alps were 'tall, upright, athletic and warlike' whereas the Pyrenean mountains were 'slimmer, more shapely and delicate . . . The Alps amaze, the Pyrenees seduce. The Alps inspire terror, the Pyrenees tenderness.' You won't be surprised at the payoff, which in the original French is *'Les Alpes représentent l'homme, et les Pyrénées la femme!'* Neither is it surprising, in the light of the man–woman classification, that Russell's cave-digging exploits have been given some Freudian analysis.

A friend of Russell's and one of the first English mountaineers to take the Pyrenees seriously and write about them was Charles Packe. His 1862 guide to the Pyrenees is stronger on fact and shorter on romantic imagery than Russell's writings but it makes great reading. It begins with this splendid, if lengthy, sentence:

> How it comes to pass that so many Englishmen and Englishwomen cross the Channel every summer for the sake of a holiday tour of a month or six weeks among the Alps of Switzerland, while so very few in proportion think it worth their while to pay a visit to the Pyrenees, that magnificent mountain barrier that separates France and Spain, has always been to me a matter of astonishment; and I can only account for it on the principle that my countrymen like a flock of sheep, love to go 'non qua eundum est, sed qua est iter' (not where they ought to go but where the road goes).

These days we'd probably change that last bit to 'qua est the no-frills airline', as these have certainly made it easier to get to any one of the four chunks into which the Pyrenees are usually sliced. There's Biarritz airport for the Basque or Atlantic end of the mountains, Pau for the central High Pyrenees, Toulouse for the most inaccessible stretch, the Ariège; and Carcassonne or Perpignan will give you access to the Mediterranean section. If you prefer the approach from Spain, you have Bilbao or Girona serving the west and the east respectively.

Another great change from the time of Charles Packe is in the status of the walker. It's only relatively recently, in the last thirty years or so, that the ordinary walker has entered the tourist picture as a force to be reckoned with. Thousands of kilometres of waymarked footpaths, plentiful hostels and refuges, dozens of published guides, ever-more detailed maps; these are the measure of the growth of walking for fun, which has replaced the more elemental historical reasons for putting one foot in front of the other: war, religious faith, smuggling, and herding sheep and cattle.

For me, it was the signposts that first sowed the seeds of walking seriously – well semi-seriously – in these mountains. About fifteen years ago I spent a holiday with a few friends in a rented house in a village in the Pyrenean foothills near a small town called Mirepoix. On a clear day you could see six distinct levels of hills, each line higher and a slightly deeper colour than the last until your eye finally stopped at the jagged horizon of real mountains. We went to visit them and drove up a valley above Bagnères-de-Luchon before parking the car and striding out. The sign read LAC VERT 7H and after two of those *heures* we were hardly out of sight of the car park, fairly knackered by the climb and the heat, and needing to start on the return journey. I realised then that mountain walking required more time and more planning, which, eventually, was what it got.

The first real guide in English to walking in the Pyrenees, as distinct from climbing up mountains, was written by Hilaire Belloc, who somehow fitted into his busy life as a Liberal MP, polemicist and best-selling author of children's verse, the time to research and write *The Pyrenees*. His book, with 46 (very good) sketches by the author, was published in 1910 and is filled with fact and description and spiky advice. He tells us – or rather instructs us – in chapter one to do both our history and our geography homework, before we take to the hills:

> The recorded history of the inhabitants lends to these hills their only full meaning for the human being that visits them today; nor does anyone know, nor half know, any countryside of Europe unless he possesses not only its physical appearance and its present habitation, but the elements of its past.

You can just see the finger wagging, can't you? Belloc might or might not have approved of the waymarked long-distance footpaths which have been created in the Pyrenees and which now provide a stiff but manageable challenge for walkers of all ages; but he would almost certainly have welcomed the recent relaxation of European border controls. Not that this border has ever been particularly watertight, but now it is possible to cross back and forth pretty much as you please between France and Spain and create an almost infinite variety of multicultural experiences, which can take as long or short a time as you have available, or that your body can take. In a nutshell, there's no need now to set aside those six weeks for your expedition, because it's perfectly possible to spend a fortnight, a week or even a weekend in the remotest of mountain landscapes and thoroughly enjoy the experience. However, if you're lucky enough to have six weeks to spare, then the great Pyrenean challenge is waiting for you: to traverse the whole of the mountain chain, from the Atlantic to the Mediterranean, or vice versa.

The best-known path along the length of the mountains is the GR10, la *Grande Randonnée Dix*, which has every reason to be considered Europe's finest long-distance walk of any kind. The first quarter of it takes you on a journey through the French Basque Country, and one warm July weekend, on the first of our

Pyrenean trips, Simon and I set out to do just that and to walk from the coast to Ste-Engrâce, the most remote of all the Basque villages.

The start of the GR10 is in the undemanding and non-mountainous surroundings (about one metre above sea level) of the French resort of Hendaye. This is a bus ride from Biarritz airport, or would have been if any buses were available. However, there is a railway station a couple of kilometres away and it seemed only right to get there on foot. There's something very liberating about picking your bag off the luggage carousel, walking through the concourse and then just keeping on walking: no need to queue for a hire car or bus or taxi. It propels you straight into your new destination and somehow helps you banish those preoccupations, which we all bring with us as excess baggage when travelling abroad. The philosopher Alain de Botton describes a memorable and recognisable travel experience in his book *The Art of Travel* in which the worries of work constantly impinge on the pleasures of his Caribbean holiday with a female companion, taking the edge off Paradise and leaving them both rather irritable and unfulfilled. Maybe if they'd strapped on rucksacks, eschewed the air-conditioned hire car and walked or hitchhiked to that beachside hotel, it might have turned out very differently.

Simon and I were still following the airport perimeter fence when we came upon a pair of shabby and abandoned walking boots, neatly placed at a slight angle to one another, perhaps waiting to be painted by Van Gogh, but looking ominously symbolic. Faced by a choice between walking down the hard shoulder of the N10, a very busy road, and cutting through a small industrial estate we chose the latter and, in the window of a DIY store, were delighted to get a glimpse of something authentic and local. Well, fairly authentic. There were a number of large granite plaques, presumably for naming your house, on which little pictures and long Basque words were carved. Among them was the unpronounceable-looking URTXINTXEKIN, which we realised instantly means 'Place of the Squirrels', although the picture of a squirrel on a branch did help a bit. Twee as it was, here was a first hint that we weren't just in France, but in a very particular part of it.

In contrast, the TGV express, which took us two stops down the line to Hendaye-Gare (having started out from Paris about half an hour before, I expect), was filled with American college boys and their surfboards, who seemed only dimly aware of their location beyond the fact it was Europe, and would presumably have thought that a Basque was some kind of cool, wave-related trick. We, on the other hand, being older and wiser, had heeded Hilaire Belloc's advice about possessing 'the elements of the past' and knew that some sixty years previously a much slower but more heavily armoured train had brought Adolf Hitler to Hendaye-Gare for a crucial wartime meeting with Franco. The *Führer* tried to persuade the Generalísimo to abandon his neutral position and join the Axis war effort, no doubt reminding him of the assistance he'd given during the Spanish Civil War, notably at Guernica. Franco was not for turning, however, and, when he went back over the border to Spain, it was still a neutral country. Hitler reportedly came away from the meeting saying he'd rather have a couple of teeth pulled out than go through that again – given the state of Hitler's teeth, this was clearly a heartfelt comment. Franco's opinion is not recorded, but who knows what would have happened if they had got on well?

Speculating on intriguing but ultimately pointless historical 'what ifs?' we made our way down to Hendaye-Plage and the sea. The Atlantic rollers were having a day off and so were the surfers, leaving the flat sea and the beach to families and their less-demanding sports of sand-castle construction and *pétanque*. You could easily see Spain and the matching resort of Ondarrabia, a mere pedalo ride away across the estuary of the river Bidassoa. Our sensible shorts, plus white knees, large rucksacks and serious boots must have looked a bit out of place among the smart casuals of the French locals and the beachwear of the relatively few foreign holiday-makers. We were also marked out by an obvious air of confusion as, for a good half-hour, we blundered around the area in front of the beachfront casino searching for the start of the GR10. Asking a gendarme '*Où est la GR10?*' only generated a look of polite bewilderment, before we finally spotted the unremarkable sign that acknowledges the beginning (and end) of the path.

From here the GR10 sets off along the length of the Pyrenees for a journey of 866km (538 miles), sticking resolutely to the French side of the frontier, towards a matching little town beside the Mediterranean called Banyuls-sur-Mer. This is more than twice the distance a pigeon would fly assuming that (a) it ignored its usual migration instincts, and (b) it avoided the guns of hunters en route. And lying in wait for the walker are enough climbs and descents to get up and down Everest two and a half times.

While we're talking numbers, it takes from six to eight weeks to complete the path in one go, although it's quite easy to chop it into sections and do it in four separate visits. We'd chosen to walk from west to east, although you can obviously do the whole thing the other way round. Mind you, there are good practical and psychological reasons for taking the former approach. Firstly, it rains more at the western end than the eastern end, a lot more, so you can get the drenchings under your belt at the beginning of the expedition rather than have them hanging over you, as it were. Secondly, nearly all the specialised guidebooks begin at Hendaye, and there's nothing more infuriating than trying to read them backwards. And last but by no means least, the essential dip in the sea to celebrate your achievement will be that much more enjoyable in the warmer waters of the Mediterranean.

Not being able to find the beginning of the walk had got things off to an inauspicious start – like Marco Polo getting lost on his way out of Venice. However, we were soon walking along leafy streets like the Rue des Citronniers in the suburbs of

Hendaye, and enjoying spotting the little red-and-white painted stripes that waymark the GR10. Some of the serious walking guides to the Pyrenees advise you to miss out this first stretch of the walk and get a bus or a taxi to the first hill village called Biriatou, but we were keen to enjoy the transition from seaside to mountain as an overture to the richer opera in store, and, anyway, even modest Hendaye is not devoid of interest. Admittedly, apart from its beach, the town doesn't attract rave reviews from the writers of guides. The 1907 edition of Baedeker's influential handbook for travellers in southern France calls it a 'large but uninteresting village', but like other frontier towns it has had its fair share of international drama, the Hitler–Franco encounter being one good example.

Nearly three hundred years before Adolf met Francisco, a more successful rendezvous took place on an island in the estuary of the river Bidassoa. This island, which goes by two names, l'Île des Faisans or l'Île des Conférences, lies just off the route of the GR10 as it starts to make its way inland. It is described by the Baedeker as, you've guessed it, 'uninteresting' and undoubtedly the little mudflat is not much to look at, but what is interesting is that the island changes its nationality every six months – from Spanish to French and back again. More interesting still, from its humble origins as a place where Spanish and French fishermen met to settle their differences amicably, it became an important venue for diplomatic meetings.

It was here in 1659 that the foreign ministers of France and Spain negotiated the Treaty of the Pyrenees, which put an end to the interminable wars between the two countries. It was ratified a year later in Llívia at the other end of the Pyrenees and then cemented by the marriage of the young Louis XIV of France to María Teresa, the Spanish princess. The marriage contract was signed on the island with appropriate pageantry and pomp. Unfortunately, while decorating the Spanish pavilion, the great Spanish painter Velázquez is said to have caught the fever that was to kill him a few weeks later. The outcome of the Treaty of the Pyrenees was that the frontier between Spain and France was set pretty much as it is today, along the highest ridge of the mountains; also, large chunks of territory that had been in Spanish or Catalan hands were returned to France, creating some territorial oddities such as the town of Llívia, which we'll be visiting later.

This political marriage led indirectly to what appears to be the maddest of all the statements ever made about the Pyrenees, beating 'The Pyrenees are a fish' or 'The Pyrenees are a woman' by quite some distance. The grand prize must surely be awarded to Louis XIV for his 'The Pyrenees no longer exist' on the occasion of his grandson's accession to the Spanish throne. Luckily for walkers, climbers and lovers of exciting but manageable challenges, he was wrong, though to be fair to the Sun King he was making a political point about the great natural barrier between the two countries, rather than a geographical one.

These days, at this end of the Pyrenees, the main political focus is not so much on the relationship between the two big countries, as on the Basque nation. The Basques have never had their own state but, despite – and some say because of – this, their culture has retained its strength and individuality. Not that it's shared out equally on both sides of the border: there are reckoned to be about eight times as many speakers of the ancient and complex Basque language in Spain as there are in France. Even so, it's not long before those walking the GR10 become aware of new sights and sounds that provide a subtle counterpoint to the usual culture of France, and will be a companion for a quarter of the journey across the Pyrenees.

Our first night's stay was to be in the Basque village of Biriatou, a couple of hours from Hendaye. On the way we walked under a motorway, the last for three hundred miles, and had to run across the N10, which – in the days before the motorway siphoned off the traffic from this busy road – would certainly have cost us our lives. A little later we spotted the first of our Pyrenean animals: a hare. Not quite as exotic as the desman, the izard or the marmot, but it was a strange enough sight seen quite close up, with its huge ears, long back legs and then its thrilling bounding run as it took to its heels.

Then, after a couple of hours, as the sun went down, prematurely erased by some ominous dark clouds, we reached our first Basque village. The GR10 arrives at the top of Biriatou, which makes you feel as though you're entering a house via the attic. Its only street slaloms down from the church past classically beautiful Basque houses with wide eaves, whitewashed facades, beams and solid wooden balconies painted ox-blood red or dark green. Over the porches are names, not in a self-conscious, apologetic English fashion, but in large bold letters, written in the slightly runic Basque script. Traditionally, the house has a significance for the Basques that goes well beyond its value as a material possession on the housing market: the members of a family belong to the house rather than vice versa, and the house shares the same name as the family, which explains why so many Basque family names contain the word *eche* (*etxe* in Basque), which means house. No question of squirrels here.

Biriatou may be at the end of the road, but it isn't as isolated as it appears to the walker. It's becoming a bit of a dormitory village for Hendaye, particularly for younger people who work in the coastal zone but can't afford a home there. This expansion is very recent and for many years Biriatou didn't even have a bakery, but even so tourism is pretty well established. There are a couple of restaurants, one of them called Hiribarren, which was a safe house for allied airmen who had been shot down in German-occupied France and were being smuggled into Spain before returning to the fray.

The themes of escape and refuge are repeated along the length of the Pyrenees, as even the highest and most forbidding ridges have provided a chance for escapees and refugees to evade border patrols in the quest for freedom. In the last century, this traffic has flowed in both directions, with many Jews fleeing Nazism during the Second World War, while a few years earlier Spanish Republicans were crossing into France in their tens of thousands to escape triumphant Francoism as the Spanish Civil War came to an end. So close is Biriatou to the Spanish frontier that in 1936 French people came here to watch the skirmishes between the Republicans and the Nationalists taking place on the other side of the river Bidassoa, which was to culminate in the capture of Irún by Franco's forces.

The hotel where we were staying was a typically beautiful Basque house from the outside, with a maze of corridors and turnings inside. We managed to find the restaurant, where the main course was *Poulet Basquaise* – chicken with a sauce of tomato, peppers and ham, served with rice. It was arranged patriotically in red, white and green stripes, echoing the colours of the Basque flag. And after dinner, as it was Saturday evening, we were in for a treat, a game of *pelote* at the outdoor village court or *fronton*. There are some sure-fire ways of telling that you're in a Basque village: the shape and colour of the houses, the names, the galleried churches; but the biggest giveaway of all is the tall pink wall of the *fronton*. It's no accident that the first new building to be constructed in the resurgent Biriatou was an indoor *fronton*. It even preceded the new bakery, which would have been the absolute priority in any other part of France.

Our match was being held at the outside *fronton*, which in Biriatou is particularly eye-catching as it's also the main square. Imagine a large outdoor squash court, whose side walls are formed by the town hall on one side and an imposing village house with red-painted shutters on the other; at the end is a tall pink wall with a curvaceous top resembling a clover leaf. It's like having your cricket pitch right in the middle of the village but more intimate. There was a small terrace at the back, where we sat alongside about fifty other spectators and watched a game between two pairs of local men. They were dressed all in white, like cricketers, and the only thing that distinguished the teams was a couple of ribbons attached to their shoulders. One pair wore red and, given the predominant Basque colours, there was only one possible shade the other two could be sporting: green.

Of the several varieties of pelote (known in Spain as pelota), this was the traditional or basic version in which you use the bare hand to whack the ball (made of a hard rubber composition wrapped around with leather, more the size of a cricket ball than a squash ball) against the big pink wall. This is not as dramatic as the variety played on a much longer court, where the ball is propelled at speeds of up to 300kmph against the back wall by means of a basket-like contraption, *une chistera*, which is attached to the players' wrists. Even so, it was surprisingly enthralling as a spectacle: apart from the striking colours and the athletic movement of the players, there was the sound of the ball, which cracked like a rifleshot against the wall and echoed around the close-packed village houses with such ferocity you could probably add it to the endless list of reasons for 'not being able to get a good night's sleep in a foreign hotel'.

There was vociferous support for both teams, who were very well matched; all four of them were from Biriatou, and one of the pairs was made up of a father and son. After a while we even began to understand the rules – much like squash but with the added interest provided by unexpected deflections off the shutters or the gable of the house-cum-sidewall. After a hard-fought hour, the parallel with village cricket was maintained when a torrential downpour ended the game with the score at an honourable 33–33, two points short of the winning number of 35.

A hat was passed round for contributions and we had the chance to pick up one of the balls, which was horribly hard, and shake hands with one of the older players, whose hands, not surprisingly, were even tougher than the ball. The only concession to protective clothing was a handkerchief, which minimally reduces the impact, but otherwise it was gladiatorial stuff, sitting well in the tradition of macho sports that characterise Basque culture, particularly on the Spanish side of the frontier. Most of these are trials of strength connected with work on the land: they involve rock-lifting, log-splitting and the like, though there's a rather less appealing pastime which features in some Basque festivals. The 'game of the goose' is a former initiation ritual in which young men on horseback compete to tear the head off a goose or duck that's hanging by its feet from a suspended cord.

It rained all night, and the next morning was not ideal either, with plenty of cloud underlining the perennial uncertainty of the Pyrenean weather. We asked the breakfast waitress, 'Will it improve?' and got a Gallic shrug in response. This wasn't so much a sign of rudeness as fair comment. The hills of the Basque countryside are a study in shades of green. It rains a lot at this end of the Pyrenees, just as it does in Ireland. And, as in Ireland, there are well-worn, homely sayings to reflect the fact: 'If it isn't raining, it's just about to,' or 'If you can see the church, the mountain, etc., then it's about to rain; if you can't see them, then it's already raining.' I've read sad tales on the Internet of walkers who've set out to traverse the Pyrenees in July and report that they would have loved to have been able to comment on the beautiful Basque countryside but were unable to do so, as three days of mist had blotted it completely from view. Those in the know recommend early autumn as the most stable and predictable time to walk in the Pyrenees, and it's also less hot and crowded than in high summer. On the other hand, in a relatively snow-free year, an expedition in late May or early June gives you the chance to enjoy the vegetation at its freshest and most vibrant.

Another important thing to bear in mind is that, above 1,500m, all bets are off, and all general forecasts are dodgy: my notes from a walk we did one year through the remote mountains of the Ariège reveal that on 5 August there was a snowstorm as we crossed the high pass between France and

Andorra called Le Port du Rat and I beat Simon in a snowball fight. This is something that he disputes, incidentally: not the fact of the snowfall but the result of the fight.

This is very good walking country and, whatever the weather, you could quite easily spend a week based in Biriatou, exploring the Bidassoa valley and the surrounding hills, with the help of the detailed walking plans provided by the tourist office in Hendaye. But the lure of the GR10 was stronger, and as a brisk wind swept the rain clouds away we adjusted our packs and retraced our steps through the village: across the *place* which had given up being a pelote court and resumed normal service as a village square, then up past the church, whose clock was striking eight to the accompaniment of swooping, screaming swifts, and on to the path that climbs through springy upland grass.

It was appropriately a morning of firsts: the Col d'Osin, which we reached after an hour, was our first col or pass, the first of very many; though at a height of 370m it was something of a midget, and demanded a lot less effort than the 2,000m-plus passes you have to scale as the GR10 gets further inland. About ten minutes later came the slightly lower Col des Poiriers, which, apart from a nice name (Pear Tree Pass), provided our first great view – a huge panorama of France's southwestern beach, which runs arrow-straight northwards from Biarritz towards Bordeaux. Even at this distance you could see the coastal fringe of white and guess that the surfers would be back in business today.

Closer to, grazing calmly, were our first specifically Pyrenean animals: little Basque horses called *pottöks*, which are about the same diminutive size as New Forest ponies. Reckoned to be direct descendants of prehistoric horses whose outlines can be seen on cave walls, *pottöks* have not enjoyed a happy recent history. Used for hauling loads in mines or as ingredients in sausage and salami, they were at risk of extinction when, in 1970, Paul Dutournier, mayor of the nearby town of Sare, set up a national association and a reserve to protect them. His venture has proved so successful that the only risk to their continued survival now is through crossbreeding. *Pottöks* (pronounced 'pochoks') come in a wide range of striking colours – creams, greys, reds, blacks – a bit like cats. Mixed in with them were less exotic reddish-brown cows, whose bells provided background music for the couple of hours it took us to reach our first frontier post.

Although the GR10 remains in France for the whole of its length, it has a number of brushes with the Spanish frontier and none of them is quite as unnerving as the first encounter at the Col d'Ibardin. One moment you're drifting along in some kind of rural daydream, lulled by the gentle clanging of cowbells, then you come round the flank of a hill and are confronted by a mad cluster of restaurants, supermarkets, bazaars, souvenir shops and coachloads of shoppers thronging the steep street. Actually, after the initial shock, it wasn't so bad, since only a few minutes previously Simon and I had been discussing the general inadequacy of the French hotel breakfast as a means of providing fuel for the walker, and wondering where lunch or brunch was going to appear from. Here, like a mirage, it was, in the form of a hefty Spanish bread roll filled with a huge slice of Spanish omelette, which just begged to be washed down with a glass of earthy red wine.

These border markets, or *ventas* as they're called, had their origins in the days when the different costs of living and rates of tax in France and Spain meant that there were plenty of bargains for shoppers, particularly from the French side of the border. In today's Europe, there aren't so many savings to be made, though there's still a lively trade in cigarettes, cheap leather jackets, various kinds of strong booze and, apparently, even plastic flamenco dancers. From an aesthetic standpoint, it doesn't do to dwell on the architecture of the *venta* at Ibardin, but a lot of joy can be had from the cultural collision of languages. The menu was available in Basque, French and Spanish, and the longest descriptions tended to be Basque: our omelette, for instance, was *arraultzopil*, which was much easier to eat than it was to say.

We escaped from the *venta* through crowds weighed down by shopping bags; many of them seemed to have bought carpets, which added a nice oriental touch to the cultural medley. At the bottom of the street there was a parting of the ways. Up to this point, we'd actually been following not one, but two different paths at the same time, which isn't quite as daft or as difficult as it sounds. This is because the route from the coast is shared between the GR10 and the Haute Randonnée Pyrénéenne, also known as the HRP.

This high path will also take you along the length of the entire chain down to the Mediterranean, but, as its name suggests, it sticks uncompromisingly to the higher ground whereas the GR10 descends into valleys and deliberately seeks out villages and human company. The HRP avoids them; so much so that early one July, while walking across the weird lunar landscape between Arette-la Pierre-St-Martin and Lescun, Simon and I met a man called Alan who seemed surprisingly keen to stop and talk to us. The reason for this became clear when he told us that he'd been walking the HRP and hadn't seen another person for five days. The HRP is shorter on variety but higher on technical demands than the GR10, and to do it safely requires a tent, an ice axe, cooking equipment and good skills with maps and compass: most of the HRP has no waymarking at all and is subject to snowfalls, even in the height of summer.

The first recorded traverse of the whole Pyrenean chain was made in 1817 by Friedrich von Parrot, a mountaineer and military surgeon of German origin. He set out from St-Jean-de-Luz, just north of Hendaye, on 5 September and arrived in Canet-Plage on the Mediterranean coast 53 days later. On the way he became the first recorded person to climb the Spanish mountain of Maladetta. Unfortunately von Parrot's account of this achievement does not make for the most colourful reading, since it's an ultra-scientific list of heights, barometric details and a record of how his pulse rate varied with altitude. Others followed in Herr von Parrot's footsteps, but it's only in recent years that the slightly odd challenge of walking *along* the length of a mountain chain instead of trying to cross it has become a feat that is within the reach of most of us.

The man behind the planning, the opening up and the promotion of the Pyrenean traverse is Georges Véron, a former teacher of biology and geology from Normandy. Holidays at the Mediterranean end of the Pyrenees kindled his passion for the mountains, which took a horizontal rather than a vertical direction. While others spent their time climbing *up* mountains, Georges and two friends made their way *along* them from east to west. That was in 1968, an experience that laid the foundations for the HRP. Véron planned the route and then wrote the first guide to the HRP in clear, sparse prose, unembellished by cultural asides and beguiling photos but a great deal more helpful than many more lavishly produced walking guides. A measure of the popularity of his *Haute Randonnée Pyrénéenne* (the guide, that is) was that in 2003 it was reprinted for the twelfth time. The new edition has nice photos, and full-colour maps have replaced the line drawings, but the clarity and occasional flashes of dry wit are still in evidence. His introduction to the eighth stage of the HRP, when you've left the Basque Country and entered the territory of the Béarn, contains the lines:

> . . . the walker will discover the cirque of Lescun, which is one of the most beautiful sites in the western Pyrenees. The perennial problems of food and lodging will drive some people towards the refuge of Labérouat or the village of Lescun; campers who still have a few biscuits left will make their way to the much-appreciated 'needles' of Ansabère (another spectacular rock-formation).

Georges Véron was also the brains behind the westernmost stretch of the GR10. Not just the brains but the hands too, since as well as the planning he also did most of the hard work: painting the red-and-white marks at regular intervals on rocks, fence posts, trees and walls. Often he did this on his own and had to improvise a special wire contraption to hold the two pots of paint, which he carried in one hand, along with the brush he wasn't using. When the inactive brush was the one with red paint on it, he had to take special care to stop drips getting into the pot of white; the opposite was not such a problem. In the early 1970s, the sight of Georges and his pots occasioned much curiosity. He remembers an old chap coming up to him and asking when his friend with the blue paint was coming along (I'll give you a clue: think of the French flag).

It's worth bearing in mind that the GR10, which is now pretty much welcomed by the farmers and villagers along its route as a nice little earner, aroused plenty of suspicion in the early days. Though it was based on existing rights-of-way and supported by the regional authorities, this was no guarantee of local acceptance. Georges decided that the most sensible approach was not to ask permission to paint his marks but just to get on with it and, if challenged, *'faire l'idiot'* – play the idiot.

The most sensitive spots, like police stations, were better left for dark winter evenings. He tells the story of returning to the gendarmerie in the town of St-Etienne-de-Baïgorry, near the Spanish border, to touch up a mark he'd painted the year before (yes – they needed repainting as well). He was approached by a local man, who asked him what he was doing, since everyone in the village, gendarmes included, had concluded that the original sign was the work of a brigade of commandoes from the Basque separatist organisation ETA, who'd marked out the gendarmerie as a potential target during a cross-border reconnaissance. In actual fact, it signals the end of one of the most stunning stretches of walking in the whole of the Pyrenees: along the Iparla crest.

I heard these tales of path-making from Georges Véron himself, when I went to see him at his home outside Tarbes. It was no surprise that from his lounge there was a wonderful view of the high peaks of the central Pyrenees. In his study were copies of the fifty-odd books he's written on the Pyrenees: guides for walkers, for cyclists, for mountain-bikers; and in collaboration with his partner, Jacqueline, he's gone beyond the mountains to write about the Pilgrim route to Santiago de Compostela.

I was drawn particularly by the shelves that were filled with bound and neatly typed accounts of every day that he'd spent waymarking the western section of the GR10. This archive, the story of a path, reveals that over four years in the early 1970s, Georges Véron spent around six weeks realising the western stretch of the GR10 between Hendaye and Larrau. These days included the Christmas festivals, for, as Georges explained, the weather is often better in late December than it is in early June.

The waymarking required 24 kilos of red and white paint, and Georges received the princely sum of two hundred French francs (about twenty pounds) as a reward for his efforts from the committee overseeing the creation of the GR10 from Pau. He was helped by a Basque man called Charles Etchpare who refused any recompense at all, saying that the GR10 had been like a dancing partner for him. On one occasion they were caught in an unexpected spring blizzard at a height of 1,400m and had needed to spend the night in a ruined shepherds' hut with no roof. Georges told me that this had brought home to him how dangerous the mountains could be and how easy it was to lose your life, even at relatively low altitudes, unless you went prepared for potential disaster with warm clothes and emergency food supplies.

After our separation from the HRP at the Venta d'Ibardín Simon and I were faced with a sharp climb, the effects of which were nicely blunted by the lunchtime wine. Drinking 'n' walking are probably rather frowned on these days unless the drink in question is water, but the early pioneers were rarely without their goatskin flask filled with the local red, and it didn't seem to do them any harm. In our sights now was the first real Pyrenean mountain: La Rhune. It's immediately remarkable because it looks like a proper mountain, just as a child would draw it with a conical shape rising to a perfect peak.

La Rhune, which means 'place of pasture' in Basque, is the first of the 'star' mountains of the Pyrenees, those that have a lot more about them than mere physical presence. The symbolic value of La Rhune far outweighs its actual stature – it's a mere 900m high, compared with the 3,000m giants of the central part of the chain. But, in the gentle, hilly landscape that surrounds it, it stands out like the proverbial one-eyed man in the kingdom of the blind and, for the Basques, it's connected with ancient rituals and the practice of witchcraft, as well as being a point from which you can view all seven Basque provinces – three in France, four on the Spanish side – weather permitting.

For the next couple of hours La Rhune remained a constant presence, becoming more formidable the closer we got. This stretch has the best and the worst of the GR10's surfaces. After the climb from the *venta* at Ibardin, there's a downhill stretch through a beautiful oak forest, which is made even more agreeable by the soft, grassy path. You pass a low wall of stone, which was once part of a military redoubt and is a reminder of another war. During the Peninsular War at the beginning of the nineteenth century, Spanish and British armies were allied against Napoleon's invading forces. By 1813, the French were on the defensive and these frontier ridges saw a bitter struggle between the Duke of Wellington's army and the forces of Marshall Soult. Wellington lost four guns here, the only ones ever lost by his army, but his eventual victory was part of the build-up to the battle of Waterloo two years later.

We soon reached another frontier *venta*, a much prettier one beside a stream. A sign promised cold drinks but the building was closed. Then, on the outskirts of a village called Olhette, there was a first sight of a *gîte d'étape*, one of the hostels with communal kitchens and sleeping quarters, which welcome the weary walker and quite often the intrepid four-wheel-drive family from Paris in the French hinterlands. We carried on towards La Rhune and now the path had become stony and painful underfoot, as well as quite crowded with weekend strollers. Griffon vultures appeared overhead and La Rhune was beginning to look a bit less perfect than it had from a distance. The summit was disfigured by transmitter masts and by a railway station for the rack-and-pinion railway that takes tourists up to the top the easy way.

We crossed the line and then waited to see one of the trains. The noise that prefaced it was an extraordinary whirring and screeching and then the train appeared, bearing a logo that will strike despair into the heart of all south London railway commuters: Connex. The train operator performed so poorly in our capital that it lost its franchise, but they seemed to be doing a good enough job down here, hundreds of miles from Victoria station: there were no obvious signs of passenger discontent or overcrowding in the wooden carriages that trundled up to the summit. This is one of four unusual railways that can be found and – if you're tired or just having a day off – travelled on in the Pyrenees. It's also a reminder that these mountains don't just preserve ancient traditions, but also have seen some highly innovative scientific and engineering projects, the most striking of which is the solar oven, high on the plateau of the Cerdagne, near the Mediterranean end of the chain. We'll be getting to that in due course.

We left La Rhune to the tourists and the vultures and followed the signs towards the village of Sare. This is one of the steep descents back to civilisation that is a characteristic feature of the GR10 and makes you wish that human beings came equipped with proper brakes; it was down a steep, eroded track with a choice for each footstep between damp, skiddy, red earth or equally unstable loose shale. The variety of path and track that you find on the GR10 is undoubtedly one of its charms: mule tracks, hunters' paths, smugglers' routes. You never quite know what's coming next, and in this case the sooner we got onto the next stretch, the better.

The GR10 is, on the whole, very well waymarked. The ramblers' organisations of the different *départements* through which it passes are responsible for the upkeep of their own particular section. However, the volunteer waymarkers obviously run out of paint from time to time or just have an off-day, and the same can be said of the people following their markings. To err, as we know, is human, and, having survived the descent, Simon and I relaxed a little and, where the dodgy path met a country lane, we erred.

Up until now we'd only experienced two of the signs in the path-makers' armoury: red-and-white horizontal stripes to show the correct route, and a red-and-white cross to indicate the wrong direction. But now a third mark appeared, looking like one of those old-style football rattles in the colours of Arsenal and whose purpose was to indicate a change of direction. I'm not sure which one of us failed to realise that we were supposed to turn left across a field. Maybe we were jointly responsible, but the net result was that, instead of taking the prettier, and shorter way to Sare, we ended up with a long hour's trudge along the Tarmac on what had turned into a hot afternoon, and plenty of time to realise that, however irritating the surfaces of some of the paths had been, they were infinitely superior to the road.

Sare was worth getting to. It's one of those villages where creators of postcards are spoiled for choice: a cluster of beautifully kept Basque houses, an interesting church, vestiges of a Roman road, a Roman bridge, and the thing we wanted most of all, a café-cum-restaurant, which was open for business. We enjoyed a slightly unusual tea of ewe's-milk cheese and Basque cake, accompanied by local beer. It was all delicious: the cheese was quite hard, and served with slightly bitter black-cherry jam and a sprinkling of sweetish red pepper from nearby Espelette, where you can see rows of the dried peppers decorating the wooden balconies of traditional houses in the centre of the village. As for the Basque cake, which is a kind of dense sponge cake filled with almond paste and/or more of that cherry jam, it was as good as it should be in Sare, where there's a museum devoted to the confection, although it was closed by the time we'd finished tasting the real thing.

Attention to detail and use of local and seasonal produce seem to underlie the spectacular rise of Basque cuisine up the world's gastronomic league tables, which is all the more surprising when you consider that the soil on the pretty green hills that we'd been walking on earlier is not particularly fertile. However, the Basques more than make up for that with products they've brought back from abroad – like the peppers – and by the cunning addition of more than a pinch of originality and creativity. The owner of the restaurant, Jean Fagoaga, talked us through his menu and, by the time he'd finished describing their dishes of fresh tuna, cod with red and green peppers, squid and ceps and wood pigeon marinated in red wine, we decided that maybe we'd done enough walking for the day and that an overnight stop in Sare would provide the opportunity for some more in-depth research into Basque cuisine.

So we booked into the only functioning hotel, which had a curious little extension like a summerhouse at the front, where a woman was selling Basque cakes of different sizes. Each one was on its upturned cake tin, like an individual plinth, and the scattering of empty plinths showed that it had been a good cake day. We walked off down the Roman road for a bit and discovered a junction of paths where the GR10 met the GR8. According to a sign, this latter path had come all the way from Bordeaux, through a landscape of dunes and pine forests, which must make the GR10 and the GR8 the chalk and the cheese of French walking. The sign also informed us that, in all, there were 65,000km of paths that were approved by the French Hiking and Rambling Association. We'd just done about fifteen of them.

Next to Sare's town hall was a small bar decorated with posters advertising cultural and political events in the Basque language, but the mainly young clientele – the exclusion being our good selves – was talking French and discussing football. We drank Basque beer and reflected on a good first day's walking. Of course, we could always have been camped beside the HRP in a small tent, surrounded by *pottöks* and cows; there would have been warm bottled water to drink and we would have been struggling to open a can of tuna, instead of looking forward to the real thing in an exotic sauce, not to mention the real beds. Sometimes, though, a man's got to do ... and although Simon claims that he prefers the simple pleasures he occasionally has his own reasons for wanting to stay where there are creature comforts rather than creatures.

2. WHERE PIGEONS DARE: THE BAZTÁN VALLEY

Simon Calder

It was on our second visit to Sare, some four years after that first one. Mick and I had decided to make up for our earlier omission, and actually reach the summit of that 'star' mountain, La Rhune. By this time we were sufficiently conversant with our adopted mountain range to become more adventurous about our walking routes. Rather than stick to a single path, within a single country, we were going to branch out. In a pub in south London we had come up with a plan for a two-day loop that promised some of the most spectacular walking in the Pyrenees. From the top of La Rhune we would descend into Spain and make our way to the remote Basque valley of Baztán for the overnight stay. Then we would leave from the far side of the valley and rejoin the GR10 as it followed the Franco-Spanish frontier along the Iparla crest – reputedly one of the finest stretches of the long-distance path. We arrived one fine May evening in Sare, intending to get a decent night's sleep in preparation for a demanding cross-border excursion. Unfortunately, for me, it didn't quite turn out that way.

Mountain air, or at least the effect of sleeping at high altitude, causes all manner of strange dreams. During our perambulations across the Pyrenees, I have experienced vivid visions of encounters with people I have not seen for years; found myself missing deadlines, broadcasts and trains; and fallen from a great height while walking in the mountains. 'Counting troubles, 'stead of counting sheep', as the country song goes. No doubt a psychoanalyst could deduce a personality flaw or two from these nocturnal revelations. But Sare is no more than 100m above sea level. And the following story was no high-altitude fantasy.

At dawn each Saturday, Studio 1H at Broadcasting House in

London runs with military precision. The Radio 2 presenter Janey Lee Grace chats to her early-morning listeners between deftly chosen discs. Her BBC radio programme includes a lively contribution about the latest films from a critic. And it also has a travel slot, which I am responsible for filling.

Janey interviews me about the latest news affecting travellers, and about the location I happen to find myself in. Sometimes this involves a high-quality audio link from the Association of British Travel Agents' annual convention (which, as you might imagine, is normally somewhere exotic), or it might be a crackly phone line from a call box in a dusty corner of Mexico. But usually I manage to find a hotel where the producer can call me with confidence that a broadcast-quality calm will prevail for the six or so minutes that the interview lasts.

When planning each of our Pyrenean trips, Mick and I carve up the accommodation bookings fairly arbitrarily. I guess that those booked by Mick tend to be about 50 per cent more expensive than the ones I choose. After half a lifetime spent trying to eke out cash to permit more travelling, I have grown fond of the lower end of the accommodation market. While Mick sees a two-star hotel in southern France or northern Spain as optimal – usually guaranteeing a comfortable bed, warm shower and cold beer – I am less drawn to stellar qualities. The Pyrenees are sprinkled with refuges where the going rate for enough space to crash out and experience strange dreams ranges from nothing to a few euros. These refuges provide shelter in anything from abandoned (and usually smelly) farm buildings to purpose-built chalets high in the mountains.

Even at the stunted Atlantic end of the range, where the hills are barely pimples on the real-life relief map, there are plenty of alternatives to a modest hotel – notably *chambres d'hôte*, the French version of B&Bs. But in Sare, I chose the relatively opulent Hôtel Arraya. Rare among hotels on either side of the Pyrenean frontier, it boasts three stars. This trinity guarantees a phone in each room, and someone on duty at reception around the clock to deal with such matters as incoming calls from the BBC. Alternative arrangements were unpalatable. In general, neither the hosts who run *chambres d'hôte* nor the wardens who manage refuges are receptive to the idea that a British hiker would like someone to call just after 6 a.m., so that he can talk intermittently but loudly. Saturdays recurred frequently during our visits to the Pyrenees, and on one ghastly occasion at Ste-Engrâce I had been obliged to walk two miles in the dark to what appeared to be the only public telephone in that particular valley (luckily, it was working). So, when you see a chance for a civilised broadcast, you should take it. Even so, Mick looked at me quizzically when I told him where we were staying that night.

I had supplied the programme's producer with the Arraya's telephone number days in advance, after dialling it to ensure it did indeed pertain to the hotel. Before retiring to bed on the Friday night, I double-checked with the hotel staff that there would be someone on the switchboard next morning.

'*Bien sûr, Monsieur.*' I was reassured, and settled down with my notes and pondered how to distil several thousand years of Basque history into 360 seconds of radio.

Like so many things in the Pyrenees, the Basque story is complex and opaque. About 2.5 million Basques live in the western Pyrenees – though the majority of them now reside in the three main cities of Bayonne in France, and San Sebastian and Bilbao in Spain. Their ancient, hazy origins are the source of some outlandish claims: Basques are said variously to be descended from Celts, Jews or Lapps, while one account insists their ancestors were survivors from the lost city of Atlantis. But, on a couple of things, there is general agreement: they have occupied the shoreline and the hinterland at the fold where present-day Spain and France meet for millennia. And they speak a language unrelated to any other in Europe (though some linguists claim to have detected similarities with tongues from the Caucasus, such as Armenian and Georgian). Evidence for the antiquity of the Basques is cited by the words *aizkora* (meaning axe) and *aitzoa* (knife), both of which have as their root *aitz*, the Basque word for stone.

The Basque language is called Euskara. It is so crucial to the community's identity that the very definition of a Basque person is *Euskaldun* – meaning one who possesses Euskara. In the unlikely event that the European Union should choose to allot funds to communities on the basis of cultural seniority, the Basque lands would instantly become the wealthiest region in Europe. But, given the turmoil that has engulfed most of Europe on and off since the Romans, how has the language and culture survived?

Some time before the broadcast, in a bid to get closer to the soul of the Basques, I had travelled to New York. I chose America's largest city not because of Manhattan's modest diaspora of people from the Bay of Biscay (numbering around 1,300, according to the most recent census), but because the writer Mark Kurlansky lives in an apartment on the Upper West Side. Since no Basque has so far chosen to set their people's world-view in print, Kurlansky decided to do so on their behalf.

The Basque History of the World demonstrates, even in its title, that this is a singular race with a particular take on events. The first achievement was to create a culture that united both sides of the Pyrenees, rather than two peoples divided by the range. 'The Basque mountains are a myth,' says Kurlansky.

It's quite right. Our earlier walk across from Hendaye to Sare had hardly been flat, but the opening stages of the GR10 try hard for dramatic effect – keeping close to the Spanish frontier, the line of most resistance. By English standards, this was high ground, but I have to concede the terrain would hardly deter a military force. La Rhune would not even qualify for Munro status in Scotland; it falls thirty feet short of the 3,000ft qualification. Kurlansky says the western end of the Pyrenees has always been the main invasion route for armies crossing between Spain and France. This perplexed me. I had assumed that the Basque culture, language and cuisine had survived because the community was cut off from the rest of Europe. But Kurlansky said the Basques' survival was 'not through isolation but just the opposite' – they had forged strong contacts with a wide range of other peoples, but had always retained a sense of confidence about their place in the world.

Partly, they defined that place through having explored quite a lot of the rest of the planet. Again, it is surprising for a mountain people to be such consummate navigators; indeed, the Basques are thought to have landed in America before Columbus reached it. Enterprising Basque sailors made the first perilous voyages from medieval Europe across the Atlantic to the cod banks off Newfoundland; the method they discovered of drying, salting and preserving the fish has survived to the present day. Later, they traded assiduously with the New World, as the deep-red peppers that ignite many dishes testify.

The Basques' economic strength has always been derived from the sea rather than the land; the soil is much poorer than in other parts of France and Spain, and so the Basques have always needed to trade for food. For the greater part of their existence, this has involved a reliance on the sea. Although we were meeting the people of the mountains, the vast majority of Basques still reside close to the coast. And, as job opportunities on the coast have expanded, there has been a definite shift away from the pastures to a more appealing life in the maritime zone.

This could explain why the Hôtel Arraya in Sare apparently finds it hard to get the night staff these days, and why early morning broadcasts can go awry.

However, fondly imagining that the broadcast technicalities would be smooth the following morning, I turned off the light. My dreamless sleep was interrupted at about 2 a.m. by someone, curiously, phoning for a cab. Judging from the background noise and accent, it was a woman from the Liverpool area calling from outside a nightclub on a lively Friday. Mobile telephones are splendid devices to have in the mountains, except when yours happens to have a very similar number to that of a Merseyside cab firm. Because of the charging rules for international calls, I had to pay for the privilege of telling her that I was about 800 miles away, and anyway had never owned a car. I hope she got home safely in time to listen to Janey Lee Grace's show.

At 6 a.m. local time, the mobile phone shrieked again. This time it was a real alert: the alarm. Radio is a marvellous medium in many ways, and I considered exercising the contributor's option of appearing naked on a national network (which happens much more than you might imagine, except in studios).

Just down the hill, the baker was already at work. Even on a public holiday, the *boulangerie* is as enshrined in French society as liberty, fraternity and equality. The daily bread is regarded as crucial to civilised life – the fuel that will see families through another day, or get hikers across another pass. At dawn in any French town, the familiar civic odours are temporarily blanketed by the smell of a thousand baguettes baking (or, in the case of Sare's *boulanger*, a few dozen). In other European countries, artisan bakers have gone the way of many other small retailers, but in France they are sacrosanct.

Experience has taught me that overnight staff in hotels are not always in such tiptop form. It is always worth giving the reception desk a gentle nudge in advance. I threw on some clothes and crept out of my room.

The Arraya is one of those fine country hotels that is enjoying a second spring thanks to the 21st-century tourists who flood in from Stansted and Paris; for the holiday weekend at the start of the summer season, business was brisk. A couple of dozen fellow guests did not wish to be disturbed, yet every step I took seemed to trigger a hotel-wide shift in the timber structure. Between creaks, I practised my little speech – not for the radio programme, but for the night porter. In a few minutes his phone would ring, the call was likely to be for me, and would he kindly put it through to my room?

Mick Webb is far too modest to say so, but he is a brilliant linguist. For someone whose home turf is the Home Counties south of London, he can make himself understood by everyone from academics in Madrid to cowboys in Peru, and disentangle heavily accented French whether spoken in Alsace-Lorraine or Martinique. Even though I come from the same area of southeast England, my language training serves me well only in Russia and a sprinkling of other Slavic states. Mick's education took place north of the Surrey–Sussex frontier; mine was to the south, in the left-wing new town of Crawley.

The Cold War barely registered in this corner of West Sussex. Crawley was twinned with Eisenhüttenstadt: an industrial town formerly known as Stalinstadt on the East German–Polish border. And, at the radical comprehensive school I attended, it was considered essential for young people to be able to converse with the people of the Soviet Union. Accordingly, for five years from the age of eleven, I underwent intensive tuition in Russian. When I finally went abroad for the first time, aged thirteen, my foreign-language skills were of little help. It was a day trip on the ferry from Newhaven to Dieppe, where not a single Russian speaker was in evidence. *Everybody's Pocket Travel Guide to France* was of some help, with its phonetic renditions of phrases like 'have you something cheaper?': 'Av-ay voo kel-ker-shohz der may-yur mar-shay?' To my embarrassment, my communication skills in the Romance languages have barely improved since then.

On this occasion, language skills, or the lack thereof, turned out to be irrelevant, since the promise of 24-hour switchboard cover turned out to be as empty as the reception area. I called out as volubly as I thought I could without waking the slumbering guests, but to no avail. All the places where I normally find dozing night porters (usually the deepest and most comfortable armchair in the lounge) were unoccupied, too.

Time for Plan B – in broadcasting, as in life, you can never have too many contingency strategies. Before dinner the previous evening, I had identified the only payphone in the village – and even written down its number, for just such a circumstance. A sprint in bare feet to the phone booth did not appeal, but there was no time to return up to my room: the interview slot was due to begin in about the duration of a hit single.

The feeling that I was merely experiencing a bad dream in which everything goes awry intensified when I studied the hotel's front door. I could open it from the inside, but to release the lock and get back in required the use of a code tapped into a keypad. The usual few minutes of concentration, to focus one's mind on the impending broadcast, had evaporated. I searched desperately for something with which to prop open the door, at the same time as calculating the risk that a rascal would sneak in for some petty larceny while I was out. Minuscule, I reckoned; the towns and villages of the Pyrenees seem miraculously free of the kind of rural crime that besets parts of Britain's countryside. But before I could get any further the hotel phone started to ring.

The first ring sliced through the silence of Sare; the second was a higher-volume, higher-pitched screech. The last thing a live phone interview needs is a background hubbub of grumpy guests wondering what all the racket is about. So I felt impelled to pick up the phone on the hotel's switchboard before too many fellow residents were rudely awoken. The electronic wailing stopped and the studio engineer asked me what I had had for breakfast (the standard question for procuring a response with which to set the level on the mixing desk). Nothing yet, I said, but with a bit of luck a coffee and a croissant should be mine in about an hour.

Andrea Corr finished singing and Janey Lee Grace introduced our man in the Basque Country. I was well into my stride, expounding the virtues of southwestern France in early summer, when I noticed a figure appear at the hotel's front door with a look of disbelief: tall, bearded and tapping urgently on the keypad. I kept talking about the unseasonal weather while the door swung open and he loomed up.

Radio 2 has a slick, upbeat presentational style. Guests on the station are not expected to stop talking in midstream. The problem was this: how to resume normal service to an audience of several hundred thousand as quickly as possible, while at the same time explaining to someone who was clearly part of the hotel staff – probably the tardy telephonist – what the heck *l'Anglais* was up to, talking in English on the hotel's main phone? He, no doubt, had the power to cut me off in my prime. *Everybody's Pocket Travel Guide to France* would have been of little use; its focus for relations with hotel staff is 'Ver-yay bee-ahn me rer-kom-mahn-day ern bon vahn, gahrson?' (Will you recommend me a good wine, waiter?).

So listeners must have been treated to a muffled and incomprehensible conversation as I tried to placate him in poor broken French. Somehow, it worked for long enough for me to finish the answer and to explain to Janey and her audience the reason for the kerfuffle. She thanked me and invited me to call next week from somewhere quieter.

The inquest lasted longer than the interview. His face comprised a mix of anger, contempt and disbelief as I pressed into service 'Zher voo fay meel eks-kuss' (I make you one thousand apologies) and tried to explain the sequence of events. Honestly, I was not making a surreptitious international phone call at the hotel's expense – they had called me. He pointed at the mobile phone peeking out of my pocket and wanted to know why I had not simply used that for the call. Explaining the high technical standards of the BBC, and the consequent need for a land line rather than a mobile, proved beyond me. But, when I produced from my notebook the number of the village payphone, he concluded that there might be a grain of truth in my implausible version of events, and finally let the matter go.

Mick, meanwhile, had enjoyed his ample rest and was happily getting fired up with a couple of *cafés-au-lait*, ready for a racing start to what was planned to be a long day. But first, I had a quick tour of the Arraya's boutique. This hotel is indeed posh:

besides Basque berets, its strongest retail offering is own-brand *salmis de palombe*. A tin containing a single wood pigeon remodelled as stew costs €7.50; a brace thus processed is €14.50. It brings new meaning to the term 'pigeon fancier'. Happily, Basque cuisine has plenty to offer those whose idea of a good meal does not include wild birds. The previous evening, the big picture windows of the hotel restaurant presented a scene to inspire the walker: hills whose deep greens gradually faded as they crept up to where the Spanish border must lie to meet a sky rapidly adopting the colour of *vino tinto*. And the same colours were reflected in the dishes set before us. My starter was a warm cod on a bed of leaves, invigorated by a piquant tomato sauce – *à la vizcaina*. The main course was a kind of Basque surf'n'turf: hake and butterbeans enlivened by a blood-red chorizo and sprinkled with parsley.

Not every Basque fish dish is red, white and green: another summer speciality is squid in its ink, which is reckoned to be the only wholly black dish in the world. I was sorry not to see *marmitako* on the menu: a stew made with fresh tuna, tomatoes, potatoes and peppers. It was originally cooked in the tiny cramped galleys of Basque trawlers in a pot (*marmita*) from which it gets its name. At St-Jean-de-Luz, the nearest Atlantic town to Sare, the dish has its own fête.

The inspirational weather of the night before was not matched by the reality of the morning after. Most mornings in the Pyrenees, the sight of the mountains is a lure, a source of energy. But that depends on being able to see the damn things. As the old clock struck an off-key 8 a.m., the big picture windows were making a terrible din as they were assailed by hail. Appetite for a long walk is dulled in direct proportion to the ferocity and temperature of precipitation.

Inclement weather was one good reason to loiter over a coffee and under the disapproving gaze of the staff. Another was the uncertainty surrounding the start of the day's journey. Before the walk we had a train to catch, and to get to the train we needed to catch a bus. But not today. The local bus company, whose name translates as 'the Bouncing Basque', was taking the day off. A public holiday to commemorate the end of the Second World War constituted a good enough reason for a day of rest for the entire bus fleet that goes by this jolly name. Not for the first or the last time, our fate lay in the hands of benevolent (we hoped) local drivers. We found a roundabout on the outskirts of Sare, dropped our rucksacks beside the road and started to hitch the meagre traffic flow. The first three cars drove past apparently oblivious to us, but the fourth motorist drew up alongside. He was a French Basque heading for the coast at Hendaye and a rowing regatta against a team of Spanish Basques. This was a far cry from our own beloved Boat Race. The vessels, our benefactor explained, were like old Irish fishing boats – more evidence of a Celtic element in Basque DNA? – two metres wide, to cope with the wild Bay of Biscay.

Each boat in a proper Basque regatta has a crew of thirteen. I speculated about an eccentric biathlon whereby the teams would, on their return to dry land, embark on a game of Rugby League – the only other sport that I know of with teams of that number. And on how Henley Regatta owes its existence to the Basques, because they invented the concept of the rowing race.

There was no time to muse more, because we had cheekily hitched for a distance of only three kilometres. In the 1970s, the Golden Thumb Club, the only association ever to have assumed the role of a governing body for UK hitchhiking, established two miles (3.2km) as the minimum reasonable distance for which to seek a lift. We undershot this, but in our defence the journey to the Col de St-Ignace was all uphill. Once there, we celebrated our flying start by seeking shelter plus more coffee and croissants in the Café Pullman, while we waited for the train.

Our sense of urgency was attenuated because we were, in fact, waiting for a train. Even though most of the public transport in France's Basque lands had shut down for the day, the invitation on the publicity material for *le petit train de la Rhune* to '*prenez de l'Altitude*' applies every day from mid-March to November. Trains depart at 10 a.m. and 3 p.m. daily, come what may. So we had over an hour to kill – until we noted, with increasing alarm, that three luxury motor-coaches had pulled up and decanted their passengers into what appeared to be a succession of garden sheds. We shot out as fast as the bill and the change and the boots and the bags would allow, and bought tickets for the most expensive railway in Europe.

Connex, the French company that runs *le petit train*, was, as Mick has pointed out, driven out of the UK national rail network partly because it ran ancient trains that showed contempt for the published timetable at ludicrously slow speeds and high fares. That combination is the antithesis of SNCF, the nationalised French Railways. Yet it proves highly successful for Connex's southwest France operation. The 4.2km journey takes 35 minutes, for a one-way fare of €9. But our demand was, as economists say, inelastic: we were desperate to buy some altitude at almost any price. And, despite the decrepitude of *le petit train*, that is what it has to offer: a height gain of 81m per euro, a bargain for any gravity-sensitive hiker carrying an improbable amount of battery-operated high technology.

High-tech does not describe the rail journey, which began twenty minutes – in a nice twist on Connex punctuality record in Britain – *early*. Work on a 1m-gauge railway to the top of La Rhune began in 1912. One reason for the project was the region's popularity among visitors from the UK. The things people do for tourists: stone for the line was dragged up the mountain on sledges. Construction was interrupted by the First World War, but, when hostilities ceased, efforts redoubled, and within five years of the Treaty of Versailles the railway was completed. It was hardly designed to bind together a Europe that had wasted four years and a generation of young men tearing itself apart. But at least the line had a certain transnational character, snaking uphill to France's frontier with Spain. In the course of its creaking, clanking journey, *le petit train* climbs 730m, across hillsides strewn with wildflowers and through cuttings sculpted from unforgiving rock. I know this because I have studied the brochure. But on this day the weather closed in on our little train, rendering almost everything invisible – especially (and I'm reading here) the 'mysterious prehistoric cromlechs and Napoleonian redoubts'. But even close-up you could tell this was an excellent introduction to the Pyrenees, slicing through meadows and ragged rocks. Halfway up, the train paused to allow a hiker to get off, presumably to pick up the GR10. A small welcoming party of *pottöks* was awaiting his arrival.

'Third class seats are padded', my old guidebook misinformed me. Our fellow passengers sitting five abreast on what turned out to be hard mahogany seats sympathised with our backpacks and our obvious intentions. But as the train rumbled across the Trois Fontaines plateau through a particularly wet and clingy cloud, I came to realise that our prospects were brighter than theirs. Most were planning to come straight down after a short stop at the top, which would mean they had little chance of seeing the 360-degree horizon from the Pyrenees chain to the Basque coast, lining the Atlantic Ocean from San Sebastian to Biarritz, as promised in the tourist literature. At least we had a good walk ahead, in theory at least.

Nearing the summit, water poured from the rocks in the frenzied manner of a theme-park ride. When the garden sheds clattered to a halt at the top of the line, I temporarily envied the way our fellow passengers could peer at the 360-degree fog then disappear into a concrete café for something warming to eat and drink.

Most of the day-trippers missed the opportunity to study the *table d'orientation*. In 1924, the year in which the railway was completed, the Touring Club de France kindly sponsored this circular plinth that indicated where, had the cloud suddenly lifted, notable features could have been spotted. The latitude and longitude of the summit were stated – the latter, relative to Paris. Even half a lifetime after the 1888 conference that placed

Greenwich at the line of zero longitude, it seemed that the French had not yet accepted the idea that they should surrender the Paris Meridian. The Spanish, meanwhile, appeared not to care much either way. All that Spain seemed to have brought to La Rhune's party was a sign announcing that this was where the province of Navarra began, or came to an end.

The absence of any kind of view drew attention to the immediate surroundings, which did not reward close study. The café is merely part of a vast concrete complex that appears to grow out of the thrust of rock at the top of La Rhune. As Mick mentioned, the summit is festooned with radio and television masts. I guess the logic from both sides of the frontier was that transmitters would blight the other lot's view just as much as one's own. But the French had at least constructed one monument that measured no more than three metres and had an historic point. An obelisk topped by an eagle commemorates the momentous last day of September 1859: '*Souvenir de l'ascension de sa majesté l'Impératrice Eugénie*'. During the Second Empire, the Empress used the rapidly expanding railway network to visit each corner of '*l'hexagone*' (a reference to the six-sided shape of mainland France). *Sa majesté* made it to the top of La Rhune – and without the help of *le petit train*.

For us, though, the journey had only just begun. Our distant objective was the village of Ariskun, which we'd calculated would take about nine hours and allow us to arrive at our *pensión* in good time for supper. We had plenty of potential energy after our motor-assisted progress to the summit of La Rhune. We had a detailed Spanish map. We had a compass. But none of them was to prove much help in getting us down the Spanish side of La Rhune.

Should, one fine day, you find yourself at almost any point astride the frontier, your eye will be seduced by Spain. The Spanish mountains reach higher and extend deeper; the landscapes are vaster and sparser; the skies are wider. And the sun burning in the south will bestow on the view a dreamy quality, shimmering and quivering through the heat haze.

Not today, though. We descended as carefully as we could, but the moisture in the air had given every stone and patch of grass a slick, slippery surface. A range of tracks – each taking a different path downhill – presented itself, but none was convincing. The map was, frankly, more trouble than it was worth. The further we went, the less relationship the chart had to what we could see. Every cartographer inserts some tiny, inconsequential error into their creations, for the purpose of detecting plagiarists. But the maker of this map appeared to have included some quite consequential mistakes as well. The first real wrong turning we took was because the little black square that represented a derelict shepherd's house was not in the correct location on the map. Or else it had moved a few hundred metres. It did not help that the paper seemed to be intended for indoor use only: any contact with the damp (of which there was plenty), and it started to disintegrate. The ideal companion, apart of course from Mick, would have been Georges Véron or at least his guidebook to the high-level route, the HRP. The path cuts right across La Rhune, and could have guided us down much more happily, by just following the stones that mark the border.

To make matters worse, a crucial signpost that was supposed to point the way had been broken – perhaps in anger by a previous hiker? We soon lost the path altogether, and were stumbling down a rocky hillside covered in foliage that seemed designed to trap the unwary walker. Progress was painfully slow and plain painful, with brambles and thorns tearing through our flimsy rainwear. It was also miserably damp, because of the frequent showers. *En Abril, aguas mil* is the Spanish term for April showers; they were a month late this year. A shed offered some shelter, which we took. I removed my backpack and placed it on a piece of farm machinery so that it would keep dry while we studied the map.

The more we had recourse to the map, the less we were inclined to trust it, suspecting it to be drawn with too much emphasis on artistic aesthetics and not enough on geographic accuracy. Perhaps Spanish cartographers are hopeless romantics, who depict their image of how the world should look, rather than the flawed, messy planet that it really is.

Our attempts to reconcile the map with reality were hampered because the compass had disappeared. I was the last to have possession of it, and there was nothing for it but to start going backwards: to retrace my tracks. Five minutes back towards France, I found the compass face down in the middle of the path. When I returned, Mick was wearing an expression that indicated something else had gone wrong during my brief absence: my backpack had toppled on to a patch of ground that was composed of a foul blend of fresh manure and old engine oil. The laptop, which had taken the brunt of the fall, somehow survived, but to this day the backpack carries a large, smelly Basque smear.

Things were, though, looking up. The capacity of the weather to affect mood was demonstrated as the sun finally cleared a way through the cloud. The brightening sky had two advantages: a psychological lift in our spirits, and the navigational bonus that landmarks were no longer shrouded in mist. Yet we were still uncertain where we actually were on the unreliable and rapidly disintegrating map. But, facing ahead, our trajectory across the corrugated countryside looked relatively clear. For an hour, we hiked through patches of woodland where weird fungi were glistening and colourful buds were unfolding. The flatter and more fertile parts of the valley had been cleared for agriculture, with some meadows sporting eccentrically constructed haystacks, like long-haired tepees.

Presiding over each dozen or so fields was a stately Basque farmhouse: a bulky half-timbered structure with wide eaves to protect against winter snows and summer downpours. Some meadows were delineated with ancient hedgerows, but barbed wire is evidently increasingly popular. In order to preserve rights of way, some ingenious Basque stiles have been created. The simplest design consists of a stump of wood on each side of the fence. The average Basque, unencumbered by a bulky backpack, could take these in his or her stride as easily as an Olympic hurdler. But it is trickier if you have to stop, clamber on to the uneven stump and lift one leg over while balancing precariously and trying to avoid a maiming from the spikes of steel.

Perhaps it was the extra stresses of such manoeuvres, or the unceremonious dunking in the farmyard, but, a few minutes after the first such stile, the entire expedition – or at least my part in it – nearly ended abruptly. The bolt that secured the frame of my backpack to the overstuffed, overweight pack came adrift. To understand the effect of this: it was as if an articulated truck had come apart. We were about fifty kilometres from the nearest outdoor-equipment supplier, which was in France and no doubt would anyway be closed in commemoration of the capitulation of Nazi Germany. Only some serious surgery by Mick and his industrial-grade Swiss Army knife restored the integrity of the pack.

An enforced stop on a long walk invariably signals a refreshment break, too, and we leaned back on the soft, grassy bank of the lane we had stumbled upon to devour the picnic. One advantage of facing southeast was that it was impossible to see La Rhune, which was an uncomfortable reminder of how short a distance we'd actually covered. When walking, the total weight carried does not vary before or after lunch, when a miscellany of bread, chorizo sausage, tomatoes, fruit and water has been transferred from backpack to alimentary canal. So it is curious that walking suddenly becomes much easier. On this occasion, the spring in our post-prandial steps became even more pronounced within fifty paces when we saw a familiar red-and-white mark. On this side of the frontier, that meant we had accidentally hit upon a *gran recorrido*, a Spanish long-distance footpath.

The Spanish have borrowed from France the idea of a national network of waymarked trails, and even imitated the initials. The GR11, on which we suddenly discovered we were walking, is a kind of homage to the original on the French side of the Pyrenees. But its route is not waymarked as conscientiously as the French GR10, thereby injecting a large dose of uncertainty into the trajectory of anyone attempting to follow it. But, while *not* seeing a GR11 marker indicates nothing, seeing the splodge of *rojo y blanco* is confirmation that you are on course, at least for the time being. The time being 2 p.m., there was not a moment to lose. Well, that was how we felt, even though we would squander many more moments that day. Much of the high Pyrenees can become mortally cold for those who are not properly prepared; but we were crossing terrain that was low and (too) liberally laced with tracks and road, not to mention plenty of abandoned farm buildings. It was not a matter of life and death – except for the wood pigeons.

National Service ended in Britain so long ago that even Mick evaded the draft by a good few years. And, with rapidly rising disposable incomes meeting the falling cost of travel, ours is the first generation to have had the freedom to go almost anywhere on the planet in peace, not war. The Woodcraft Folk, to which I belonged as a child, insisted that the world citizen should travel widely but in accordance with pacifist principles. All of which is fine and dandy, but it means, when confronted with structures that evidently have some military purpose, I tend to be mystified about exactly what that might be. For example: the gunmetal-grey tower ramming through the beech trees and topped with a cabin big enough to hold two men brave enough to climb up the flimsy ladder. But you do not need to be a military genius to work out that this was an offensive structure against an enemy woefully lacking in any kind of fire power of its own.

Each autumn, millions of pigeons take the fast track to the sun from northwest Europe. They fly in squadrons across the western Pyrenees, or at least across part of them. Once they get within range of the *palomeros*, the massacre begins.

Two million or so unfortunate migrants are trapped and slaughtered each year in the Basque Country. Many of the victims are caught in nets that are strung between trees. The trick is to persuade the pigeons to fly low enough to become trapped.

The path led us past a massive stone tower, which echoed the shape of the obelisk to Empress Eugénie at the top of La Rhune but was a good twenty metres high. It was a particularly fine specimen among many towers that dot the forests in this part of the Basque Country. The door was locked and bolted; I guessed it led to a staircase for the hunters to climb to their look-out. They get a predator's-eye view as wood pigeons approach from the north-east across a broad valley. The birds choose this route across the Pyrenees to fly south each autumn because the relatively low terrain makes the migration easier. They naturally stay above the tree-tops, unless there is a very good reason to descend. And that is where the secret weapon of the hunters comes in. It is a table-tennis bat, or something that looks very much like one. When a flock of pigeons approaches, the high-level hunter launches this decoy skywards. To the migrating birds, the spinning bat looks dangerously like a bird of prey. They instinctively dive – straight into the waiting nets, where they are finished off in a variety of unpleasant ways by the ground staff. In Sare, which supplies some of the manpower, they call the annual slaughter *enfer des palombes*: 'pigeon hell'. Were Disney ever to make a film about the ritual, perhaps involving an escaping wood pigeon, I know what they could call it: *Where Pigeons Dare*.

If you ignore the fact that this is a killing forest, this section of the walk rates as excellent: the late afternoon sun filtering through leaves still bursting with the intensity of spring. Better still, enough mulch from the autumn leaves remained to provide a walking surface of rare comfort (or perhaps it was decomposing pigeons underfoot). Even the gradients felt reasonable. Now we were making the kind of progress that had eluded us all day, ascending to the rim of the valley of Ariskun. Our average speed actually increased – an unusual event so late in the day. But by the time we looked down upon the Baztán

Valley, a tranquil bowl of land, ringed by uncompromising hills, we were already late for dinner.

Ascents are usually journeys into the unknown. Your eyes concentrate on finding safe footholds (and, *in extremis*, handholds). On the odd occasion when you glance upwards it is usually tricky to make out precisely where the path leads. Speculation about what lies beyond the next ridge is generally pointless, though a fair bet is ... another ridge. Descents are more aesthetically satisfying: so long as the path is not smothered in clammy Basque mist, you can enjoy the view as you follow the track downhill.

That assumes you can find the track. Standing on the cusp of this Basque Country micro-republic, it was clear where we needed to go: for once the map and the clusters of houses in the Baztán Valley agreed, and the evening light was shining on the village of Ariskun, seven kilometres away. On a good day a fit person could reach it in ninety minutes, but only if they knew the way. All that we knew was that the GR11 headed away south. But it was hard to tell the correct route down towards Ariskun, at the heart of the valley.

The usual walkers' comradeship was beginning to wear thin. Sure, we had made a slow and lazy start to the day, but for the past eight hours we had barely paused for anything other than backpack repairs or disentangling ourselves from a barbed-wire fence. Had it been the start of the day, the view beneath us would have been inspirational: directly in front was a series of narrow valleys divided by muscular hills; beyond them, the flat, inviting land of Baztán with a scattering of white villages, one of which was ours. The sheep had dinner sorted; they scuffled noisily around to find the most tender shoots of grass, but were silent about which way was down. With neither the map nor waymarking providing any help, we would have to depend on our navigational instincts. And, this evening, they were differently calibrated. Mick was convinced that he could detect a path making a long arc around the outcrop to our left; I perceived a lower track heading steeply down along the line of a stream that was powered from the spring just beneath us. We tetchily decided to set off in different directions.

Walking alone has many advantages. Without a companion as distraction, you can feel at one with your surroundings – appreciating each nuance of your surroundings, from the ground underfoot to the birds overhead. You move at your own pace, and pause whenever you wish to rest, snack or listen to the sounds of the planet uninterrupted by the grunts and grumbles of a fellow human. So why was I walking (apart from right now) through the Pyrenees with Mick? Oh yes – besides his sparkling wit and repartee, profound understanding of European cultures and salacious stories involving people we knew in common, there were definite practical advantages. Just as civil aircraft have a flight crew of two, it is valuable (apart from right now) to have a second opinion on the best course to take. On physically demanding stretches (apart from right now), a certain amount of mutual support can help one partner or the other through patches of exhaustion. And, crucially, if one were to be hurt, the other can go for help. But right now, geological faults in our relationship had been exposed by fatigue and frustration, or maybe we were simply both feeling that our conflicting senses of direction outweighed any consensus.

Over the hill (and we certainly were), the two paths converged; we were both right and both wrong. The terrain was a muddle of billowing meadows, shady groves of beech trees and even a car park, signifying reconnection with the 21st century. My mobile telephone reconnected with the globe, and Mick readjusted our arrival time with our host for the evening. 'No later than nine if you want some dinner,' she had insisted.

This was an unwelcome surprise. We'd become well used to the tyranny governing the French evening meal: in France, the dinner plates would be en route to the sink by now. Elsewhere in Spain, restaurants would barely be limbering up for the evening, with only tourists ordering a meal before 10 p.m. But the Baztán valley was obviously a law unto itself.

The worst thing about the Baztán Valley is the name, which translates as 'Rat's Tail'. Most other facets are positive. Baztán is an example of how the world could be if only everyone lived in isolated valleys with no apparent threats. Each of the fifteen villages has an informal power structure, and decisions about matters that affect the whole valley are made in a consensual, collegiate fashion. Mick and I would obviously fit in well there.

The path became a track and then a road, threading elegantly through slumbering hamlets. We shuffled along uncomfortably. If the world were to be redesigned to suit long-distance walkers, then the last segment of each hike would be across compliant, springy grass. Negotiating a busy road (busy for the deep Basque Country, that is) and a complicated route that appeared to disappear behind a carpet warehouse did not enhance our moods. We were, after all, following part of the (famously unmarked) HRP high-level route across the Pyrenees, a trail that is supposed to eschew the trappings of the 21st century. The final furlong involved clawing our way up an unexpected final slope to the main street of Ariskun. Here, a bunch of local kids pointed the way to the Pensión Exteberría. It turned out to be opposite a *fronton* that was much bigger than the village church, which was noisily striking nine. After painfully peeling off boots and surgically removing socks we walked in and started coughing.

Whatever your needs in the Basque Country, if you can't find it at the Pensión Exteberría, you're probably better off without it. If you fear for the future of diversity in a continent that is becoming increasingly homogenised, pay a visit to the commercial hub of Ariskun. No Ibis hotels, Tesco supermarkets or McDonald's fast-food outlets here: the Pensión Exteberría performs all these functions and more. First, it was necessary to fight our way through the Saturday night fug of cheap-cigarette smoke. Though the bar had a population of only three men (apply any of the usual adjectives: gnarled, wizened, timeworn), they were smoking for Spain. Or was it for the Basque Country? None of them looked as though they would be ready for the apple dance (*sagar dantza*), the autumnal ritual that was born in this town. This men-only event is part of the carnival (*ihauteriak*) celebrations that include a bear and his trainer; these days, the unfortunate beast is represented by a human. During the rest of the year, the more athletic men busy themselves with the wooden-shoe dance (*eskalpoin dantza*), which celebrates the traditional Basque footwear.

When the coughing stopped, we announced ourselves to the ancient and imposing Señora who ran the *pensión* and betrayed her scary phone persona by taking our boots away to a drying room, which I hoped was lead-lined. We promised to be down in ten minutes and went upstairs to our rooms – though not to put on our dancing shoes. The *pensión* had everything a weary walker could want from a hotel (except, perhaps, an in-room phone on which to conduct radio interviews). The rooms were generously proportioned, with wooden furniture stained by time and probably worth a fortune if you could get it down the precipitous stairs and drive it to an auction house. The communal baths were huge, though luckily Mick and I did not have to share. Therefore I could dab away in privacy at the cuts sustained on the inept scramble down the thistle-clad slopes of La Rhune.

In doing so, I felt an honorary Basque; they have an implausibly high incidence of people with rhesus negative in their veins, matching the blotch of dried blood I was wiping away from my left shin. Surprisingly, the thistle is venerated by Basques; it is known as *eguskilore*, which translates as 'flower of the sun', and forms an important part of the pre-Christian traditions that have endured in the region – being nailed to the door of cattle sheds, for example. But it also represents a good reason to wear long trousers, or to carry a supply of B-rhesus-negative blood.

I walked downstairs carefully to avoid another injury, and

found more blood on the menu. The epicentre of Basque cuisine is on the Spanish side of the frontier, and two of its standard dishes are chorizo and black-and-white puddings. The further you get from the ocean, the more the emphasis on meat with dishes such as grilled mutton or lamb with peppers and tomato. I settled for a fiery stew, which was just what the doctor ordered after the day we had experienced. The fire was due to the peppers that came back from the New World with the conquistadors and are now used with abandon in many Basque dishes. They rate 4 on the Scoville Index – the Richter Scale of peppers, which peaks at 10. Peppers were originally used to add bite to chocolate recipes in the seventeenth century, but have since become an important ingredient in many great Basque recipes.

Not every Basque made it back from the New World. Indeed, travelling around Latin America you will often encounter Basque names such as Echeverría. Even in the United States, Basques constitute a significant and identifiable minority. Like most Iberian emigrants, the Basques initially settled mainly in places like Cuba, Mexico and Argentina. But, as the West was won in the US, demand for food among Anglophone settlers in Idaho, Nevada and California increased. Basque shepherds were ideally qualified to raise livestock in the newly opened lands, whose thin soil was a good match for that of the Basque Country. They brought their tradition of transhumance – moving animals from lower to higher ground in summer – and helped the West develop.

Ironically, this way of life was jeopardised by tourism, or at least the embryonic movement to preserve wilderness for future generations by creating National Parks. In addition, immigration quotas were introduced in the 1920s, limiting the number of arrivals from the whole of Spain to just 131 people a year. But nearly 20,000 Californians still regard themselves as Basque, as do 6,000 Idaho residents and 5,000 Nevadans.

Basque links with America's gambling hub are so strong that Senator McCarran (after whom Las Vegas international airport is named) sponsored legislation in the 1950s to make a special exemption for shepherds to enter the US. Today, the Center for Basque Studies is part of the University of Nevada at Reno, the state capital. Revenue from gambling helps to fund research into American Basques, though the Center can probably do little to help preserve the ethnic group in the New England state of Vermont (which at the last count had just two Basque residents). Instead, it focuses on Basque society in the West, such as the extraordinary role played by women who moved to America to run Basque hotels. The typical Basque woman acted as a surrogate mother to the young Basque men working in the West, and would do everything from looking after their possessions while they roamed the hills in summer to cooking, cleaning and washing their clothes for them during the winter. An academic at the University of Nevada has made a study of them, called *Home Away from Home*; her name is Dr Jerónima Echeverría.

The woman running the Basque hotel in Ariskun was like a mother to us, fussing to make sure we had eaten and (especially) drunk enough to make up for the rigours of the long and winding path. Ariskun's Saturday night excitement does not exactly match that of Las Vegas, so we took the excuse to head for bed. I did not, thankfully, experience an anxiety dream of hotel staff interrupting live broadcasts.

Next morning, the Basque mother figure force-fed us with breakfast, sorted out a taxi to ease us to the start of the Sunday stretch and enquired what kind of picnic we would like. One of the recesses of the *pensión* doubled as the village general store, selling everything from agricultural implements to bread, chorizo and water. Totting up our bill for board, lodging and shopping took a while but cost a modest €70 (about £50) – less than the cost of a Basque dinner alone in Reno. Mark Kurlansky, the American author of *The Basque History of the World*, points to the role of Basque entrepreneurs in creating modern capitalism. At a time when restrictions on trade were the order of the day –

for example, allowing only certain ports to trade in particular commodities – the Basques had already caught on early to the economic theory that free competition benefits both the consumer and the supplier. Prototype Thatcherites they may have been, but Basques have proved extremely successful in business. During the stultifying days of Franco's dictatorship, Spain's most economically successful city was Bilbao.

The proprietor of the *pensión* declined to capitalise on her monopoly, as did the taxi driver. He transported us 18km along and 500m up the pass of Izpegi – also known as the Col d'Ispeguy, since it divides Spain from France. Eighteen euros saved us a day's hike, and put us in prime position for an excursion that promised to be as gentle as Saturday's was demanding. At 10 a.m., under blue skies and with bellies full of breakfast, we started up the path that would lead us up the highly rated walk along the Crête d'Iparla, the Iparla crest. It led sharply up a flaky hillside, with thin grassland, underfed trees and scraggy patches of gorse. An hour later, the vegetation had thinned still further, yet we were still going uphill. Our tempers were not improved by watching a group of students from Pamplona disappear into the distance. They had caught up with us shortly after we started. Unencumbered by baggage (or years), they raced ahead to join what is certainly one of the finest stretches of the GR10.

Watching the four of them skip along as if they were on a Sunday stroll (which, I suppose, they were) made matters worse. Adding 25 per cent to one's body weight and carrying the whole lot through the Pyrenees is especially arduous on steep uphill stretches. There are many of these, naturally, but the gradient of this one was particularly effective at creating the impression that the backpack was crushing me into the mountain. The grass was slippery enough to make the most nimble Basque shepherd slip, and patches of loose gravel added a Sisyphean edge to the proceedings (Sisyphus was the Greek god punished with the perpetual task of pushing a stone uphill, only for it constantly to slip back).

By 11.15 a.m. the Pamplonans had no doubt reached Paris, while we finally reconnected with the GR10, which had appeared from the west. We were actually tackling it the 'wrong' way, in the direction that you would normally take when walking from the Mediterranean to the Atlantic. Maybe this is why things turned out the way they did.

Self-justification with the benefit of hindsight is never an attractive trait, so I shall get my excuses in early. Like the rest of my immediate family, I am terrified of heights. This is not, though, an altogether irrational fear, because it kicks in only when it is clear that putting a foot wrong could end in disaster. I readily admit that susceptibility to vertigo is not an entirely helpful characteristic when walking in the mountains, but for most of the time it stays quietly in the compartment of the brain marked 'phobias'. Too much research can be a dangerous thing, though, and leafing through books containing photographs of the GR10 turns up several patches where straying from the path could be hazardous to your health. The Crête d'Iparla, the cliff face that defends the Baztán Valley from the rest of the world, was one such. The heights reached are nothing out of the ordinary, barely exceeding 1,000m, but anyone tumbling from the precipice would have quite long enough to fall. 'Path runs along cliff edge', our guidebook notes helpfully.

I did not trouble Mick with my concerns, because he already had plenty to contend with. 'Equipment issues' occur with impressive frequency when walking with Mick. The fleece/no fleece decision, in particular, proves constantly problematic. Air temperature declines rapidly with height, increasing the need for the strange mauve fleece that he insists on wearing despite its effectiveness at scaring off interesting wildlife (and, when hitching, prospective lift-givers). Once on, the extra layer quickly raises his body temperature to the point where the fleece has to come off. The very act of stopping long enough to disrobe causes a sharp fall in temperature, and so the cycle repeats endlessly. A corollary is my self-unlacing boots. They are, as the song goes, made for walking, not standing. As long as the laces are subject to the extra stress provided by constant movement, the double bow stays taut. But a pause to check the map, snap a picture or gasp for breath relaxes the tension. When I start walking again, one lace or other quickly unravels and poses the sort of health hazard that the EU is always seeking to outlaw. I studied once again the alarming picture of the Crête d'Iparla while Mick attended to the fleece; I nervously retied those wayward laces.

Before we saw the real thing in all its fearsome glory there was work to be done. A short, sharp ascent led to the Pic Buztanzelhay. At 1,029m, this was more of a ruffle in the rocks than a serious summit, but it had two interesting features. First, in profile it looks far more like a breast than most of the mountains that are usually celebrated for this trait; second, it was our earliest encounter on this particular trip with snow that you could crunch around in (or fashion into non-lethal missiles). Best of all, the view was the finest so far. To the east and south, the Basque Country rippled away until it merged with the misty mountains. The valley in the foreground appeared more fertile than the norm for the region; this is one of the rare areas where vines thrive, and we were peering down at the source of rich, earthy Iroulèguy reds. To the west, the Baztán Valley looked so placidly perfect that it could be the setting for a children's story book (the carpet warehouse was not obvious from this range); and, beyond it, La Rhune at last looked a respectable distance away.

Only the north provided cause for concern. Tiny figures – probably the Pamplona students on the way home from their sprint to Stockholm and back – were silhouetted against the clinically blue sky. They edged along the *crête* almost imperceptibly slowly. I just hoped their laces were tightly done up.

We faced a solid hour's trudge to the start of the crest. Pyrenean time has a knack of catching up on you, and then overtaking while your attention is elsewhere. What had started as an unchallenging schedule to reach the station at Pont Noblia by 5.30 p.m. (when the last train of the day was due to leave) suddenly looked tricky with six hours to go. Our hiking guide book calculated a time from the *pic* to the station of five hours, forty-five minutes. In our favour was the fact that we were travelling in the opposite direction. Between here and the railway station, we were set to descend nearly 1,000m – about the height of England's highest mountain. Against us was the ambitious nature of the timings given in the book. I sometimes felt the guide had been written by a Pamplonan athlete charged up with performance-enhancing substances and carrying no baggage whatsoever. Completing a section in anything less than one-quarter more than the stipulated time was almost beyond us.

Perhaps this was our day. The terrain was manageable enough – sparse grass punctuated by randomly scattered boulders. A few *pottöks* added an element of equestrian cuteness, and an explanation for the sparseness of the grass. A grove of trees provided a brief respite from the noonday sun. For a moment I thought the fleece was going to go back on, but we pressed on – hopping from France to Spain and back again with every couple of steps – to the Pic de Tutulia, at the threshold of the *crête*.

Fear is a curious phenomenon, but usually a healthy one. The Pic de Tutulia provided an excellent viewpoint for what faced us. This was a classic example of an escarpment, where a gently rising hill suddenly stops in midair and falls vertically like a clumsy hiker to the valley below. If anything, the reality was scarier than the photograph in the book. I took one of my own for good measure.

The advantage of the gently shelving ground on which we were standing was that mistakes were punished only gently. At school, I was the kid who attracted PE reports that ranged from a polite 'faces challenges on co-ordination' to the brutally accurate 'clumsy'. While Mick played amateur football at a reasonable level – demanding a certain degree of balance and agility – I seem destined always to be tangling with a shoelace, slipping on a patch of frozen snow or tripping on a small but sharp outcrop of granite lurking beneath the grass – often, all three at once. That is why he looked upon the Crête d'Iparla as a bracing, breezy ramble while I felt faintly sick: one foot wrong and it would be all too easy to breeze through hundreds of feet of thin air.

We ticked off the red-and-white markers on the shallow descent to where the cliff edge took shape. A track meandered off to the left, but the proper path then climbed steeply. The incline of the cliff increased towards the Pic d'Iparla, resembling the jagged bit at the top of a sorely decaying tooth. Without wishing to mix oral metaphors, the track led along a lip of rock just beneath the summit. It didn't help to see a distant group of elderly ramblers negotiating the path from Hell with no apparent difficulty. The surface was rough and loose and I quickly became convinced that my backpack – which usually was merely a dull, constant aggravation – had become a danger to life and limb. It was inexpertly packed, with a lot of weight (such as the laptop on which I am writing these words) towards the top. The effect was to raise the centre of gravity, which is exactly what you do not need when sneaking along the edge of calamity. Mountaineers and rock climbers can do amazing things with mass, gravity and footholds, but the only solution that made sense to me was to crouch lower and lower.

One of the stranger sources of income that I enjoy is from the *It'll be Alright on the Night/Auntie's Bloomers* genre of television programmes. In case you are not familiar with these shows, they comprise a series of clips of people being filmed doing dumb things. Those school reports were right about clumsiness: I have made a profit stream out of walking into doorframes and ending a piece-to-camera from the driver's seat of a sports car by roaring off backwards. Someone with a video camera who had caught my sorry high-altitude performance in the Pyrenees frame by dismal frame could now be making a decent living flogging DVDs entitled *How not to walk in mountains*. I could not properly take in the amazing sight of the world falling away into a distant, verdant valley for fear that I would become part of the view.

The longer I prolonged the agony, the more it hurt. The onset of vertigo can be fatally self-fulfilling: the lower I crouched, the more unwieldy the backpack became. The more unwieldy the backpack became, the lower I crouched, until I was crawling along the ledge. Simultaneously, I was keeping as far from the edge as possible, which meant scraping painfully against the rock face and running the risk of rebounding from an obstinate outcrop over the precipice.

Looking back objectively on that beautiful, terrifying afternoon, the solution was obvious: to stop messing about and do what Mick was doing so adroitly, skipping purposefully across the lip of the crest as though he was advancing on goal. Thanks to the miracle of digital photography, I have studied at length the photograph of the *crête* that I took from the Pic de Tutulia. Using this laptop, I can zoom ever closer on the crucial ledge and the precipice I perceived. The more intense the close-up, the more pixelated becomes the image – until it looks just like a staircase. And guess what: just like the staircase in my house, the average gradient is no more than 45 degrees to the horizontal. It just goes on for a lot longer.

In the unlikely event that Mick ever contemplates another joint hike across the Crête d'Iparla, I know exactly what to do: print out those digital images and look at them for reassurance as I stride purposefully to the end of the crest. But on that sunny Sunday afternoon, I did the next best thing: stopped in my tracks and cried out plaintively for help.

You know what men are like. They rarely share their fears or volunteer reassurance to each other. We worry too much about our emotional image, in a curious parallel to the way women fret about their physical appearance. Until each sex can come to terms with looks and hearts, our true colours will manifest themselves only in extreme situations (usually, of our own making). Mick would have had right on his side had he told me to stop messing about and get my backside in gear. Instead, he suggested I abandon my backpack and scrabble across the worst thirty metres or so unencumbered until I reached a surface I regarded as secure. He would then retrieve the backpack, and no doubt remind me of the event at regular intervals for years afterwards. It struck me as a good deal. I scampered, with all the grace of a mortally wounded Pyrenean bear, to the safe ground.

At last I had a chance to appreciate the view. Because the land dropped away precipitously, the image was a work of art. A patchwork of meadows gave way to one mountain ridge after another, disappearing into an afternoon haze that blurred the horizon. But even so you could make out the dramatic, jagged top of the Pic d' Anie, which was on our route and looked quite awe-inspiring. Perhaps risking life and limb was worth it after all.

'What the hell have you got in here?' enquired Mick as he swayed unsteadily towards me bearing a backpack with its own eccentric sense of direction. 'The centre of gravity's all wrong. It's all over the place.' An idea for a new make-over show for travellers called *How Not to Pack* flashed before me, but I suppressed it in favour of simple gratitude to the man who, so it seemed, had risked his life for a backpack full of socks, maps and consumer electronics. However dazed and amazed I was to be alive, the practicalities of life rapidly took over. Mick slung down the backpack while I made some time-and-motion calculations. We could expect to see the last train of the day to St-Jean-Pied-de-Port arrive at 'our' station, pause and depart any moment now. As the song goes, 'Who knows where the time goes?' Consumed by terror, that's where. The 5.30 p.m. duly came and went.

Mick wore a classic 'that's another fine mess you've got me into' expression as we scampered downhill. Soon we reached a junction of tracks that merited a warning in the guidebook for people heading in the opposite direction: 'Path heading off to right; it's easy to get side-tracked onto this.' You did not need to be a world-class explorer or cartographer to realise that this was the very track whose other end we had encountered on the far side of the *crête*. In other words, there was a non-threatening bypass around the back of the peak that sensible Basque sheep and their shepherds no doubt took, all the while sniggering at the antics of the fools on the dangerous side of the hill. Between us and the village of Bidarray, the map in the guidebook carried no fewer than three double-chevrons, indicating a trio of stretches with severe gradients. Normally these would signify an impossibly steep climb against us, but on this occasion they were all downhill.

Gravity is your worst enemy when climbing, but that does not make it your best friend on descents. We were physically depleted from yesterday's exertions and (at least in my case) emotionally stressed by a brush with death – though with every stumble downhill I had to admit that the actual danger ranked lower than, for instance, cycling around the Place de la Concorde during rush hour. Furthermore, we were out of water. When fear steps in, physical necessities take a hike. Only when the world (or at least your role in it) has not ended do you realise that the hot and cold sweats of the past few hours have left you seriously dehydrated. These were not the marvellously leaky hills that were to sustain us further east. We would have to rely on human kindness and Basque plumbing.

Many things amaze me about the Pyrenees in general and the GR10 in particular. The source of wonderment this precise afternoon: that there exists a single Basque dairy farmer who is not weary of hikers descending from the hills to plod along the lane that he relies upon for his livelihood, and asking for water to replenish their supplies. We stumbled across Alain as our spirits sagged. He was at the door of the first structure we had seen close up since the *pensión*. *Oui*, we could of course help ourselves to water from the tap.

Some people have the knack to mould themselves to circumstance. Mick has an uncanny ability to get on the right side of people through a combination of humour, empathy and linguistic ability. I did not follow every nuance of the conversation, but as Alain grabbed his keys I could see where it was leading. Not only had we successfully negotiated some water but also Alain was prepared to drive us down to the main road. I happily bundled myself into the back of an ancient Simca van, along with a couple of imperfectly packed rucksacks, and gleaned what I could from a whizz through Bidarray. The village is on two levels, with the cluster of *l'église*, *la poste* and *le fronton* well above the corridor shared between the Nive river, the now-silent railway and the D918 to St-Jean. Alain agreed to take us to the Pont Noblia, the bridge across the river where the now-useless station was located, whence we could plan our next move to cover the 25km to St-Jean. He clearly did not rate our chances, because he took the opportunity to introduce us to the *patronne* of the Hôtel Noblia. In Basque, he assured her that we would be back within the hour looking for a place to stay. Well, I reckon that is what he said.

Standing on the fast, long curve of the main road, I was inclined to agree with his prediction – not least because both of us were caked in the muddy dust that clings to people who sweat a lot in the mountains. Still, as a means of attracting drivers it was better than the sight of Mick's purple fleece.

While we waited, Mick told me that what had seemed to me a generous and relaxing lift from our friendly shepherd had in fact been as terrifying for him as my traverse of the Iparla cliff. Alain had actually been rather the worse for his Sunday glasses of Pastis and had negotiated the very tight bends at some speed while rolling a cigarette with one hand and waving out of the window at his many friends with the other. Hitchhiking lore is clear on a few things, and one is that mothers with young children never stop – especially for two bedraggled blokes on a darkening Sunday evening on a fast, bendy road in southwest France. But stop she did, and somehow found room in the Renault Espace for ourselves and our bags without turfing out any of the three children, who were clearly unimpressed with our arrival. She was bringing them back from a 'Basque day' of song, fun and games, whose aim was to promote the Basque language among the younger generation.

Mick weaved his usual verbal magic as we raced up the Nive Valley, which meant that we were dropped within a totter of our hotel. The two lifts embodied a principle on which Mick and I have placed rather too much reliance: that, for each bad travel experience, there is an equal and opposite good one.

Usually.

Six weeks later, at a refuge further east, we learned some sad news on the hikers' grapevine. A solo traveller had slipped from the Crête d'Iparla. His body was not found for three days.

3. WAR AND PEACE: THE PASSES OF THE BASQUE COUNTRY

Mick Webb

If there's such a thing as a walkers' town, St-Jean-Pied-de-Port deserves the title. For 800 years its cobbled streets have felt the footsteps of pilgrims on the renowned route to Santiago de Compostela and, more recently, their numbers have been supplemented by secular trekkers like ourselves, who are following the GR10 along the length of the Pyrenees. As well as being a crossroads for the long-distance walker, St-Jean-Pied-de-Port is a very photogenic little town beside the river Nive, with well-restored medieval walls of pink granite, punctuated by ancient gates. Simon and I arrived here on a chilly evening in May, and decided to take on the mantle of honorary pilgrims and try the first stage of the Chemin de St Jacques (French), or Camino de Santiago (Spanish). On the French side of the frontier it's called the GR65, an unromantic, official designation for a walk which is as packed with historical interest and human drama as a walk can be; and the stretch that leads across the Pyrenees presents quite a physical challenge during winter and spring.

In the twelfth century, pilgrims coming from northern Europe followed four major routes through France. Three of these converged just north of St-Jean-Pied-de-Port, making it an ideal place for them to gather their strength before crossing the Pyrenees on their way to the great abbey at Roncesvalles in Spain. They arrived in their hundreds of thousands each year and were welcomed by the clamour of church bells as they appeared over the crest of the hill and made their way through the gate called the Porte de St Jacques. Simon and I made a slightly lower-key entrance, through the side gate by the car park after getting out of a Renault Espace in which we'd hitched a lift, after missing the last train of the day from our previous walk.

May is not the best month for mountain walking, but at least there's no difficulty finding accommodation, in this case a half-timbered Basque hotel with two stars. Then it was off with the packs, down with a beer and time for a wander up to the citadel for a view over the town and the surrounding mountains before it got dark. A colony of small hawks whirled excitedly around hunting for insects while the mountains gradually turned black and merged with the sky. In a distant suburb there was a floodlit game of pelote in progress: you could hardly make out the figures of the players, but the whiplash crack of the ball on the wall carried quite clearly through the cold evening. The citadel itself has now become a college, but its impressive fortifications are a reminder that St-Jean isn't just a pretty face, providing a haven for peaceable pilgrims: it's also had a serious military role to play over the centuries.

St-Jean's suffix, *pied-de-port*, means 'at the foot of the pass', and the pass whose approach it guards is one of the most important crossing points in the Pyrenees. Before the advent of tunnels, passable routes through the Pyrenees were few and far between, particularly those that could accommodate an army. The pass of Roncesvalles, at a relatively low altitude, was less likely to be blocked by snow than nearby Somport and therefore a prize worth protecting. This was not such a problem during the early years of the pilgrimage, when St-Jean was comfortably placed at the centre of the independent kingdom of Navarra, which stretched across from Spain well into France.

But, after four centuries of intrigue, dispute and strategic royal marriages St-Jean finally became part of France in 1589, which is when its defensive frailties became evident. In the early seventeenth century, it was described in an official report as 'cowering rather than nestling' at the bottom of the Pyrenees. The ubiquitous military architect Vauban, the brains behind France's powerful system of seventeenth-century fortifications, was brought in to assess the citadel's defences and suggested a number of improvements, which turned it into a defensive stronghold with a permanent garrison.

The citadel is at the top of the Rue de la Citadelle, which was the main artery of the original walled town. Halfway down the steep cobbled street, at number 30, is the *Bureau d'Accueil*, the welcome centre where the pilgrims can get their all-important 'credential'. This document is a passport-cum-record that lists all the refuges and hostels along the Camino where pilgrims can spend the night at a very reasonable cost. As long as the record is stamped and authenticated at churches and refuges along the way, the bearer qualifies for a certificate called a 'Compostela' to mark the achievement of completing the pilgrimage. On top of this, there's the chance of a free meal at Santiago de Compostela's luxurious Parador de los Reyes Católicos. There is a catch, though, as only the first ten arrivals each day are eligible; and, in case the lucky few fancy the chance of making up for those days on the road by eating their way through the menu in the Parador's sumptuous restaurant, I'm afraid that pilgrims are sent to an outbuilding with their food tray.

The pilgrims' reception centre in St-Jean-Pied-de-Port also has a dormitory with accommodation for a small number of people, but only if they're genuine pilgrims who have arrived on foot. So how do you tell a *bona fide* pilgrim from a phoney one? We put the question to a smartly dressed Frenchwoman in her sixties, who was sitting at an official-looking desk. 'By the size of their packs,' she said. 'Genuine pilgrims have to carry a lot of things; and we also keep an eye on the time when they get here.' Hardly relevant, you might think, until she went on to explain that the daily train from Bayonne arrived at 1 p.m., and half an hour later, without fail, groups of dodgy pilgrims who'd let the train take the strain began to turn up.

I can vouch for the fact that the volunteers who staff the centre make sure that its facilities are not wasted on undeserving cases. They have an Internet connection here, and, as St-Jean's only Internet café had apparently closed down, Simon asked if he could log on to check his e-mails, but was politely refused permission.

Another of the voluntary helpers was Alfred, a German from the Bavarian city of Nuremberg. This is a journey of 1,600km from St-Jean, twice the distance remaining between here and Santiago de Compostela. Alfred had walked the whole way a couple of years previously. This year he'd returned, sensibly taking the train, to assist the German- and English-speaking pilgrims with any problems they might have when they get to St-Jean. These were mostly to do with health: visits to the doctor for various ailments, to the chemist to deal with the much-underrated affliction of blisters and even to the vet. Plenty of pilgrims bring their dogs with them, and a number make use of donkeys to do the heavy carrying, in which case it's the donkey that is likely to need attention by the time they arrive in St-Jean-Pied-de-Port.

On the wall of the reception centre were charts filled with details of the pilgrims who'd been welcomed here over the past few years. The numbers have been rising steadily since 2001 when there were 13,799 arrivals; this increased to 17,241 in 2002 and 18,196 the following year. In terms of nationalities, 2003's gold-medal position was occupied by France, the host nation as it were, with 5,892, followed by Germany (2,488) and Spain (2,379). The UK was placed fifth with 604. There was a multiple tie for last place, with Bolivia, Thailand, Turkey, Peru, Bulgaria and Nepal providing one pilgrim each. I wondered what the Nepalese representative thought of Europe's puny peaks. Maybe he or she wouldn't have considered the Pyrenees worthy of the description 'mountains' at all. On the other hand, those from Holland might well have had a bit of a shock in store for them. Wherever they come from, there are rarely more than 350 pilgrims a day, even in summer. In the heyday of the pilgrimage in the twelfth century it would have been around ten times that number.

Also on view was a framed copy of the Pilgrim's blessing:

May the road always rise to meet you,
May the wind always be at your back,
May the sun shine warm upon your face,
The rain fall soft upon your fields,
And until we meet again
May God hold you in the palm of his hand.

There was an unfortunate error in the original typescript, which had rendered the word 'back' as 'beak', and, though this had been corrected afterwards in pencil, it did rather undermine the tone of the otherwise generous and lofty sentiments. I pointed it out to Simon and we struggled unsuccessfully to hold back attacks of schoolboy giggles. And, while we're being childish, that phrase about the road coming up to meet you seems to conjure up the image of falling flat on your face, presumably squashing the aforementioned beak: not at all what the pilgrim ordered.

The bureau was housed in a beautiful building – la Maison Labourde – one of many such houses in the Rue de la Citadelle. They date from the sixteenth century when St-Jean was part of the kingdom of Navarre, and their half-timbered facades, and solid wooden eaves, shutters and balconies gave them the look of stately galleons. They also had very informative lintels, which tell you when the house was built and sometimes who it was built for, and what their job was. The most striking example was at number 32, which was built in 1510 and all of whose wooden features are painted in a deep ox-blood red.

These days number 32 is an art gallery, but lots of its neighbours offered accommodation for pilgrims – presumably the ones who failed the authenticity test to get into the Bureau. Signs in the window announced the following kind of invitation: *CHAMBRES CHEZ L'HABITANT: PELERINS 7 EUROS*, which is a pretty good deal in anyone's currency. One landlord had upped the marketing stakes by displaying a neat installation on his doorstep: it featured a red rucksack, a larger blue one, a staff and a water gourd. Present in all the windows and on all the signs was the image of the scallop shell, the ubiquitous symbol of the pilgrimage.

Simon and I were staying in a hotel that backed on to this delightful street, but which had failed to be influenced by its very economical B&B rates. Still, we had the advantage of a little bar, where we met a group of what you might call modern pilgrims. They were eight Dutchmen, middle-aged or older, and they were cycling to Santiago. They also had a back-up crew in the shape of their wives and partners, who were following them in a couple of minibuses to help deal with punctures or attacks of exhaustion, and would be driving the pilgrims back from Santiago at the end of the trip. Receiving the benefits of this extra support was going to disqualify the group from gaining the prestigious Compostela certificate when they eventually got to Santiago, but that didn't seem to be troubling them unduly as they celebrated their rest day with lager and cigars. This wasn't their first experience of the Camino, as four years previously they'd run to Santiago. But, because they had done so in relays, that didn't count either.

Another guest joined us to report that she and her husband had been for a drive into the mountains and had been forced to turn back by thick snow. We checked her route on a map and found it was exactly where we were planning to walk the next day. Our landlady then joined in the conversation and showed us a photocopied flyer put out by the pilgrims' bureau, strongly discouraging anyone from taking the high-level route and proposing instead a low-level winter alternative, which seemed to run alongside the main road to Roncesvalles. It didn't look much fun, wasn't the genuine article and was hardly in the adventurous tradition of the pilgrimage, but as this was a crucial decision we decided to do the sensible thing and postpone it.

The next morning I was woken by church bells and eagerly listened for the clumping of pilgrims' boots down the Rue de la Citadelle, which my room overlooked. But the only other sounds besides the bells were of rain lashing against the window and someone coughing and sneezing, then swearing. I quite like the discipline of packing a rucksack, trying to get all that stuff into such a small space before realising you've left out the maps or the socks or the hip flask; but it's much more fun taking nearly all of it out and going off for the day with the very, very barest of essentials. Light as feathers, we almost flew down the Rue de la Citadelle and out through the Porte Notre-Dame. On either side of the gatehouse there were stone benches, shiny and worn from use; according to an informative panel on the wall, this is where the poorest pilgrims sat, while they waited for the doors to open so they could find themselves a bed in the hospice that had been built outside the town walls. It was part of a commercial sector which grew up in the seventeenth century to meet the needs of the local populace and the pilgrims: there were cobblers, weavers, goldsmiths, stone-cutters, chocolate makers. In the mid-eighteenth century there were 64 master craftsmen in this quarter of the town and 2,000 soldiers in the garrison.

After a few minutes we reached a crossroads and it was time to take the big decision we'd postponed the day before. A large sign pointed out the options in a no-nonsense and geometrical fashion: there were two arrows at ninety degrees to one another, labelled Route 1 and Route 2. IN CASE OF BAD WEATHER TAKE ROUTE 2 it advised in several languages. As the weather *could* conceivably have been worse we opted for Route 1.

For the first couple of kilometres of the walk there's no shortage of information: not just signs but quite lavish information panels. One of them shows a stylised panorama over St-Jean-Pied-de-Port and the surrounding mountains with an accompanying quotation from the twelfth-century guidebook that is presumed to be the first such book ever written. It's attributed to a certain Aimery Picaud:

In the Basque Country, the way of St James crosses a remarkable mountain called the Ports de Cize. To surmount it, you have eight miles to climb, and the same number again to descend. In fact this mountain is so high

that those who have made the ascent can touch the sky
with their hands.

The Ports de Cize are a sequence of four elevated passes, well
over a thousand metres high, which during the centuries have
seen the passage not just of pilgrims but also of shepherds,
smugglers and soldiers. Roman legions came this way, as did
Napoleon's army. It's hard not to feel the cloak of history
gradually enveloping you as you trudge up the unremarkable
country road from St-Jean.

We spotted a couple of slower-moving walkers ahead and, in
our new jet-propelled incarnation, soon caught up with them.
They weren't pilgrims either but turned out to be a charming
retired couple from St-Nazaire, at the mouth of the river Loire in
northwestern France. They were very fond of the mountainous
landscape, they told us, as it was such a contrast with the flat
terrain around their home. The previous year they'd come here
in early July when unseasonably hot weather had made it hard
to walk after ten o'clock in the morning; this year they'd decided
to come a bit earlier to avoid the heat and had coincided with
this unseasonable spell of late winter weather. We chortled over
ways of saying Sod's Law in French. The appropriate translation
seems to be *la loi de l'emmerdement maximum*, 'the law of
maximum bloody nuisance', which doesn't trip off the tongue
quite like its equivalent.

Farewells were said at a scattering of houses called Honto,
where our friends were staying at a farmhouse B&B, in what
seemed to be the last outpost of civilisation. The rain had
become a thick mist, which was as cold as it was damp. At least
there was no trouble finding the way, which was marked with a
kaleidoscopic array of colours and symbols: blue splodges,
yellow marks, the familiar red-and-white stripes of the GR; and,
of course, the scallop shell symbol, which was carved elegantly
into stout wooden fingerposts.

At one of these we met Felix. If you applied the size-of-pack measure of pilgrim authenticity, he was clearly the genuine article. On his back, sensibly covered with a blue cape, was a rucksack that would have given Simon's a run for its money, and dangling from it was a bedroll. He was peering alternately at a map and the signpost with a furrowed brow and was clearly lost.

We were able to reassure him about the direction and discovered in the process that he was Spanish, from Orense in Galicia, which meant his pilgrimage would be in the nature of a long walk home. Felix was dark, aquiline-featured, about forty years old, and appeared to be a man of very few words. Without any kind of discussion, in a tacit display of solidarity we all set off into the mist together and for the next six hours we were fellow pilgrims on the road to Roncesvalles.

As I speak Spanish and Simon doesn't, I tended to walk next to Felix, who didn't seem to speak any English. Being on the loquacious side myself, I found it odd to be walking alongside a total stranger who didn't want, or feel the need, to talk. I'd rather hoped to discover, for instance, whether this was a religious undertaking for him. There have been many different reasons for doing the pilgrimage. Atoning for grave sins or the chance of receiving a plenary indulgence from the Catholic Church are probably a bit less popular than they were in the Middle Ages, but the spiritual side of the journey is still in evidence: pilgrims tell you that they're hoping to get in touch with their inner selves, that they're getting over the loss of a loved one or maybe doing the walk for charitable purposes. But all I found out from Felix was that, like me, he had two children and that he enjoyed doing the occasional 50km trek, which was a good job as this one would be around 500km.

The road continued to climb and the mist had got thicker; from time to time you'd spot a vague shape, which would only gradually turn into a horse or a tree. Round about lunchtime an authentic miracle occurred, and this after only a couple of hours of pilgrimage: a building loomed up on the right-hand side and we'd almost walked past it before we realised that it was a refuge.

The Refuge-Auberge Orisson was brand new; it had been open for just three days. We draped our very damp waterproofs on hooks specially placed next to the roaring fire, ordered drinks (beer for Felix, coffee for the more wimpish members of the party) and chatted to the proud proprietor. For many years, Jean-Jacques Etchandy had run a bicycle shop in St Jean, which he'd sold in order to realise his lifetime dream of setting up a hostel on the pilgrims' route. As well as the bar and restaurant there were also three bedrooms, each with six bunk beds. He was hoping that the year 2004 would bring him good fortune: it is one of the so-called Holy Years, which occur when the feast day of Santiago (St James) falls on a Sunday; these years are marked by the granting of Plenary Indulgencies and the number of pilgrims increases fivefold as a result.

Meanwhile, without any preliminary comment, Felix had produced a large Spanish roll filled with ham and cheese from his pack, cut it expertly into three pieces and handed two of them to Simon and myself. We had another round of beer and coffees to put off the evil moment of leaving the warm, welcoming refuge. Hanging over us was the threat of the snow up ahead, but no one at the refuge seemed to know how deep it was, or whether we'd be able to find our way through it.

Back on the road, we walked in virtual silence for half an hour; I'd got used to it by now and began to enjoy the basic rhythms of walking: the muffled thump of moulded rubber soles on the tarmac, the sound of our breathing, the clicking of Felix's walking pole. There was an occasional purple orchid in the roadside grass. On one side, the fields sloped away abruptly, suggesting that there would be great views, if only we could see further than five metres. Felix's phone rang; he tersely told someone at the other end that the weather was crap and he was walking with two French people. Then the snow began to appear; at first in patches, then in banks, and by the time we'd reached our first landmark, a roadside shrine surrounded with little tributes and offerings from pilgrims, we were crunching through the stuff.

We reached a critical point, where the path left the road; at least the signpost suggested it should have done, but snow had obliterated all traces of the track that was undoubtedly there, while the mist made it impossible to spot any helpful features in the surrounding landscape. For a few minutes we were very disconcerted, until Felix, who had eagle eyes to match his aquiline nose, spotted a red-and-white mark. Into the white unknown we plunged. The snow was about half a metre deep, mostly, though there were occasional deeper drifts. We had a compass and a good, detailed map (1:25,000) but being a French map it was only interested in the land on this side of the frontier, about halfway to Roncesvalles, after which we would be in alien territory and at the mercy of our own resources and navigational expertise.

The fact that there were three of us was both comforting and extremely useful. Apart from the extra pair of eyes for finding marks and checking directions, there are other reasons why three is company rather than a crowd in these conditions. If, for instance, you're tackling very tricky terrain and need a rope, ice axe and a pair of crampons, the weight of these can be shared out among all of you. If someone falls and breaks a leg, then the second person can go for help while the third stays behind with the casualty. And last but by no means least, if you come to a place where a tricky choice has to be made about which way to go, at least there's the chance of voting on it and reaching a majority decision.

We found traces of boot prints in the snow, which showed that someone else had been this way. At first this was very encouraging, but after a while doubt set in: what if the owner of the boots was completely lost and was leading us towards an unexpected ravine? Were we trudging and slipping to our doom? It was only later we discovered that in the winter of 2002 two lone pilgrims who'd been following this route had died after being caught in blizzards.

We carried on upwards for half an hour, following a kind of gully, which struck us as being the way a sensible path would go, if only it were visible. At least the snow didn't get any deeper and the only brush with disaster was an ironical one when Felix tripped over his helpful walking pole and almost disappeared down a steep bank. He had the bit between his teeth now and was setting a cracking pace, which we only just about managed to match, despite our much lighter loads.

We came to a wood of beech trees, tiny and disfigured at this altitude, with just the hint of buds on the gnarled twigs; 200m lower down, the beeches were in full leaf. In the relative shelter of the trees the snow was beginning to melt and turn into a horrible gluey mud. An unseen bird gave an eerie and repetitive peeping call, the first living thing we'd come across for a couple of hours. At the Fontaine de Roland, which marks the Col de Bentarte (1,240m) we drank icy water and took some team photos. The Roland commemorated by the fountain is the single most famous name in this stretch of the mountains. He was a commander in the army of the emperor Charlemagne that had crossed into Spain to take part in a factional dispute between warring Moorish forces. On his way home, Charlemagne stopped off to plunder the town of Pamplona, and the Basques avenged themselves by ambushing the rearguard of the army as it crossed the Pyrenees. This eighth-century battle would have left little mark on history if it hadn't been for the medieval troubadour who wrote an account of the battle with plenty of poetic licence and more than a twist of 21st-century spin. 'La Chanson de Roland' embroiders in particular the part played by Roland, who of course died heroically defending himself against an enemy that he conveniently changed from Christians into Saracens or Moors, who were followers of the Islamic faith.

The legend of Roland became part of the publicity around the Camino de Santiago and it was exploited by the Catholic Church, in particular that handily inaccurate detail which attributed the ambush to the Moors rather than to those really responsible, the Christian Basques. There is some doubt as to where the attack actually took place and, though some think it might have been up here at Bentarte, it's usually reckoned to have been in the woods around the lower pass of Ibañeta.

Our trail took us uphill for another half-hour to the highest pass of all – la Collada de Lepoeder, which is over 1,400m high. The snow was at its deepest here and a sudden vicious wind got up. It was the only place where we needed to call on the democratic process to decide on the route, as the signposting was ambiguous to say the least. I lost, two against one, and accepted defeat graciously (well, that's how I remember it), and in any case the two routes rejoined after a few minutes, so there was no chance of an 'I told you so' outcome.

From the pass it's downhill all the way to Roncesvalles, through a real beech forest with tall handsome trees. Skis would have been an advantage in the conditions, but I found that a stout branch was nearly as helpful; you could leap down the hillside and use a combination of the snow and the stick to slow you down and make sharp turns. The mist began to disappear as did the snow; in the space vacated, clumps of bluebells appeared and very pretty pyramidal white flowers, which I think were a kind of saxifrage. Felix increased the pace even more and we were almost trotting when the sound of traffic began to intrude and we came out of the forest to find ourselves right behind the vast grey stone complex of religious buildings that is Roncesvalles. It was half-past two and we'd done the whole journey in a very fast time of six hours, though, with full packs and without our doughty pacemaker, I suspect it would have taken us a couple more.

The centrepiece of Roncesvalles is the collegiate church of Santa María, with its impressive cloister, founded early in the thirteenth century by the Navarrese king, Sancho the Strong; there are also a couple of chapels, the residence for pilgrims, a library with a collection of invaluable manuscripts, and a museum whose exhibits include a rather beautiful chess board which is supposed to have belonged to the emperor Charlemagne.

It was the parting of the ways for Felix and us; after handshakes, he disappeared towards the dormitory area reserved for genuine pilgrims. I felt we should have recited the pilgrims' creed, but I couldn't remember it and I'm still not sure about that line in which the road comes up to meet you. The institutional welcome for the pilgrims was muted, to say the least; a sign laid down the rules in no uncertain terms: *SOLO PEREGRINOS CON CREDENCIAL – UNA NOCHE* ('Only pilgrims with a credential – one night') and this was repeated in French and German, but not Nepalese. There was a vast bar, almost completely empty, but a sign on that door warned us *ONLY PILGRIMS, NO TOURISTS* followed by two exclamation marks.

We sat outside La Posada, the inn where the unworthy and nonspiritual *are* allowed, and ate our own ham and tomato rolls, feeling a bit guilty that Felix wasn't there to have his share. I wonder to this day whether his silence might have been due to an overwhelming sense of guilt brought about by some great sin, which he was hoping to expiate through the pilgrimage. But maybe he was just a quiet kind of chap. Light relief came with the appearance of four Americans, dressed for a Florida golf course, who made their way past us into the Posada and came out again two minutes later exclaiming, 'Oh my God, everyone's smoking in there – how can these people allow that?'

It was now raining heavily again, and a couple of bedraggled pilgrims appeared along the main road from St Jean, having obviously taken the boring route. Rain was dripping from their matching grey ponchos and running down their noses – they looked like an illustration from *The Pilgrim's Progress*. A coach bringing a Spanish version of a Saga trip from nearby Pamplona pulled up in the car park, whose great size showed that Roncesvalles was not entirely uninterested in the higher-spending, non-pilgrim sector. We walked past the line of old ladies as they got off the coach and one of them said loudly to her ancient companion, 'Look, dear, pilgrims!' They all smiled sweetly at us and would almost certainly have given us money if we'd been quicker on the uptake.

The choices facing the authentic pilgrim in Roncesvalles are not overtaxing: after your night in the pilgrims' accommodation (only one, don't forget) you just hit the road to Pamplona. But, for part-time pilgrims like ourselves, there are several options – one of them is to walk back into France the very pretty way, starting by heading east on a path towards a place called Fábrica de Orbaizeta, and then finding your way back over the frontier through the Iraty Forest. This had been our original plan, before the late spring snowfall had intervened, but, as most of our possessions were now back at the hotel in St-Jean-Pied-de-Port, that's where we had to go; and since by now it was raining even harder, we weren't going to walk.

The tourist office was open and the very pleasant woman working there seemed delighted to get any custom on such a grim day. Unsurprisingly, there were no buses across the frontier into France; this left taxis, which would have to come from the border village of Valcarlos (fifteen kilometres away). We couldn't help asking her about the weather – was it always this awful in Roncesvalles? Yes, was her candid reply. We all agreed that an umbrella might be a more appropriate symbol for the pilgrimage than a scallop shell.

This was a mobile-phone-free zone, as befits a place where the simple life is paramount, so I went to find a public phone and ring one of the distant taxi operators. Meanwhile, Simon stuck out his thumb and a white van appeared from nowhere and stopped. It was another miracle. We both sprinted towards it and the driver indicated that there was only room for one person. Infused with the selfless spirit of the pilgrimage, Simon offered me the lift. At least, that's what I thought he'd done, and, being extremely cold and fed up, I accepted with alacrity, only realising my mistake when I saw his amazed expression as we drove away.

My saviour was a French fisherman on his way back from a

day trying his luck in the trout streams of Navarre. 'The water's much cleaner in the Spanish rivers than in France,' he said. Even so, melting snow had chilled the water and discouraged the fish from taking his flies, so he'd returned with *nuls poissons*. The road connecting Spain with France twists through the bottom of a valley, following the course of the Nive d'Arnéguy. It wasn't built until 1884, replacing the route which we'd been walking on three hours previously, high on the sheer cliff that now rose spectacularly on our right-hand side. I told the fisherman about our day with some pride. Being a native of these parts, with fifty years of hunting and fishing in the mountains behind him, I'm not sure whether he was particularly impressed, but he did agree that the pass of Lepoeder was particularly treacherous: the southerly wind that had surprised us had apparently blown a pilgrim off the track the previous summer and she'd broken her ankle.

Back in St-Jean, the market was still functioning, though most of the stallholders were beginning to pack up. It featured the usual combination of local food and handicraft-cum-tat that you find in most French markets, but it gained in authentic atmosphere from being arranged alongside the ancient town walls. I was admiring some bright-red Basque berets as possible presents and deciding that I couldn't think of anyone who would be seen dead in one, when a coach pulled up and a single passenger got out. It was Simon, who had hitched a lift back in the empty vehicle when it had dropped its load of pilgrims who were even less authentic than us at the inn in Roncesvalles.

Our early return had given us plenty of time for an evening out in St-Jean. A few years before, on a previous walk, we'd arrived here late in the evening and only had time for a quick drink, but this time we were able to start off in a restaurant recommended by *Le Guide des Routards* – a French guide to cheap and cheerful places to eat, sleep and drink. I was slightly put off the place by its door; actually they were those half-doors, the kind you find in stables to allow you to talk to the animals without them getting out. In this particular case, the main purpose seemed to be to entertain a group of locals, sitting on high stools at the bar, as unsuspecting diners like us made clumsy attempts to get in.

It didn't take much to put things right: in fact, a bottle of Irouléguy from the local vineyard, one of the highest in the Pyrenees. The label calls it robust; actually the taste is earthy to the point that you wonder whether any fruit has ever been near it, but it's just the job when you've been pounding the trail for hours in rain and snow. The food was quite adequate, and we chatted to a couple of pilgrims, Swiss women, who were sharing the trestle table. They were interim pilgrims really, as they'd only just got off the train from Geneva and hadn't started walking yet. They'd certainly come the pretty way – via Paris and Bayonne, like going from London to Cardiff via Edinburgh, but assured us it was the quickest way to do the journey thanks to the great speed of the TGV trains. Their approach to the pilgrimage was quite interesting too – they were going to do it in two-week chunks, picking up where they left off the previous year and arriving in Santiago de Compostela . . . somewhere around the year 2010, I suppose.

The post-dinner entertainment was on the limited side – only one of the town's bars was showing any signs of life at all – and most of the clientele were watching a TV programme about swimming with sharks, off-piste skiing and other such dangerous pastimes. Extreme walking didn't feature, though we both felt we'd done a bit of it that day. One of the locals spoke very good English, which she taught in a local school. She was originally from around here but had moved away to Bordeaux to go to university and then even further away to the north of France in order to get her first teaching job. This has been a pretty typical route for young people to follow, given the lack of career opportunities in the region, outside farming and tourism of course. So why had she come back? 'For the quality of life,' she said. 'The mountains, the sea, the fresh air.' She also felt strongly about the local culture: the ancient Basque songs and dances that, she said, were kept alive by young people. By prevailing European norms, you might expect that the fandango or the Basque whistle would be considered a touch on the uncool side, but that didn't seem to be the case here. She even had a teenage younger brother who was proud of singing in the church choir, and no one seemed to find that odd either.

An important ritual, which often signalled the end of our walking day, was the award of *le con du jour*, the twit of the day. Given our relatively disorganised approach to the business of travelling, as well as our idiosyncrasies, very few days went by without one or other of us – or possibly both – committing an outrageous *faux pas* or making some potentially catastrophic blunder with map or compass. The good thing about the process was it stopped any rancour building up over the long term; on the negative side, if there hadn't been a reckoning for three days, as was the case now, it was quite possible for old wounds to be reopened. On this occasion, there was no doubt about the identity of today's *con*: I proposed myself, seconded by Simon, for getting in the car that he'd flagged down, and taking the only free seat, leaving him open-mouthed and frozen by the roadside in shock at my inconsiderate effrontery. The previous day's winner was also uncontested: Simon – for his attack of vertigo on a path across an awkward rock face, which was admittedly steep but had held no terrors for a group of elderly ramblers from Bayonne.

We walked back to the hotel. The streets were empty and damp, but more welcoming than the English author H.G. Wells had found them a hundred years previously.

St-Jean-Pied-de-Port is a lonely frontier town and at night its deserted streets abound in howling great dogs to whom the belated wayfarer is an occasion for the fiercest demonstrations. I felt like a flitting soul hurrying past Anubis and hesitating at strange misleading turnings on the lonely Pathway of the Dead.

In case you didn't know, and I certainly didn't, Anubis was the Egyptian god responsible for conducting the dead to their final judgement. Wells had come to St-Jean-Pied-de-Port to tend to his friend and fellow writer, George Gissing, who was dying from pneumonia. Maybe this coloured his harsh verdict on what is actually a nice little town.

Four years previously, in July 2000, Simon and I had left St-Jean from the opposite end of town, this time following the GR10. It was mid-July and the weather was appropriately warm, though a few small white clouds were floating in a slightly hazy blue sky. Our aim was to get to Ste-Engrâce, which is a remote village at the easternmost edge of the Basque Country, in two days, breaking the journey at a place called Chalet Pedro, an oasis in the middle of a vast forest.

The first half-hour was a stroll down a country lane to a village called Caro, then there was a bit of a climb until we arrived at a ridge, la Crête d'Handiamendi; the path stayed just below the ridge, and was bordered with gorse bushes, which were decorated with some splendid spiders' webs. This undemanding stretch of walk brought the memorable experience of being able to look down on vultures flying, instead of having to crane your neck and peer up at them as they circle miles overhead. Griffon vultures in military formations would appear like stealth bombers: huge, silent, flying at speed with absolutely no effort, close enough to see their beautiful tawny plumage. After a couple of hours during which all we saw were the vultures, a yellowhammer and a man with a dog, we left the ridge and walked down to a village called Estérençuby.

A convenient auberge provided *une assiette de crudités, une bière* and a very clear stream to lunch beside. This is the life, you're tempted to think, and even a glance at the map, where the word *sommet* (summit) featured for the first time since we'd left the coast, didn't spoil the occasion. This is the walk where I became properly aware of the ups and downs of the GR10. The word *dénivelé* occurs frequently in French walking guides: it tells you how far you have to climb or descend on a given stretch, and it's a better indicator of the time it will take you than simple distance. The *dénivelé* on the next stretch of our walk – from Estérençuby to Chalet Pedro – was in the order of 1,400m going up and 700m down. It's reckoned that a reasonably fit person can do about 350m an hour on an ascent, which suggested that we would be pushed to get to our dinner in Chalet Pedro by the witching hour of half-past seven.

All was fine while the post-lunch glow lasted, but, as the afternoon wore on and the sun got hotter, so the climb got steeper, in reality as well as psychologically. The gentle, grassy hillsides that had characterised the previous Basque stages of the GR10 were now pierced by sharp, angry-looking outcrops of rock. The morning's amiable chatter about the landscape and the weather gave way to terse practical comments about which direction to take or whether there was any more water available, as we concentrated on dragging ourselves and our packs up the slopes. Around teatime, we reached the top of a particularly steep one, only to discover a Tarmac road. I remember feeling quite cheated: you expect to be rewarded for such an expenditure of effort with a particularly fine view and/or the triumphant feeling of having arrived somewhere dauntingly accessible, but a road . . .! This happens quite frequently in the Basque Country, where shepherds have given up the old custom of spending the summers up in high hills with their sheep and now need roads to drive up from their homes in the valley to check on their flocks. Very inconsiderate of them.

This particular road also had a farm beside it, with a sign saying *FROMAGES À VENDRE*, but, tempting as a nice fresh cheese would have been, there was more hill to be conquered and time was marching on – rather quicker than we were. What's more, the morning's small clouds had begun to join forces to become large billowy blobs and they'd changed colour too, from white to grey. It wasn't long before the drizzle started and as we continued our endless ascent the clouds came down to meet us so that by the time we reached the Sommet d'Occabé we could hardly see a hand in front of our faces. We couldn't see the cromlechs, the prehistoric standing stones, and could only guess at the beasts – cows, sheep and *pottöks* – whose bells jangled eerily. Suddenly a huge black witch took to the skies from her perch on a jagged rock right beside the track. When we'd recovered from the fright we decided it was more likely to have been a raven.

By paying careful attention to the guidebook and the compass, we passed round the correct side of the summit and also managed to get through to the Chalet Pedro on a mobile phone to say we were a bit delayed, but on our way. 'We'll keep your rooms till half-past seven,' was the not very comforting response, 'and dinner's at eight!'

The path now entered a beech wood – actually it was the edge of the vast Iraty Forest – and a bit of a poem by Robert Frost got stuck in a loop in my head and fitted itself to the rhythm of our descending footsteps: 'The woods are lovely, dark and deep but I have promises to keep and miles to go before I sleep.' To try and escape from it, I asked Simon what the time was, frequently and, no doubt, irritatingly. This kind of walking is supposed to be relaxing, a chance to escape from the time pressures of urban living, but not in France, when dinner is imminent. 'And miles to go before I sleep, and miles to go before I eat.' We started to take shortcuts across the loops of the path, skidding dangerously through the damp leaves until eventually, at a quarter to eight, we reached flat ground and a clearing where a group of buildings huddled together, smoke rising from chimneys. In one of the outlying huts, our beds were still waiting for us and, in fact, there were no signs of any other travellers at all.

There followed the curious incident of the shower. This was in another hut, requiring a rapid traverse with towel across open ground, before a welcome encounter with a stream of hot water. My turn passed uneventfully, but Simon came back to report that he'd been interrupted by a knocking on the door and someone who claimed to be the chef, shouting, 'Hurry up, Monsieur. Dinner is ready; come now or you will miss it.' We never managed to confirm if this was the chef, a joker or an admirer hoping to get a glimpse of Simon in the altogether. But strange things can happen in the forest.

After dinner we talked to the owner of this oasis. Isabel – vivacious, late twenties, single – seemed an unlikely candidate for such a job. She'd taken over the business from her father, who'd bought it in the 1960s when it was a hunting lodge. Now it was more of a destination for ramblers and day-trippers. Isabel herself was passionately interested in nature, as you'd need to be if you lived here, and her particular love was for the vultures, for the effortless ease of their flight, she said, and, rather more worryingly, because of the fine job they did cleaning up the corpses on the mountainsides.

The next day was 14 July – Bastille Day – and the unofficial opening of the French holiday season. It was pouring with rain. I can't remember having got so wet on the way *to* breakfast before; the hundred yards between the hut and the restaurant was enough for a thorough drenching and for the rest of the day we remained soaked through. If the weather was bad news for us, with a twelve-hour walk ahead, it was even worse for Isabel, as this was a bank holiday on which people would, in theory, come out in large numbers to enjoy a walk in the forest and lunch at her restaurant. A wonderful aroma of vanilla and almond wafted from the kitchen as dozens of Basque cakes baked in the oven. But would there be anyone to eat them?

We splashed away from Chalet Pedro through large puddles, ready for the first climb of the morning. It was a forest stage, so at least the massive beech trees provided protection from the rain. Iraty Forest is thought to be the largest broadleaved forest in Western Europe, though only 2,300 of the 17,000 hectares are on the French side of the frontier, the Spanish majority being wilder and, in the main, less exploited. After a couple of hours we emerged from the forest onto a grassy hilltop. It was high enough to be in the cloud rather than underneath it, which meant that interest was provided by the guess-the-shape game as objects appeared indistinctly in the thick mist. The large triangular things turned out to be wooden chalets. These are holiday homes rented in summer and also during the winter, when they're used by skiers at the nearby resort of Chalets d'Iraty, and this was the next thing to loom in front of us.

Ugly and purpose-built it may have been, but there was a café with a scorching fire and hot vegetable soup – *garbure* – both of which we took full advantage of. We met a couple with a baby who were walking the GR10 weighed down by a tent, the baby (obviously) and a vast rucksack filled with nappies. They'd actually been staying in the nearby *gîte d'étape* and told us they'd been very impressed with its state-of-the-art fittings; mind you, anything would seem good compared with a night in a tent in the rain with a baby.

Dragging ourselves away from the fire, we resumed the journey. Just after Iraty there's a choice of paths to the next place, Logibar: the pretty way across the hilltops or the ugly one, which more or less follows the road. The French *topoguide* to the GR10 has a warning for anyone choosing the former route.

You are reminded that passing or stopping by the shooting platforms when they're occupied during the wood-pigeon hunting season in October and November can present certain dangers for walkers.

It's no accident that the hunting season coincides with the autumn migration season. Birds, like humans, make use of mountain passes to cross the Pyrenees: as Simon has pointed out, it saves them from having to gain extra height during their exhausting flight to warmer countries. French hunters take full advantage of this to wreak havoc, in particular, on the flocks of migrating wood pigeons; but here at least they don't have it entirely their own way.

A short distance from the ski resort of Chalets d'Iraty is a pass called the Col d'Orgambidexca. It's the most important crossing point in the Pyrenees for birds, particularly birds of prey, and since 1979 this pass has been rented during the migration season by members of an environmental group called Col Libre, who observe and count the migrating birds, in order to monitor the health of their populations. They also lead campaigns to try and reduce the scale of the hunting of wood pigeon, nearly two million of which are shot or caught in nets every year in the southwest of France. Jean-Paul Urcun of Col Libre told us that the task was an uphill one in a region where the traditional approach to wildlife was summed up in this homely saying:

Tout ce qui vole, au casserole,
tout ce qui court, au four.
(If it flies, into the pan,
If if runs, into the oven.)

This was neither the weather nor the time of year for migration or hunting. As we walked down the series of hairpin bends we did at least see a yellowhammer sitting on a gorse bush; a camper van came by and I'm sorry to say we stuck out our thumbs and I'm glad to say that it stopped. The young family were returning to the inn at Logibar as one of their little daughters had left a sandal there the previous day – a case of an ill wind blowing us a bit of good. The father was a keen bird-watcher and we were able to establish that the yellowhammer is called *un bruant jaune* in French, though its characteristic song, 'a-little-bit-of-bread-and-no-cheese', does not apparently translate into *un bout de baguette et pas de fromage*. This is a shame, but the whole concept of bread without cheese is probably incomprehensible to a French ornithologist in any case.

The lift was handy as we were behind schedule for an early-evening arrival in Ste-Engrâce and once again there was the looming threat of being late for supper and the chance that we'd be the ones getting the little bit of bread and no cheese. Beyond Logibar, the GR10 really takes to the hills, but first there was the climb out of the valley, through a forest, with the rain showing no sign of letting up.

After an hour or so we met a couple of young women from Bayonne and discussed the foul weather with them – *temps pourri* was their description. They had had enough, and were walking back down to Logibar to get their car and return to their campsite at Ste-Engrâce, which was our destination as well. They offered to take us there; reluctantly but heroically we said 'No, thanks' and squelched onwards. At the next pass a sign read: STE-ENGRÂCE 7H. It was now one-thirty and I don't know about Simon, but I was already regretting the decision about the lift.

In the Basque Country, you rarely seem to get higher than the sheep. We were on a plateau, walking along a dirt road, and on the adjoining hillside a vast flock was being expertly marshalled by a couple of border collies. It would have been nice if they'd been Pyrenean mountain dogs but, as the shepherd explained, since in this part of the mountains there are no large predators like bears to be scared off, the smaller, more agile collies are more useful. They were obviously intelligent enough to have learned Basque and responded instantly to the shepherd's shouted commands. Twenty years ago this shepherd would have spent all the summer up here in his hut – tending the sheep, milking the ewes and making cheese. Now he commutes to work by car from his farm in the valley and the milk is taken away by tanker to be turned into cheese in a dairy.

My abiding memory of the next four hours is of total all-pervading wetness. The rain undertook a searching examination of us and of our equipment, most of which was found wanting. We'd had the forethought to put rubber waterproof bags inside our rucksacks, which kept essential clothes dry, but anything not protected by this was gradually and completely soaked; maps suffered particularly badly in one of the outside pockets and my mobile phone, inside my supposedly 'waterproof' jacket, developed some strange digital pneumonia in which the numbers dripped down the screen like the opening titles of the film *The Matrix*, before it finally died. This was particularly unfortunate as we looked destined for another late arrival, and a call would almost certainly have lessened the risk of us losing our place at the *gîte d'étape*. The descent from the hilltops towards Ste-Engrâce is down a sequence of sunken lanes, which on another day would, I'm sure, have been enjoyable and relaxing. Unfortunately the lanes had become a series of streams, knee high in some places, and we had no alternative but to paddle through them; the experience was not one I'd particularly want to repeat.

It was eight o'clock in the evening when we slithered down the last of these watery channels and emerged like newts onto a Tarmacked road, beside a sign announcing STE-ENGRÂCE. The bad news was that we'd happened on one of the longest villages in Europe and there were still three kilometres to go to reach our accommodation in the centre. There was good news, though, in the shape of an unvandalised and functioning public phone-box and, when we rang to announce our impending arrival, the landlady said she'd send one of her sons to pick us up. Opposite the phone-box was one of the great attractions in this part of the Pyrenees. The Gorges de Kakouetta were formed by a river slicing down through its limestone bed to form a narrow rift, whose vertical cliff walls are in parts over 300m high but only a few metres apart. Inside the gorge, the relative warmth and the damp from the waterfalls has allegedly created a virtual rainforest; we had to take their word for it, because we were too wet for tourism and anyway, at eight o'clock in the evening, the gorges were closed.

Ste-Engrâce is a sequence of three hamlets – a straggle of three hamlets would be a more accurate description. We passed a hotel that was closed, and a scattering of houses and farms. Its heart is provided by the church, the auberge and its neighbouring *gîte d'étape*, and, unlike anywhere else we'd been for some days, both auberge and gîte were throbbing with activity. The gîte was a large converted barn, with a unisex dormitory and a kitchen–dining area with a fearsome stove. A group of cave-divers was stripping off their wetsuits and hanging them on a guard in front of it; a couple of French women were conjuring a lavish meal for their families from two electric rings, and as for us, after a pit stop that Michael Schumacher would have envied, we were out of our wet clothes, into dry ones and making a dash through the continuing rain to the inn's restaurant.

The last thing you need after twelve hours of walking in the rain is to have to make any decisions about food and drink, and there was no such problem at the auberge: water and red wine appeared seconds after we sat down, and they were followed at regular intervals by plates of food. I remember in particular a large pot of excellent *garbure*, a great slab of home-made pâté and a plate of wonderful ewe's-milk cheese.

Our table was in the bar, as the restaurant upstairs was occupied by a group celebrating a birthday, so, when the dishes stopped arriving, we got up and joined a jolly and motley collection of drinkers at the bar. Some of those present were walkers: a British couple were describing the dreadful time they'd been having on the high-level route, the HRP, which is not waymarked; they'd spent the first three days being almost permanently lost, they said, and so they'd found themselves a guide, who'd got lost as well. This was an atypical experience, however; despite the bad weather, everyone else seemed to have enjoyed themselves, including a French photographer from Bordeaux called Yannick, who was also walking the HRP. A couple of years previously he'd been sent to take photos for a French magazine feature on the life of a Pyrenean shepherd. The experience had so captivated him that he'd decided to traverse the mountains on his own. English football fans would have been amazed at the facial similarity between Yannick and London football's combative midfield player Dennis Wise.

Back in the gîte, the cave-divers' wetsuits were steaming gently in front of the fire everyone else seemed to have gone to bed and we had to stumble blindly to our own bunks. I was sandwiched between Simon and one of the cordon bleu cooks; it was extremely hot. In the small hours an alarm went off close by, waking me as well as some of the others. I was then amazed to see Simon get up, get dressed and go out. Was he sleepwalking? About an hour and a half later he came back and I had to restrain my curiosity and irritation till the morning proper.

'Sorry, I meant to tell you; I do this interview for Radio 2's early-morning show on Saturdays and I had to go down to the phone-box.'

'You mean the one right down by the Gorges?'

'Yes, but it wasn't raining; it was a nice walk.'

Hmm. I made one mental note not to share a room with Simon again and another one to seek an order banning him from all communal sleeping quarters, with immediate effect.

The next morning, no one except me seemed at all put out by Simon's nocturnal wanderings. While struggling, unsuccessfully, to get dressed with a modicum of decency, I noticed that the French women who'd been cooking in such an unhassled way the previous day seemed equally unfazed by the demands of staying glamorous and decent in a crowded communal setting. Is it part of their school curriculum?

We delayed our departure to have a look around the church, which dominates the village from its position on a slight plateau. From the outside, against a grey sky, it looks squat, forbidding and a bit lopsided, but concealed within are some authentic architectural wonders from the twelfth century. The tops of the supporting columns are decorated with *chapiteaux romanes* – sculpted Romanesque capitals. There are a dozen of them, featuring small groups of animals and people, whose oversized heads and exaggerated features make them look rather like the puppets from the TV show *Spitting Image*. Among the varied scenes are groups of musicians, hunters and a Nativity in which the three Wise Men seem to have caught an early train and arrived in time for the birth of Jesus. The best known of the decorated capitals is, unsurprisingly, the sexy one, which shows King Solomon and the Queen of Sheba very erotically entwined. An animal, obviously an elephant, which has transported the queen to her rendezvous, sports a ridiculously long tongue in place of a trunk, presumably because the sculptor had never seen a picture of the original beast.

Sainte-Engrâce, whose name the church bears, was a Christian martyr and her story dates back to 300 BC, during the reign of the Roman emperor, Diocletian. A native of Braga in Lusitania, now northern Portugal, she was on her way across Spain to be married to a Christian noble in Roman Gaul when her party was attacked near Zaragoza. Eighteen of her relatives were killed, as was Engrâce, whose body was hideously abused. How her sanctified name then came to be attached to this isolated mountain church is open to question, but the legendary events surrounding it include a severed arm filled with precious jewels, a bull with glowing horns that knelt down each day at a hollow oak tree by a fountain and other such storylines that would not have been out of place in the *Lord of the Rings*.

Ste-Engrâce, the village, is at the very limit of the French Basque Country and until recently it really was the end of the road; it was only in 1987 that a new road was built, connecting Ste-Engrâce with St-Martin, in the next valley to the east. This is also the most remote of the three French Basque provinces – La Soule – which has its own dialect of the Basque language, and where ancient customs have survived in their most undiluted forms. The tradition of the Pastorale, once widespread in rural Europe, is still strong here; whole villages take part in these open-air plays that combine age-old plots of good against evil with contemporary local stories.

Back at the bar of the auberge, a newspaper headline displayed a reminder of current Basque politics and concerns. A car bomb had exploded in Madrid's Puerta del Sol, right in the heart of the city. As it was early in the morning the casualties were limited: eight people had been injured. The Basque separatist group ETA had claimed responsibility. The locals we spoke to in Ste-Engrâce denied having any sympathy for ETA. They told us that unemployment was the issue of greatest interest, particularly for young women like Sylvie who was working in the bar at the auberge. Not attracted by the prospect of a job in agriculture or in one of the few modern firms that had replaced the decaying espadrille-making industry, she felt she'd have to leave the mountains and go off, against her will, to Pau, Toulouse or one of the other non-Basque cities on the plain.

The weather had improved slightly. At least the mist had disappeared, which was important for walkers, as the next stage of the GR10 comes with a weather warning: it is only too easy to lose your way when visibility is bad, unless you're very good with a compass, which might have put us at some risk, I reckon. Move on four years, and we were here again, setting out for la Pierre-St-Martin, a stone in the middle of a pass between France and Spain.

4. ON THE EDGE: CROSSING THE BÉARN

Simon Calder

When you leave Ste-Engrâce on the GR10, you're faced with the usual stiff climb – and a change of territories. The first quarter of the Pyrenean walk, and the first three of our chapters, have covered the Basque Country; now we cross into the ancient kingdom of the Béarn. Celebrated in the gastronomic world for its *sauce béarnaise*, the Béarn has had close links with Britain ever since a number of Wellington's soldiers settled here after their successful campaign against Napoleon's forces. By the second half of the nineteenth century, one in six of the residents of the main city, Pau, was British. The railway arrived in 1866, and with it the usual consignment of writers and intellectuals seeking relaxation and inspiration; Pau's position, on a bluff above the Gave de Pau river, provided a fine vista of the mountains for those who were not up to walking through them.

The Pyrenees started to form about eighty million years ago, when the Iberian tectonic plate collided with the European plate and was subducted – forced under it. About forty million years ago, the Bay of Biscay began to expand, creating the pressure that lifted the earth's crust and layers of sediment. The process began at the Mediterranean end of the chain, where the rock is granite and gneiss. On the western side, where we were, the main layers of rock at lower levels are limestone, while the peaks are of granite. This is highly resistant to erosion, so the view from Pau should endure for eons, and the Boulevard des Pyrénées is the ideal place to enjoy it.

Our own experience of the mountainous parts of the region, the Haut-Béarn, was fairly brief but included a walk through one of the weirdest stretches of landscape I've seen and then confronted me with a challenge I had been dreading for months, an encounter with the terrifying cliff path, *le Chemin de la Mâture*. In fact, it's only when you leave the Basque Country that the Pyrenees begin to show that they are a serious chain of mountains. The first major pass, or col, after Ste-Engrâce is at a height of 1,760m. This is nearly twice the height of La Rhune, which looked such a mountain in the context of the Basque Country but here was a mere pimple. The Col de la Pierre-St-Martin is an unlikely high-level crossroads. The highway from Pamplona, the road from Pau, the international frontier, the GR10 *and* the HRP converge at a broad, open area which has been colonised by a car park, so the col has become a favourite starting point for day hikes. No barrier marks the frontier, but a triangular concrete pillar proclaims 'E' on the face that looks out over the misty valleys of Spain and 'F' on the side leading to a mountainside that looks freshly skinned. Look more closely and you might spot a smaller tablet of stone, poking out of the ground at an oblique angle.

Archaeologists a millennium from now should be intrigued, just as we were, by the symbols etched in it with less-than-total geometric accuracy: a simple cross at the top; the word *PIEDRA* (stone); another line reading *STMAR*; and the conclusion *TIN1858*. The map proves more help: this is evidently the famous stone that marks the site of one of the more curious and enduring traditions of the Pyrenees.

On a sunny early evening, the col presents views that could be of two different planets, not merely countries. For once, Spain's side of the frontier looks much more enticing than France: seductive green folds, rather than a gaunt, bare valley. In the fourteenth century, herdsmen from north of the divide wanted, understandably, to graze their cattle on the grassy, southern side. Farmers on the Spanish side were understandably reluctant to let them, until they were offered a tribute of three cows each year for the privilege. The livestock was handed over each 13 July amid much ceremony. Today, the ritual continues, though the cows are brought up by truck and return whence they came, while the ceremony is accompanied by much razzmatazz and plenty of partying, with onlookers and tourists significantly out-numbering the farmers.

The cash crop of the 21st century is all too visible in the valley on the French side. It looks as though some cataclysmic event has occurred – the event being tourism.

To the south, the ski resort below the col, on the French side, has the appealing name of Arette-la Pierre-St-Martin. That is where the appeal stops. It could conceivably look attractive under a heavy cloak of snow, but summer reveals a ski resort in all its ugly nudity. The land has been stripped of its trees, its foliage and its decency. In their place stands a ghostly collection of machinery for lifting people and their skis, plus the inevitable ski-slope suburbia such as military-looking snow-making machines and sad little huts for employees to shelter in when checking the lift passes of skiers.

They may not be employed much longer. The resort has suffered a series of poor snowfalls and higher-than-average temperature. Natural snow can be augmented by the synthesised variety, but if the prevailing temperature is too high then the white stuff turns grey and slushy – as does a resort's reputation. Arette-la Pierre-St-Martin has a mix of skiing customers. Some own or rent apartments in the awesomely ugly blocks in the valley; others drive up from Bayonne or Biarritz or even Bordeaux for the day or weekend; but many are, or were, package holiday-makers from northern Europe. And, in the relatively small world of skiing, views about a resort's potential spread rapidly. Climate change may mean that the geology that makes the western Pyrenees such excellent walking territory renders it inadequate for skiers and snowboarders.

Perhaps the resort of Arette-la Pierre-St-Martin should change its name (its acronym approximates to Alps) or change its focus, and pay more attention to its summer clients. Mick and I grumbled about the mess that summer revealed at ski resorts, as we half-skipped, half-stumbled down the hillside with the temperature sinking as quickly as the sun. Following the precise course of the GR10 – rigorously adhering to a track littered with ski-season detritus – was dreary and time-consuming, putting an extra half-hour between us and a bottle of beer.

The drink in question is a Basque brew, the label in red and green, the flavour much more bitter and intense than the average French lager – perhaps like some Basques themselves. We had learned about the possibility of refreshment in an oblique and curious reference from our guidebook. 'Be slightly wary,' it warns, 'of false hospitality. Being offered a cold drink as you collapse on to the bench outside isn't just a show of spontaneous generosity: you'll be charged for it when you leave.'

Sure enough, as we collapsed onto the bench outside and began the sorry business of untangling our feet from our boots and the most unsavoury socks north of Burkina Faso, Jean Hourticq appeared on cue with an invitation for refreshment. Not being from the universe where hikers are welcomed at the end of each day with free beer, we weren't at all unhappy with the notion of paying for our drinks. If this was false hospitality, let's have more of it.

The little, nineteen-bed Pyrenean universe that M. Hourticq runs may not boast complimentary *consommations*, but it is the kind of place that instantly relieves the pain and weariness of a long day's walk. A handsome wooden chalet, it stands aloof from the gloomy structures that comprise the ski resort. It has what, in more proprietorial circumstances, would be termed a front garden, which merges with the grassy hillside. On this have been planted a range of brightly coloured tents for those who decline the comfort of a more permanent structure.

I was surprised Mick didn't bid for a berth in one of them, since he has a curious craving for life under canvas. We once set off for darkest Peru, where refuges – like everything else – are in short supply. We, or more accurately I, carried a borrowed tent that, for reasons that escape me, we had not checked before we flew to South America. Only as night fell several thousand metres up in the Andes did we discover that the tent had not been dried before being packed after its last outing, and was in an advanced state of decomposition. Furthermore, it was several tent pegs short of an effective erection. But, making do is part of life in the mountains, as demonstrated by the writer and explorer Hilary Bradt: on her first trekking expedition to Ecuador, all her equipment was stolen on the first day in Quito and she camped her way around South America using a tent fashioned from a shower curtain. Anyway, after many miserable nights we found ourselves in a village where a new school building had just been completed, and in which we were welcome to stay. Mick insisted, though, on pitching the tent in the middle of an Amazonian-scale rainstorm while I bedded down near the blackboard.

On this occasion, with characteristic unpredictability, Mick declared 'Good job we've booked places inside – looks like rain.' Indeed, after a long, hot, humid day, the Pyrenean clouds were clearly cooking up something dramatic for sunset. But the small population of tent city went about their ablutions and laundry with the quiet confidence of those who have not borrowed a mate's old tent that he probably got in a Millets sale circa 1970. We placed our boots in the pigeonholes in the porch, and went inside to evaluate our new refugee status.

'Convivial' is an overused word in brochures and guidebooks, but wholly appropriate for the Refuge Jeandel. The permanent residents appeared to number five: M. and Mme Hourticq, plus three polite and strapping children who could no doubt clear a couple of cols before breakfast. In addition, there appeared to be some family friends staying, along with a dozen hikers, all of whom were chatty and forthcoming.

It was easy to understand why. Hiking, even in company, can be a solitary experience: Mick and I seemed rarely to be in conversational range when walking, because there was always some good reason why one of us was unable to make progress at a sensible speed. But at least we could talk, or curse, or grunt monosyllabically when resting and at the start and end of each day. Some of the solo walkers who we met in the mountains proved extremely talkative, through simple craving for human company.

At the Refuge Jeandel, conversation flowed as easily as the Basque beer and brusque red wine. A hubbub of English and French reverberated along a table that stretched almost the length of the building. The guest list for 4 July 2004 was about evenly split between British and French, with the surprise guest addition of an American couple. They were from Chicago, and made a habit of walking in France rather than the US. Given the way that American visitor numbers to Europe have dwindled in the past few years, I was intrigued why they should spend a fortune – and their precious two-week annual vacation – walking through a region that, scenically, was easily matched by the mountains in one of America's National Parks.

'Sure, it's beautiful, and you can wander for weeks without seeing a soul. But there's nowhere like this, where you can come down from the mountains and find a place to stay and eat.' That wasn't the reason why villages first grew up in the valleys of the Béarn. They early settlers ventured further and further upstream, balancing the advantage of access to land with the adversity of coaxing a living from increasingly unyielding terrain (as the ski industry was having to do). When France industrialised, the attractions of the city – jobs, homes, culture and climate – drew many downstream away from the valley. This story is repeated in valleys all the way along the Pyrenees.

Happily, we were playing a small part in bringing life back to the valley. The bunch that was gathered around a table on America's Independence Day represented a 21st-century solution of sorts for the valleys. 'Eco-hotels' are typically located on coasts or in jungles accessible only by long flights and long drives in 4x4s. Sustainable tourism does not reside in such places; instead, you need to look to the valleys of the Pyrenees, where farmhouses are augmented by low-impact buildings like the Refuge Jeandel. No roads need to be built: almost everyone walks in, and walks out.

You may have spotted a logical inconsistency hovering like a griffon vulture over this self-congratulation. None of us had walked from our home towns. The American couple had taken a series of three flights to cross the Atlantic, and the rest of us had hopped in on low-cost airlines. Indeed, at one end of the table a conversation was taking place of the kind that has replaced house prices at middle-class dinner parties in London: how little each had paid for the Ryanair flight to the Pyrenees.

Low-cost flights are partly so cheap because no tax is paid on aviation fuel. Regional governments recognise the economic benefits of access to a rich travel market such as southeast England, and subsidise airlines to fly in. As a result, Mick and I are among millions who fly frivolously. Some say that the increase in flying is contributing to global warming, and will detect a link to the sinking fortunes of the ski resort just below the refuge. But lower down the valley, there are few doubts about how radically the Irish no-frills airline has transformed the region. Pau is the commercial and cultural hub for the valleys in this stretch of the mountains, and has been a destination for Ryanair since 2003. The traffic is almost all one-way, reported the latest edition of *Pyrénées* magazine.

A storm was looming over Arette-la Pierre-St-Martin. The few boots and socks still outside the refuge were brought safely inside as supper began. The general atmosphere at the refuge was of a jolly, if authoritarian, holiday camp. M. Hourticq brought out a series of serving dishes and instructed us as to how many pieces of meat we could have, and how much bread. In case the English contingent hadn't understood, a charming French walker called Claire was called on to translate the message and make sure we didn't overdo it. In fact there was bags of food. We were offered seconds, thirds and even fourths of soup and tagliatelli. The host's genial and eccentric disposition was welcomed by most of the refugees, except a couple of Frenchmen at the end of the table who, after a couple of carafes of the local red, made no secret of the fact that they found him something of a pain. They'd clearly not got over their own welcome, when alongside the offer of the not-free beer, they'd been told, 'We do have ash-trays here, you know', as they stubbed out post-walk cigarettes on the porch of the refuge.

By now even the cruellest of the day's ascents or descents had mellowed into a valuable experience or mutated into an implausible story as we shared our common affection for the mountains. I was sitting next to a father and son team who were doing the whole GR10. Dad was an extrovert who was not ashamed of his very ropy French, leaving his 18-year-old son to be quietly embarrassed for both of them.

A man in his early 50s turned out to be a teacher from the school where David Beckham had 'studied', which made him an immediate celebrity. For years, he (the teacher, not the footballer) had nurtured a dream to walk the length of the HRP and had finally decided that this was the summer. Nearby, a huddle of Londoners were discussing ways of generating some euros, because the ski-resort cash machine had not been refilled since the last snows melted. The standard technique employed by travellers with a cash-flow crisis is as follows. You identify a restaurant popular with rich tourists, ideally American. They are the nationality most likely to take large, expensive meals. The traveller waits until the group is about to settle up, and explains his or her predicament and the solution: that he or she would like to pay with a credit card, and that only after the payment has successfully been transacted will they collect the cash. This strategy would not work on a Sunday evening high in the western Pyrenees – strictly a cash society. Various denominations of sterling, dollar and euro notes circulated the table until a suitable fiscal solution was reached.

'Portugaaaaal!' Time to settle down to watch the final of Euro 2004, enlivened by a French guest temporarily adopting the nationality of the home team. Their opponents were Greece. I would not normally pass an evening watching a football match between two minor southern European nations. The last time I saw such a team play in the flesh was at Wembley, when England trounced Albania 4–1 in a World Cup qualifier. It was a dreary game in which the biggest cheers were for the Albanians' single goal, and for the banner my parents had impressively made reading 'Crawley Town FC salutes Albania'.

The Béarn has a similar size, terrain and individuality to Albania, without the wanton internecine violence. Albania v. Basque Country: now that's a game I'd watch. But on this occasion I chose not to stay and cheer for either team. Since my excuses would not have been heard, I did not bother giving any, and wandered down to the ski resort. OK, I admit it, I had a phone interview with BBC World Service about the new generation of long-haul aircraft and their effect on the environment. To prepare for it, I needed to find a telephone. And that involved going into the strange world of the ski village, Arette-la Pierre-St-Martin.

The neutron bomb was big in the 1980s. Its specialist subject was to destroy human beings and other animals, while keeping buildings intact. Arrete la Pierre St-Martin had evidently been the test bed for the weapon.

Once upon a time, when it opened in the 1970s, this labyrinth must have gleamed when the late afternoon sun crept over the mountains. The main body of the resort is an implausibly long apartment building that, with the patina of age, looked as sad as a rusting limousine. Yet it was not completely derelict and redundant. Indeed, absurdly jolly music trickled out of loudspeakers all the way along the commercial corridor, a space as endless as the typical GR10 climb. Just two of the enterprises were open, though: an Indian restaurant with a diner population of zero and a mock-Mexican café, population three.

The tremendous din emanating from the barren bar was due to the television being turned up to the threshold of pain for the football commentary.

Between roars, I talked to a couple of students from Bristol University who were conscientiously making their way across the Pyrenees a week or two at a time, and clearly with more determination to proceed in a logical manner than me and Mick. Being students, they were having to do this on the cheap, which is why they had negotiated with the bar owner to pitch their tent outside his premises in exchange for some custom during the evening, rather than stay up at the refuge where a nominal charge was levied for camping.

That absurdly jolly music rendered all the phones in the commercial corridor unusable for broadcasts, so I ended up talking to the World Service from a payphone in an underground car park. Yes, the new A380 aircraft – assembled just along the Pyrenees and up a bit at Toulouse – was more fuel-efficient than other aircraft, but aviation as a whole would need one-quarter fewer air movements for the same number of travellers if only airlines would fill every seat on board. Which would only be a good thing for the planet.

As I climbed the hill back to the refuge, the first drops of rain the size of ripe Irouléguy grapes splashed down. I crept back into the now-silent refuge (Portugal having lost) in a hopeless attempt to avoid disturbing the inhabitants. A design fault with every *gîte d'étape* and refuge I have stayed in is their propensity to creak at the slightest movement. I squeaked and graunched upstairs and into the four-bedded dorm that M. Hourticq had kindly assigned to just the two of us.

Talking about the walking you've done is often a lot more fun than actually putting on yesterday's socks and boots and putting one foot in front of the other. Breakfast was a much more sombre occasion than dinner had been, with everyone quietly preparing themselves for the next stage of the journey. There was another reason for the subdued atmosphere: a mild, generalised hangover I had contributed to quite unwittingly.

Outside, the camping contingent resembled those terrible images of Bangladeshi flood victims surveying the latest deluge. Inside, the endless resupplies of supper were not repeated the morning after, and I chewed the last crumbs of bread knowing that our food supplies were poor. Then *Madame* totted up the damage. I still have a copy of the bill, which appeared to involve Mick buying everyone in the gîte a drink during the second half of the match. We operate on a strict pooling policy, whereby every expense is split down the middle; so I had shared the round, without knowing it. But, in the accounts of gallantry, Mick was soon to be in credit.

The next leg of the GR10's eastward journey begins dismally: a gravel track winds up something approximating to a skier's green run, and gets tangled with the skiing equipment. And then you arrive at the moon, or at least the closest thing to it in this part of Europe. Karst country is limestone landscape that has been partially dissolved and distorted by brutal weather of the sort that had battered the campers overnight.

You can find similar landscapes in the Burren of western Ireland and in the former Yugoslav republic of Slovenia. And, as with those locations, the karst country in the Pyrenees is riddled with holes. Just across the Spanish side of the frontier above us was one of the biggest caves in the world. The Gouffre de la Pierre-St-Martin was discovered only in 1950, on an expedition organised by the legendary French caver, Norbert Casteret. One of the chambers is vast enough to hold a fleet of Airbus A380s – it measures 270m by 230m by 180m. By all accounts it is a magnificent, though treacherous cave system.

On the surface, the eroded limestone was giving us problems. It resembled a freshly fried popadum in texture, perforated randomly with holes. You can imagine how difficult and dangerous it would be in snow, or even a thick mist.

The GR10 leads a tricky course across and around the chasms, with an occasional waymark painted on the few trees that manage to scrounge a ragged existence on the fringes of the limestone. Despite the surface being mostly level, it also proved some of the most stressful walking on the trip. Suggesting that every step could be your last is an exaggeration, but you have to stare down at the ground and concentrate at every moment rather than let your mind wander to the surroundings and beyond.

At this point, the city-dweller becomes closely acquainted with the concept of the cairn – the world's oldest and simplest form of waymarking. On an otherwise featureless spread of crazy paving, some good soul has painstakingly piled up small stones to form a series of rough cones. They are just high enough to catch the eye in a sea of stone, and to lead you across difficult terrain. I like to think that I was following a trail laid centuries ago, but in fact I was following Mick rather than the cairns. Being second has many advantages, not least that your partner will provide an early indication of any threats with a verbal warning, or by falling over, or by sinking without trace. We both survived.

At the end of the giant sieve section, the GR10 climbs to a bare shoulder of rock that turns out to bear yet another array of ski-machinery blight. It then bears south to hug the bottom of a cliff face – better, in my view, than teetering along the top of one. The path then scissors its way up what looks like a continuation of the same cliff face, which struck me as silly, because paths don't go up cliff faces, do they?

The last six metres or so was a breathless scramble up it – the closest the GR10 gets to rock-climbing in its entire course. This was to reach a *pas*. Until this point, I had wondered how this term differed in meaning from *col*. As I looked up at a ridge that sharpened to a point, it was about to become painfully clear. A *pas* seems to be a notch in a knifelike spur of rock, and describes the only place at which it is, at least in theory, possible to cross.

I could still climb but, on reaching the ridge and the equally precipitous drop on the other side, I froze.

Mick saw my expression of fright, sighed and offered to take my pack down the tricky part – but not before sipping some water, and drinking in the staggering view that awaited us. The Pic d'Anie, a majestic molar of a mountain, is the first 2,500m peak you reach from the Atlantic. Mick had suggested a side trip to the top, on which I had been noncommittal. Several reasons militated against such a plan, not least our lack of food – our supplies of muesli bars and dried apricots were running short.

The nineteenth-century writer Frank Tatchell suggests you should 'chew pieces of your boots' when lost. There would be nothing left of mine. But Mr Tatchell's advice is not necessarily to be followed rigidly nowadays; he also notes that 'on the Continent, poor men only get shaved on Saturday', and, if confronted by a brigand, you should 'finger an imaginary revolver in your hip pocket'.

I had no gun in my pocket, just my heart in my mouth as I slid down from the *pas*, taking half of it with me, while Mick stumbled down much more heavily yet also more steadily and sure-footedly. An easy day's walk was turning into the kind of adventure that is better in the telling over vast, vinous meals than in the doing.

The good thing about a *pas* is that there is guaranteed to be a downhill stretch immediately afterwards, giving your legs the chance to shake off the wobbles and perhaps even offer an opportunity to savour the view. The southern side of the cliff turned out to be very different terrain from the skeleton section: a smooth semicircle reining in the next valley to rise up from the French side. The next *pas* was almost the same altitude, but far less daunting, curving gently up to the ridge. And then the sort of view appears that makes everything worthwhile: a panorama crowded with geological interest from mighty mountains to placid lakes, laced with just enough human traces to make it clear that we had pulled clear of the moon's gravitational field: a shepherd's hut, and a few tiny human figures making their way down the path that tacks patiently back and forth, lazily making its way downwards.

A couple of men were working inside the shepherd's hut that was perched on the plateau. This *cabane* turned out to be a popular destination for people walking up from the nearest vehicle track, 4km distant horizontally and 500m vertically. The Cirque de Lescun, a perfect parabolic termination of a glacial valley, is a big draw. I stuck my nose in the door to ask for some water, and saw some gleaming stainless-steel dairy equipment amid a dark, dank interior. At 1,689m, this must be a contender for the highest dairy in France; *fromage de brebis* – sheep's-milk cheese – is made on the premises and sold to hikers and the daytrippers. In addition, there was a small pen of large pigs, who presumably provide prime bacon to the *boucherie* down the valley at Lescun. No water here, I was told by the man standing closest to the tap, and was directed to a *source* nearby.

After a steeply shelving open hillside, the GR10 disappears into a wood of pine and beech for a throwback to the Basque Country: shady, gentle underfoot and with a none-too-taxing gradient. It emerges at a car park. The traditional Béarn way of life – coaxing a living from the mountains – is only 75 minutes' hike from a connection to mainstream Europe. These days, the living is likely to be made from tourism. But the building at the top of the track, the Refuge de l'Abérouat, made a sad sight. We were there in early July, when the *juilletistes* (French holidaymakers who take their annual *vacances* in the month of July, rather than August), should have been packing the place out. But instead the refuge was empty and locked. In the porch were some mouldering posters – about the cloud formations that hikers might see. It spelled out the danger signs that should alert one to (a) a deluge, (b) a lightning strike or (c) impenetrable mist, presumably of the kind that had cloaked La Rhune on the morning we spent there. Curiously, the porch also had a functioning France Télécom payphone. Some communications reach this far into a remote valley. We both took the opportunity to call our respective families, and both felt strangely downcast afterwards, as though one of the lighter clouds on the poster had briefly blotted out the sun.

The closure of the Refuge de l'Abérouat did not post a danger to any hikers hoping to stay there, because it is a relatively short walk down to the village of Lescun. 'Can be a quagmire in wet weather. This bit of path can be extremely muddy after rain,' reported the guidebook about the next step. I can confirm that the steep descent on a heavily wooded hillside can be a quagmire after days or even weeks of dry weather. The addition of, at the very worst, half a kilogram of wet mud adding itself to boots increases the total walker-plus-kit weight by only one half of one per cent, yet the leadening effect on pace and morale is far greater.

Mick and I sport a variety of gaits, from brisk high-stepping to an almost terminally slow trudge. The prevailing one depends on a wide range of variables: strength – physical and emotional; how recently we have eaten and/or drunk a strong coffee; the weather; and the proximity of shelter, showers and beer. Back on the road, I watched a procession of cars taking the easy route as I scraped off as much as I could of the sticky Béarnaise soil before resuming a heavy slouch. It was enlivened by much flailing of limbs, in the manner of a skier caught in an avalanche. The reason: the woodland hereabouts is inhabited by swarms of insects for whom you comprise a tasty mobile snack bar. Whatever itch you have, the Pyrenees will scratch it, and if you don't have any itches, the stretch between the refuge and Lescun will give you some.

Like much of the Pyrenees, on both sides of the frontier, Béarn has an anomalous status *vis-à-vis* central government. The medieval *comté*, corresponding to an English county, was ruled as an independent fiefdom by a succession of viscounts. Under the expansionist Gaston Fébus, count of neighbouring Foix, fortifications were built at strategic points on the valleys and his control extended into the Basque Country and what is now the Navarra region of Spain. As a trans-Pyrenean venture, the kingdom of Navarre – as the entity became – proved remarkably robust. In the 16th century, its king, Henri IV, manipulated his way to the throne of France – or France and Navarre, as it became in 1594. He was assisted by Dianne Corisande d'Andoins, an artful, young and aristocratic widow with whom he had an affair.

Possessions on the Spanish side of the mountains were shed under the 1659 Treaty of the Pyrenees, but even in its reduced form Béarn had an impact on Europe – notably Scandinavia, where descendants of a low-ranking soldier from Pau still rule Sweden. Jean-Baptiste Bernadotte was born in 1764, and aged 16 became a soldier in Napoleon's army. He rose to become imperial marshal, and led many European campaigns. As a result of one such excursion, he became crown prince and later king of Sweden, Norway and Eastern Pomerania. The Swedish empire has shrunk since then, but the line of Bernadotte still reigns. His birthplace is now a museum. The 21st-century Béarnaise are very proud of their land. Indeed, they could be accused of trying too hard to trumpet its virtues by, for example, proclaiming the capital, Pau, to be 'the South-West's third main economic centre', whose civic arena was opened by the singer Johnny Halliday. But beyond the tourist blurb, there is much to recommend the Béarn: copious vineyards in the north (including a cluster around the village of Bellocq, pronounced identically to the godfather of the mountains, Hilaire Belloc); a town named Bruges after the Flemish city, to commemorate a medieval excursion from here led by Gaston Fébus; and Pau itself, one of many pretenders to the title 'gateway to the Pyrenees' but which has a better claim than most.

On a sunny summer's day like this, hundreds of day-trippers are drawn to one of the Béarn's natural wonders – the cirque of Lescun. The wiser weekenders find rooms in Lescun's solitary two-star hotel, the Pic d'Anie; we met a British couple who had joined the mass movement to south-west France and were living near Toulouse. They had come up for the weekend, but like us had made some foolish assumptions about the ready availability of bread. Happily, we were correct to assume that hitching between Lescun and Etsaut ('gateway to the Pyrenees' worst walk', as I was pre-supposing) would be manageable.

Public transport is understandably sparse and sporadic here, as in any remote rural community in western Europe. The spiral is the same everywhere. Increased incomes allow greater car ownership, which depresses demand for bus services. Depleted public transport forces people who might not want to drive to buy a car, reducing use of buses still further. The services that do exist are heavily subsidised, and must surely be vulnerable to further cuts – pressurising yet more car ownership, and heavier congestion on unsuitable roads. Lescun's last bus ran decades ago.

The farmer who squeezed us into the cab of his pick-up was off in search of a stray cow, but happy to take us the tightly curved, steep five kilometres between Lescun and the main road linking the Valley of the Aspe with Pau, the N134. This junction is no nearer to Etsaut than is Lescun, but at least the valley has some buses, even on a Sunday. I know this for a fact because my waving-off of the motorist who had dropped us was taken as a request to stop by the driver of the SNCF bus. You might have imagined that the business of the Societé Nationale des Chemins-de-fer Francais is to run trains. Yet the philosophy of French Railways is so radically different to that of the British railway network that the state enterprise supports a vast range of bus services, too – and even, when a fifty-seat coach is plainly disproportionate to demand, taxi services at railway prices. Maintaining tens of thousands of miles of track is an expensive business, so the farther-flung reaches of the French Railways empire are regularly pruned. The line along the Vallées d'Aspe has a special reason for being abandoned: it used to be a second trans-Pyrenean track to parallel the route through La Tour de Carol, using the Tunnel du Somport to reach the Spanish city of Huesca (where George Orwell once served during his futile Civil War episode). A collapse in the 1970s cut the railway permanently. When it re-opened, the tunnel became part of the N134, cutting out the tortuous climb to the 1,632m Col ¿ Somport. Yet a narrow, twisting highway and an old railway tunnel is considered inappropriate infrastructure by some on both sides of the road debate.

The bus that I had inadvertently hailed was going the wrong way. We could have walked along the cycle path that has replaced the railway (theoretically, we could have covered the entire stretch between Lescun and Etsaut in a touch over four hours). But in the interests of what we would claim to be energy-conservation, though others might see it as sloth, we hitched.

Etsaut has a railway station whose time as a transportational terminal has passed. Instead, it has become a shrine to the spirit of Eric the Red – an environmental campaigner last heard of consigned to a psychiatric hospital. In the 1980s and 90s, Eric Pétetin fought a series of legal and political battles against plans by the local and national authorities to build new roads in this part of the Béarn. Assisted by ecologically-minded supporters (a surprising proportion of whom appeared to be young, attractive females), he succeeded in delaying or defeating road-construction projects. But some of his tactics strayed beyond the legal. He was imprisoned, where he acquired the status of a martyr, but upon his release behaved ever more eccentrically to the point where he was pronounced clinically insane. Much of his support faded away, but the spirit of Eric still resides in the caravan parked in the grounds of the station, bearing slogans such as 'our valley is being massacred by the trains of lorries'.

The issue of a new tunnel under the mountains is still a live one, to judge from posters on display in the main square of the innocuous small town of Argelès: *Traversée Centrale des Pyrénées*

= *mort aux vallées*. They warn of the dangers that a new, fast crossing of the mountains would bring to the communities that cling to the valleys.

The TCP, as the trans-Pyrenean project is known, has been discussed on and off for at least forty years. The idea is to link Tarbes and Lourdes in France with Zaragoza and Huesca in Spain. At the heart of the plan is a tunnel even longer than the Channel Tunnel, forty-eight kilometres in total, to be dug between France and Spain passing beneath Gavarnie. You might imagine that consigning all the cars and trucks to a hole in the ground would be an aesthetically pleasing idea. But Argelès would suffer from greatly increased traffic because it is the last significant settlement north of the proposed tunnel mouth. Happily for opponents of the scheme, it is currently more 'off' than 'on', having been put on hold by the European Commission in 2002.

The Béarn, like the Ariège further east in France and the Ariskun and Baztán valleys in Spain, is impoverished by geography. A glance at a road atlas of Europe reveals that the Alps are far more porous than the Pyrenees in terms of transport. Dozens of road and rail tunnels burrow through Europe's highest mountain range, supported by impressive engineering projects carrying roads and railways above ground. From the Mont Blanc tunnel to the Brenner Pass, vehicles and high-speed trains need barely slow to cross the mountains. But the main routes between France and Spain cling closely to the coasts. In between, the Pyrenees – much lower than the Alps, remember – are traversed by some pretty mediocre links, by European standards.

The only railway of any note to attempt the crossing is the line from Toulouse to Barcelona, which performs some impressive tricks on its ascent to the border station at La Tour de Carol – such as completing a 270-degree turn inside a mountain just north of L'Hospitalitet. But the standard railway gauge in France differs from that in Spain, so everyone has to change trains at the bleak and chilly station whose main point of interest is a plaque to the memory of Spanish Republicans who fled north via La Tour de Carol as the Civil War ended.

Long-distance truckers would choose almost any other route than one of the mountain passes across the Pyrenees. A good mountain crossing for anyone who is less concerned about scenery than speed is a good, gradual approach on a fast dual carriageway or motorway, with the edge taken off the mountains by a twin-bore tunnel. The few tunnels that exist are dangerous single-carriageway affairs, and the approaches are slow and tortuous, clinging to the steep sides of narrow valleys. Which is just how hikers like it. The Pyrenees comprise one large speed bump, which slows traffic to a relative crawl and champions the rights of the hikers.

Due south from here, across the border in Spain, the ancient villages of Ansó and Hecho occupy parallel valleys of upper Aragon – yet with each standing on a separate cul-de-sac, they have little contact with each other; the dialect of *cheso* is still spoken in Hecho, while mountain Spanish prevails in Ansó. Both valleys give access to the bizarrely sculpted limestone shapes of the karst landscape that straddles this part of the frontier, but few hikers take the opportunity to make the international crossing.

Across the Aspe from Etsaut station is the parallel medieval village of Borce, which has an *Espace animalier*. Here, it is asserted, you can *Contemplez les animaux des Pyrénées en toute liberté*. A 10-hectare enclosure is hardly the stuff of total freedom, but at least the deer, goats and marmots enjoy more independence than Eric the Red.

Etsaut is, in theory, one of the stops on an alternative pilgrimage route to Santiago de Compostela. I find it difficult to understand why a pilgrim would decide to take a less direct and higher route than the main pilgrimage highway through St-Jean-Pied-de-Port, but perhaps that is just evidence of pagan values.

One good reason for pausing here for the night is the Hôtel des Pyrénées, planted squarely on the village *place*. We were glad to have booked rooms; the hotel and the square were packed for some sort of government-sponsored cultural manifestation.

We were in the mood for some non-subsidised dinner on the *terrasse*. A single, young and pretty waitress – who might once have campaigned with Eric – whirled among the tables serving weary, muddy and hungry hikers with cold beer and hot stew. The worst busker in the world – who had evidently somehow negotiated a deal with a tone-deaf functionary in the Ministry of Youth, Sport and Culture – spoiled the calm of a warm summer evening. I wandered off to bed, to sleep a fitful sleep punctuated by incidents involving falling. Mick stayed behind, and in the morning swore that he had detected touches of the Belgian genius Jacques Brel in the musician's performance.

'We had joy, we had fun, we had seasons in the sun,' goes the Anglicised chorus of one of Brel's songs. When the day of the Chemin de la Mâture finally dawned, I wondered if the past tense would prove to be appropriate. This leg of the GR10 is both a novel transportational solution to the challenges of the Pyrenees and, if you believe hikers' lore, the most dramatically dangerous day's walk. Mick and I are both Capricorns, but it has failed to bestow me, at least, with a goat-like ability to climb. Nevertheless, it makes light work of consulting our horoscope in *L'Express*. *Belle Vitalité*, it promised. But the positive feelings that are necessary at the start of any day's slogging up hill and down *val* were erased by a companion at breakfast. Three British men had descended, the previous afternoon, from the same stretch that we planned to tackle. How was it, I enquired by way of conversation. 'It's a bit narrow', replied the youngest. I pressed for more details. 'I suffer a bit from vertigo.' And thus was triggered an inevitable downward spiral (hopefully psychological rather than gravitational) about my own tendencies in that direction. But at least I was required to carry only my backpack along the Chemin de la Mâture, rather than help lug a tree trunk on the most terrifying walk in Europe.

At the time Jean-Baptiste Bernadotte was growing up in Pau, the French navy was trying rapidly to expand. Late eighteenth-century rivalry with the English for military supremacy depended partly on France matching their naval firepower. The most suitable trees to use as masts on warships were, it was generally agreed, grown in the forests of the Béarn – and specifically in the mountains between the Aspe and Ossau valleys. Then, as now, no roads could be built through such terrain. The masts (or *mâts*) could successfully be floated down the Aspe and onwards to the shipyards on the Atlantic coast. But a sheer-sided gorge lies between the forests and the river. The solution was one of the strangest infrastructure projects in history: a one-kilometre path was to be hewn out of the cliff face to allow the masts to be carried.

Starting opposite the formidable fortress of Portalet – where Marshall Pétain was later to be imprisoned after the Second World War – convicts carved a path just wide enough to carry a tree trunk, provided the bearers were as sure-footed as Pyrenean goats. The Chemin de la Mâture did not ultimately confer France with naval supremacy, but today provides the GR10 with a way between the valleys without deviating a long way north. The standard photograph in guidebooks shows just how precarious it is: a mere notch in a wall of limestone, with a couple of tiny figures so far from the lens that it is impossible to tell their precise expression. The particular guidebook I was using also has some helpful phrases in French and Spanish: 'Help! Au secours! Socorro'. As we began the *chemin*, the last one would have been the most appropriate, because we met a bunch of Spanish tourists.

Sometimes I wonder how Spain has managed to sustain its population, given the average citizen's propensity to tackle dangerous pursuits using inadequate equipment. They looked as though they were out for a gentle ramble rather than the most treacherous part of a long-distance path. In the event, the only help we requested was for them to take a photograph of us before the great adventure.

The reputation of the Chemin de la Mâture goes before it. Besides my vertiginous compatriot in the hotel, a lift-giving driver had whistled when told of our plan to tackle this stretch of the GR10. 'Five hundred metres,' he had insisted, when describing the extent of the drop. If Isaac Newton dropped an apple off the edge, an easy calculation using the motorist's estimate and the scientist's gravitational formulae reveals that it would accelerate to a top speed of 100 metres per second in slightly less than ten seconds, whereupon it would smash to pieces on the rocks. Now that's what I call 'terminal velocity'. What concerned me was how long it might take to walk along the *chemin*. Calder's First Law of Vertigo holds that the degree of fright is proportional to the narrowness of the path, the angle of the drop, the depth of the chasm and the duration of exposure to these fearsome statistics. The needle on the vertigometer was already bending off the end of the scale, and was scheduled to remain there for fifteen minutes – the length of the path was just over one kilometre – so long as nothing untoward happened.

A sign pinned to a tree close to the Chemin de la Mâture did not soothe my anxiety. It was a home-made, computer-printed sign showing a picture of a young Frenchwoman who had set out on a journey here from Pierrefitte, a town several valleys away, and had not been seen since.

An older German woman who we had met some days earlier had proved a source of some consolation. She had described the walk in as matter-of-fact terms as she might a journey along the pavement to the local shops. When I asked how easy it would be to tumble over the edge, she looked at me as a judge might regard Eric the Red, and asked 'Why would you want to do that?' Her solution reminded me of one of the Top Tips that feature in the magazine *Viz*, such as 'Why waste money on expensive binoculars? Simply stand closer to the object you wish to look at'; it was just 'Keep away from the edge'.

I had already worked that one out myself. For fear of being locked up with the unfortunate Eric, I will just describe my preparations for the Chemin de la Mâture, which stretched back months. I tried to convince myself that I had spent many years successfully walking along a pavement without falling into the road. Sources describing the *chemin* differ, but it appeared that the narrowest part of the path was 1.8m – over five feet. Whenever I found myself walking along a pavement, I visualised a line on the ground five feet from the edge, and made sure I stayed within the two bounds – until one morning, beside Westminster Bridge Road in London, when I lost concentration and did, indeed, fall off. But a 5 cm kerb is a different matter from a 500m drop. (In fact, the drop is nearer 200m, reducing the velocity on impact to just 55 metres per second. But since this equates to about 125mph, the speed of the fastest domestic train in Britain, it would still be enough to spoil the walk.)

The Chemin de la Mâture climbs steeply from west to east, adding another dimension of danger. And the forced labourers who built the *chemin* were not unduly concerned about creating a flat, smooth walking surface. The path turned out to be strewn with boulders, rendering one of my many plans for dealing with the challenge unwise. This particular coping strategy involved pressing one hand hard against the wall of the rock, and closing my eyes. So long as I could feel the wall, I would be all right, I reasoned. Mick regarded this plan as completely mad, as he did my thought about singing my way through the Tim Hardin songbook during the ordeal: with lines like 'Someone like you makes it hard to live . . .', I was obliged to agree. He thought that visualising a glass of beer and a glass of Madiran at the end of the day would prove more effective, though I felt focusing on such trivialities would not address the profound problem of propelling myself and my pack along a Pyrenean mountain ledge. Neither was I convinced by his argument that it would be unfair to fall off and leave him to write the whole book. So I did the only sensible thing: I summoned up a vision of my wife, Charlotte, and our young daughters Daisy and Poppy. While tumbling to an early grave would be uncomfortable for me, it would prove downright inconvenient for them. I imagined them waiting at the end of the *chemin*, and set off to meet them (trying to suppress the thought that the two toddlers could probably manage the ordeal without the sort of fuss that I was making).

At the start of the Chemin de la Mâture the ledge narrows as it is forced out to turn a corner. Soon after this, the gradient slopes down towards the edge on another narrow stretch, while the overhanging rock forces you closer to the drop. I paused to look back, during which time my bootlace worked itself loose. I was caught between trying to tie the thing while, as I saw it, teetering on the brink or shuffling dangerously for ten metres or so to a point where I could more safely make repairs. Foolishly I chose the latter, but I survived the half-stumble, half-crawl anyway.

A surprising amount of the upper part of the *chemin* involves a degree of protection from the worst excesses of gravity. Some of it has been dug quite deep, with a lip of rock acting as some kind of guard rail. A few scruffy, spiky plants have staked a claim to this lip, which in the long term could undermine it, but, in the very short term on which I was focusing, it was reassuring to know that there was something to cling to in the unlikely event that I toppled sideways and over. It gave the occasional chance to take in the surroundings. An equally sheer cliff shot up on the other side of the gorge. The two must be like mirror images, though our one bears a scar administered by man halfway up its face.

Suddenly, in no more than the allotted fifteen minutes, you find yourself at the end. Wow, I thought. One day I may even feel strong enough to tackle the stretch of the GR10 along the Corniche Alhas north of Gabas, where there is a sign that promises (or threatens) *passage vertigineux*. In retrospect, I'd say that completing the Chemin de la Mâture made me feel more, well, mature.

The British get everywhere. At the top end of the Chemin de la Mâture the countryside suddenly steps into serenity. Where woodland had been cleared – presumably as part of the ship-building effort – tranquil farmland has taken its place. A sign indicates the entrance to Grange de Perry, presumably a holiday home for a family of that surname. Higher up, the GR10 leads through a young forest, then into a high, broad and bleak valley. It seems a world away from the valley in which Etsaut shelters. The high ridges separate and preserve the valleys that run like veins through the Béarn – and also test the calf muscles. Somewhere along the way, shortly after we had entered the Parc National des Pyrénées, my rucksack zip had decided to unburden itself, and my washbag and computer power supply fell to the ground. Thank goodness that did not happen on the Chemin de la Mâture, I thought to myself as I zipped them back in.

At a couple of refuges – with stone walls and steeply raked slate roofs, in the Béarnaise style – early arrivals had already quit walking for the day. They were lazily staking their claim to the beds while lying in the sun on the banks of the stream that carves through this valley. The GR10 heads due south – a fact which helps when sunbathing beside it – towards yet another *cirque* that marks the end of the valley, and of France. Cols at over 2,000m are commonplace by this stage in the Pyrenees, and are prone to be both cold and spectacular. At the 2,185m Col d'Ayous, we shivered as we looked down upon South America. Not the continent that contains an even more challenging hike, the Inca Trail, but the largest of the Lacs d'Ayous. From above, the shape looks just like the southern portion of America, with a suitable bulge on the top right representing Brazil and a narrow, tapering lower portion corresponding to Patagonia. Beneath a benevolent blue sky, the largest *lac* – and its smaller siblings, doing impressions of Ireland and Africa – gleamed. Above, yet another jet flew overhead, making a mockery of the plans to bore under or over the mountains. A quarter-century earlier I had hitch-hiked across the Pyrenees, this being the only way to reach Spain without breaking the Post Office Savings Bank. The jets streaking across the sky were full of people paying a pittance to reach Malaga or Madrid. Most of the traffic is between northern Europe and Spain's Costas, but some of the planes that are being turned out by the dozen along at Airbus in Toulouse will find themselves employed on relatively short flight sectors that cut out disproportionately long land journeys. From Toulouse, the road or rail journey to Barcelona or Bilbao takes half a day; a flight on easyJet would last barely half an hour. At present, routes to and from Britain are the most profitable but, with competition intensifying and new Airbuses arriving every fortnight, the no-frills airline could soon comprise the answer to Eric the Red's increasingly incoherent prayers.

Our cheap flight to London was on Ryanair, departing from the Béarnaise capital, Pau. The city reinforces its claim to be the gateway to the mountains by naming its airport 'Pau-Pyrénées'. The last part could legitimately be disputed by Biarritz and Perpignan but, for any adventures in the Béarn, Pau is the place to start, or end. Neither of us had been there by air before. While I found a payphone for an interview with Radio Five Live about easyJet's plan to abolish cabin-luggage limits, Mick (whose complete backpack would barely test the existing limits on hand baggage) called in at the tourist office for instructions for reaching the airport. 'Meet me at Place Verdun,' he said before we split up again to research the city. 'I'll already be on the bus.'

Four out of five passengers flying on Ryanair's route to Pau from Stansted are British. Some have bought up cut-price property in France, but many are drawn either to the mountains or to a new city they didn't know they wanted to visit until Ryanair started flying there. The citizens (known as *Palois*) are catering for the average of 150 visitors who each day are funnelled into their town with a range of handy tourist information in English. The *History and Heritage* guide opens with a section entitled 'Walking around the city'. Circuit Three is called 'Pau Today', and suggests you 'chart the ascent of Pau by wandering from one modern building to the next'. Your appetite for a rewarding stroll thus whetted, it is somewhat disappointing to be told the jaunt is 'best done in a car'.

Pau, though, does provide an appetiser for the mountains. Plenty of people walk to the promenade overlooking the railway station (to which it is connected by a free funicular). On a monument, a poem is inscribed that extols the beauty of the mountains and a nineteenth-century panoramic map recites the names of the peaks that are visible on days when the storm clouds are not massing.

Along the Boulevard des Pyrenees the guard rail bears small plaques with the names of significant peaks. Anyone armed with a profound knowledge of the mountains, or a map, might be confused by the apparent reverse order of these. The secret is to look for the highest chimney in the valley below. When you are standing at the plaque marked Pic d'Anie, the chimney should be lined up so that it points to the mountain.

Equally unhelpfully, the city map issued by the *office de tourisme* manages to omit Place Verdun, where I was to rendezvous with the airport bus (and Mick). This is odd, since the square in question is surely the largest in south-west France. So vast is the former military parade ground, that should the authorities decide to build an airport closer to the city, this would be the ideal location.

Helpful locals pointed the way to the *place*, but no one could suggest from where in this expansive quadrant the bus might depart. 'Opposite the army barracks,' asserts the timetable – a loose description that could apply to almost any point. I began a circuit of the perimeter of Place Verdun with plenty of time to spare; by the time I had completed one orbit, only a few minutes remained before the appointed time for the bus. Eventually I spotted a stop marooned amid hundreds of parked cars in the middle of the square. This was, indeed, the *arrêt* for the *navette* – the airport bus – but the schedule pinned to it announced a radically different departure time, which showed the bus arriving ten minutes after check-in for the flight closed. By this stage, the only solution was a taxi. The ten-minute cab ride cost a non-negotiable €20.

At the airport, Mick was, as usual, calmly sipping a coffee and wondering what all the fuss was about. The stop in the middle of the square was the right one; it was the timetable that was wrong. He had convinced the driver that his *ami* was about to arrive, but eventually they and a navette full of passengers had agreed it was time to leave.

When it was time to take off, we were still drinking coffee, and I could have saved my taxi fare. The Ryanair plane from Stansted had arrived on time, but the usual 25-minute turnaround had extended to nearly an hour. A team of airport workers had carefully helped off a woman in a wheelchair, and had eased another such traveller aboard before the ordinary passengers could get on. Pau is the main airport serving Lourdes, and these were people seeking a miracle in the mountains.

5. MOUNTAIN PASSION: IN THE HIGH PYRENEES

Mick Webb

The most exciting, challenging and romantic part of the Pyrenees is to be found in the central section, within the French departments of Les Hautes-Pyrénées and La Haute-Garonne. The mountains are twice as high as their counterparts towards the two ends of the chain; the valleys are much more remote and the animals and flowers more unusual. What's more, visitors will be following in the footsteps of the great romantic writers like Tennyson and Victor Hugo, who were among the elite tourists that the Pyrenees attracted in the nineteenth century.

To reach the heart of the mountains will take about a fortnight if you're following one of the long-distance footpaths from the Atlantic coast. On the other hand, a no-frills airline will deliver you here in a few hours, but there is a third way, which is more leisurely and more civilised, particularly during the summer holiday period, when Simon and I tried it: the overnight train from Paris to Lourdes. Among the nocturnal pleasures were downing a couple of midnight Leffe beers at the station bar in the Gare d'Austerlitz, before entering the odd twilight world of the *couchette* and a night of relative intimacy with a couple of complete strangers, who left the train at Pau before we'd had any kind of conversation with them.

We arrived in Lourdes at eight in the morning, feeling not exactly refreshed. However, just across the road from the station is the vast Café de la Gare where we sat for an hour, soaking up the coffee and the atmosphere of this small town that underwent a miraculous transformation to become a very holy city. Already the trains and coaches were rolling in, bringing groups of pilgrims, the extremely unwell and the simply curious to Europe's most marketed religious shrine. It's no surprise to discover that, among French cities, only Paris can boast more hotels than Lourdes which, with 240, is just ahead of Nice.

It was a Sunday morning in early August and as the bells rang out from every direction we sought out one of the few secular buildings of any interest. Perched imposingly on a crag in the centre of town, the *château-fort* (the castle) houses the small but engaging Museum of the Pyrenees. Its main focus is on the literary mountaineers who first brought the Pyrenees to the attention of a wider public in the nineteenth century through their writings. Among its exhibits are the goatskin wine flask carried by the charismatic and eccentric Franco–Irish aristocratic, Count Russell, as well as a first edition, dated 1862, of the then definitive guide to the mountains, written by Charles Packe.

Maybe Lourdes is an appropriate location for this museum. The strength of the sentiments expressed by the early explorers, and by the Romantic writers who followed them, for the natural wonders of the High Pyrenees has more than a touch of religious fervour about it. If those gruesome corporate slogans had been around in the nineteenth century, 'passionate about mountains' would have applied to Russell, Packe et al. Then, as the word spread beyond the aficionados and the literary classes, the first mass tourism to these mountains was provided by the faithful who had originally flocked to Lourdes in search of miraculous cures. After visiting the sacred grotto, where in 1858 the peasant girl Bernadette Soubirous received her first visitation from the Virgin Mary, many of the pilgrims then took excursions to visit a natural wonder, the Cirque de Gavarnie. This vast and spectacular geological amphitheatre rapidly became the most-visited natural site in Europe and in 1997 its importance was recognised by UNESCO, when it was listed along with the adjoining Spanish range of Monte Perdido as a 'Natural Treasure' and 'Cultural Landscape'.

Outside the museum, from the ramparts of the castle, you can look down on the world's greatest religious theme park, whose long and aptly named Boulevard de la Grotte is lined with shops bursting with kitsch religious curios; alternatively you can look upwards towards the jagged line of mountains, thirty kilometres away on the southern horizon. There's one of those orientation maps, much favoured by the French tourist authorities, where on this sunny morning, a basking lizard obscured some of the names of the featured peaks. Somewhere up there, nestling in the mountains, was the spa town of Cauterets, the starting point for a three- or four-day circuit that is a classic and, if the weather is right, enthralling introduction to high mountain walking.

In fact, the weather couldn't have been better as we boarded a bus in Lourdes and then had to change to another one in the small town of Pierrefitte-Nestalas, whose main claim to fame, apart from the length of its name, seems to be a sprawling chemical works. After this the road climbs steeply, following the course of a mountain river, the Gave de Cauterets. The closer you get to Cauterets, the narrower the valley becomes, and the slopes, covered in chestnut woods, tower overhead. You can imagine the powerful impact that this landscape would have had on the eyes and minds of the nineteenth-century writers, unprepared by photographs or television: George Sand, Alfred de Vigny and Victor Hugo were among the French authors who summered here, and the best known of the English contingent was Alfred Lord Tennyson, who first came in 1831 with his great friend Arthur Hallam. The reason for their visit was an idealistic and romantic one: not just to admire the scenery, but to lend support to a group of Spanish rebels who were seeking to overthrow the dictatorial King Ferdinand. This was like a nineteenth-century rehearsal for the volunteers who joined the International Brigade in the Spanish Civil War.

Hallam died not long after their Pyrenean visit, and, when Tennyson returned to Cauterets in 1862, the fast-flowing Pyrenean streams like the Gave de Cauterets gave him inspiration for the poem 'In the valley of Cauteretz' which commemorates his friend and begins:

All along the valley, stream that flashest white,
Deepening thy voice with the deepening of the night,
All along the valley, where thy waters flow,
I walked with one I loved two and thirty years ago.
All along the valley, while I walk'd today,
The two and thirty years were a mist that rolls away.

Victor Hugo also loved the drama of these mountains, which he described as more than a landscape; he called the torrents workmen, *des ouvriers*, in the workshop of the mountains. He came to Cauterets in 1843 with his mistress Juliette Drouet, having told his wife and family that he was taking the trip on his own in order to do some serious work and to 'drink some sulphur' at the spa. By then, Cauterets had become *the* place to be seen as royalty, aristocrats and writers congregated here to enjoy the wonderful scenery and bathe in the sulphurous waters that poured from underground springs. The word *cauterets* means 'springs of hot water' in the ancient dialect of Bigourdain. The temperatures haven't dropped over the years – between 45 and 60 degrees Celsius at source – and are supposed to be particularly effective in treating rheumatism and ear problems. This seems a curious pairing, but not as odd as the specialism of the spa town of Barèges, two valleys to the east. In the nineteenth century, it was where soldiers went to have their gunshot wounds cured.

The spas still function in Cauterets but nowadays the *curistes* have been joined by *touristes*, who come here for the skiing in winter, the walking in summer and because Cauterets is a gateway to France's most important National Park, the Parc National des Pyrénées. Even so, a walk down the Boulevard Latapie Flurin, with its grand but slightly fading hotels, suggests to the visitor that the great days of Cauterets are behind it. During our brief stay, we certainly found the atmosphere on the sedate side even though it was early August and the height of the summer holiday season. The highlight of a very quiet evening was provided by a minor traffic accident involving a scooter and a bus in a narrow street, which had not been built with the needs of modern transportation in mind. And, while not wanting to have a go at Cauterets, which is a nice enough place, I couldn't help but notice the all-pervading and slightly menacing smell of sulphur that takes the edge off the otherwise fresh mountain air.

The next morning, the sky was again clear and blue, and we were both unusually keen to don the rucksacks and get walking. However, we were staying in a 'traditional' variety of French hotel, the kind with alarmingly large-patterned floral wallpaper and where the serving of breakfast proceeds in an unhurried fashion. The upside of this was that the bread was fresh, the coffee newly made, and we had the time to enjoy the walkers' morning ritual: studying the map. All maps have something intriguing about them but those of the IGN 1:25,000 blue series are indeed works of art. The dark shading of the steepest of gradients brings a 3-D effect and contributes a slightly sinister touch to the pinkish patches of rock, the green swathes of forest and the blue spots that represent the lakes. Marked with a bold red line, our path struck boldly southwards into the mountains through a slightly worrying pack of contour lines, but we were kept from it for a few minutes more; the lethargic breakfast was followed by a funereal bill-paying procedure, during which the very ancient *propriétaire* wrote down, in painstaking longhand, every item of food and drink we'd consumed.

The walk finally began in a positive cloud of sulphur in the car park of the Centre de Rhumatologie, where you can be immersed in, sprayed with and filled full of the curing waters. We had an appointment with a real French rambler, who was going to accompany us on the first stretch of the walk. There he was, Monsieur Lebeau, a retired head teacher and philosopher, who was also a leading light on the local ramblers' committee. If we'd had any doubts about the professor's walking credentials, these were immediately dispelled by a glance inside the boot of his car. Alongside his small, neat day-pack were two cans of paint, one white and one red, as well as a bottle of white spirit and an array of brushes and scrapers: in short, the essential tools for maintaining a French long-distance footpath.

'Il y a deux GR10 ici,' M. Lebeau remarked.

Two GR10s! No, this wasn't a philosophical statement about the inherent dualism of walking; he was just pointing out that the path we were intending to follow was a diversion, *une variante*, from the main route. While the real GR10 continues on the north side of the mountain range towards the town of Luz-St-Sauveur, our *variante* describes a loop, making its way up into the high mountains before coming down again and reconnecting with the GR10 at Luz. This morning's stage would take us to one of the best known of the Pyrenean lakes – Lac de Gaube – and, showing a proper French sense of life's priorities, M. Lebeau told us that he'd booked us all in for lunch at the lakeside restaurant.

The path climbs steeply beside the river; it was hard to talk over the noise of this mountain torrent, which thundered down the hillside in a welter of foam. The surrounding forest, *la forêt domaniale de Péguère*, was one of a number that were specially planted in the nineteenth century to stabilise the mountain sides and protect villages like Cauterets from the effects of avalanches, rock falls and landslides.

To begin with, there were none of the customary red-and-white marks to guide us, though M. Lebeau explained that it was the policy of the Ramblers' Federation not to paint the symbol where it was not needed. If there was no possibility of losing the track, the marks were omitted, and I must admit even Simon and I would have been pushed to take a wrong turning on this particular stretch.

After half an hour or so of constant clambering, our efforts were rewarded by a sequence of stunning waterfalls and pools, the most dramatic of which was the Pas de l'Ours, named in honour of the Pyrenees' best-known inhabitant – the brown bear – though what the bear had to do with it, I'm not sure. The water poured down across a tongue of overhanging rock, turning into a liquid chandelier. By this time we'd entered the territory of the National Park of the Pyrenees and the first creatures we met were a cloud of horseflies, which attacked Simon and me with unrelenting viciousness. As we danced about in a futile attempt to shoo them away, we discovered that the French word for these unpleasant and noiseless insects is *taons*.

M. Lebeau remained quite undamaged and observed with a sly smile that *les taons* seemed to prefer *la viande anglaise* to *la viande francaise*, an ironic reference to the unforgotten cross-Channel dispute over British beef. To even things up and score a point for Britain, we pointed out a rather amateurishly executed splodgy waymark on one of the pine trees. '*Ce n'est pas de Francis Bacon*,' M. Lebeau said drily, continuing the meat references, then rising to the challenge he went on to describe the ideal waymark, as prescribed in the rulebook of the French Ramblers' Federation. 'It's seven centimetres long and one centimetre wide, with a centimetre gap between the red stripe and the white one.' Game, set and match to M. Lebeau.

An hour and a half from Cauterets, we arrived at a large and crowded car park, which was a bit disappointing, but on the other hand gave us the chance to feel sweatily smug. The cars and coaches had taken the softies' approach to one of the most-visited parts of the National Park, the Pont d'Espagne. The *pont* in question is an impressive stone bridge crossing a gorge, where the Gave de Marcadau meets the Gave de Pau. Its name derives from the fact that it was once the route taken by Spanish shepherds on their way to trade in France. Nowadays it's the site of a bar–restaurant, a visitor centre and a cable car, which gives the very young, the very old and the plain lazy the chance of an easy ride up to a high mountain valley which shelters an equally popular attraction, the Lac de Gaube.

Of course, we eschewed such assistance and tramped resolutely up through the vegetation levels. The forest of beech and fir gave way to mountain pine and then the trees disappeared altogether as we reached a beautiful open grassy valley, generously sprinkled with wild flowers, mainly purple and blue. The track was softer and flatter, so we had enough breath to talk as we walked. The professor told us a bit about the work of the waymarker. He explained how it's particularly important in late spring, when the rigours of winter have taken their toll on both paths and painted marks. The marks are easy enough to repaint, but the repairs to the paths are often serious jobs; groups of volunteers are needed to cut up and remove large fallen trees or to deal with sections that have been washed away by rivers swollen by melted snow.

Now, you can't go on a walk with a philosopher and not talk about the more cerebral side of walking. Did the professor make use of his long and often solitary journeys to solve complicated philosophical problems? The answer was quite long and in French, but the main concept could be summed up in the words 'L'esprit se vide' – the spirit empties itself. Although as a student I was mostly asleep during 'introduction to existentialism', I took this to mean that a good, demanding walk empties your mind of weighty preoccupations, making it easier to think them through when the physical exertion is over. I have since put this into practice during some of our long walking days and I think M. Lebeau has a good point: any serious hassles that are on your mind at the beginning of the day are battered into submission by the insistent rhythm of footsteps and then replaced by very immediate demands on the senses: great things to look at, directions to find, the pain in the knee to worry about, etc., etc. As far as part two of the therapy, the resolution, is concerned, I suspect that the necessary reflective state can only be attained if you forgo the post-walk glass of beer and bottle of red; but I'm sure it would be worth the sacrifice.

Our philosophical musings were interrupted by an extraordinary noise. It was a piercing, whistling screech, which ricocheted off the surrounding slopes and stopped us, as well as a number of other walkers, dead in our tracks. The nearest group to us was gathered around a bronzed, bearded man with a pair of binoculars. We followed his pointing arm and spotted a beaver-like animal standing on its back legs and emitting these extraordinary calls. The bronzed man, who turned out to be a park ranger named Marc Empain, explained that we'd just seen a male marmot giving a warning signal to his mate, who was 'sunbathing like girls do' on a flat rock nearby; and if she hadn't heard that piercing sound she'd have been in serious need of some of the water treatment down in Cauterets.

The marmots' story is one of the Pyrenees' ecological triumphs. Originally indigenous to the Pyrenees, they became extinct ten thousand years ago but were successfully reintroduced in the late 1940s to the nearby valley of Barrada and now, at altitudes between 1,400m and 1,800m, are among the most commonly seen of the mountain's wild animals, and certainly the most commonly heard.

'The marmots hibernate for five months of the year,' Marc told us. 'They dig tunnels where they shelter from the snow, and during this time underground their temperature drops from forty degrees to four and they lose half their body weight.'

Simon, M. Lebeau and I tagged on to the ranger's group and, in the hour or so that it took us to reach the Lac de Gaube, we were treated to a most informative and entertaining crash course in the ecology of the National Park. Marc was a ranger of the old school. Not a university-educated Parisian but a local man, brought up in these mountains and as much a part of them as the marmots. He filled us in on the Pyrenean animals we were likely to see, might possibly see and definitely wouldn't see.

The izard is another creature that has benefited from the creation of the park: a relative of the Alpine chamois, it has been saved from extinction at the hands of hunters. There are now five times more than there were when the park was created; and their graceful silhouettes can be spotted quite frequently these days in the higher valleys.

The brown bear, on the other hand, is not doing so well; it's at the heart of a ferocious debate between environmentalists and sheep farmers, and there are now only about ten left across the whole of the Pyrenean chain, half of which have been imported from Slovenia. They don't help their own cause by venturing into territories outside the park boundaries, which exposes them to constant disturbance and worse at the hand of hunters and foresters, while their occasional attacks on sheep create huge political rows. At this rate, the Pyrenean brown bear will soon go the way of the Pyrenean ibex, which officially became extinct in January 2000 when the last of the species was killed by a falling tree – a sad and ignominious finale, but at least a hunter didn't get it.

Then there's the desman; 'our own little elephant' was how Marc described it. Was this an unexpected descendant of the animals that Hannibal brought with him across the Pyrenees on his way to Rome? Not quite. The desman does have a trunk, but it's actually a tiny, web-footed, molelike creature that lives beside the swift-flowing streams, where it hunts for grubs and small insects, using its trunk like a snorkel. The only places you'll find the desman are here in the French central Pyrenees and the region of the Upper Aragon on the Spanish side, although the chances of actually seeing it are remote, as it's almost entirely nocturnal, as well as being very small and retiring.

And after the desman, there's the dahu. 'It has legs shorter on one side than on the other,' Marc explained, to the accompaniment of muffled titters from the French members of the group, 'so that it can run more easily across steep hillsides. It used to be hunted with a frying pan and a ladle. You'd creep up on it and bang the ladle on the frying pan and the noise would make the dahu turn round quickly and run away with its shorter legs on the lower part of the slope, so it lost its footing and tumbled down the mountain to its death.'

By this time even Simon and I were beginning to suspect a joke. We discovered that the prospect of seeing a dahu is used to encourage reluctant French children to keep on walking during country rambles, though whether it's something that they will be desperate to catch sight of, or desperate to get away from, I'm not sure. But there was more to find out about the dahu: 'To cook it, you need a cauldron filled with water and you boil it, along with a quince. After a week, when the quince is cooked, so is the dahu.'

Talking of lunch, at exactly one o'clock we reached the Lac de Gaube. Picture a large lake, an incredible blue-green in colour; behind it is a semicircle of towering snow-topped mountains and beside it a little restaurant, with a terrace of welcoming tables. Paradise? It would certainly be a strong runner. M. Lebeau ordered a refreshing Perrier-Menthe drink that was exactly the same colour as the lake and took from his backpack a bottle of extremely good Madiran wine. 'Ninety-one, a good year.' It certainly was, and went extremely well with the roast pork and courgettes in cheese sauce.

It's not surprising that the Lac de Gaube is a very popular spot, but it's been given an extra *frisson* by a tragedy that occurred here in 1832: a young English honeymoon couple, the Pattisons, came to enjoy the view and took a rowing boat out onto the lake. Somehow they fell in and both of them drowned. Those are the bare bones of the story, but a whole host of unofficial versions have grown up around the incident suggesting lurid twists and sinister motives. For instance, while they were out on the lake, she accused him of having an affair and he threw her into the lake and then drowned himself out of remorse; or she confessed to being pregnant by another man and then tried to commit suicide and he tried unsuccessfully to save her; or maybe one of them fell in and the other drowned while trying to effect a rescue. Whether it was murder, suicide or accident, you couldn't imagine a nicer place for it.

The lake owes its extraordinary colour to the melted snow from the mountain glaciers, and on some days you can see the mountains reflected on the surface, which has led to the Lac de Gaube's nickname, 'the mirror of Vignemale'. Vignemale, the name of the highest mountain on the Frensh side of the Pyrenees, is more than a mountain; it is actually a massif of eight separate peaks, which straddles the frontier with Spain and includes its little brother, Petit Vignemale.

The Lac de Gaube was an essential shrine for nineteenth-century writers: Victor Hugo wrote a poem about it and drew a very fair sketch of it, with Vignemale towering in the background. In the 1860s the British poet Algernon Swinburne caused almost as much stir among the locals as the poor Pattisons, when he actually dived into the deep freezing water and swam across it. He recalled the moment in his poem 'Lac de Gaube':

> The spirit that quickens my body rejoices to pass from the
>   sunlight away,
> To pass from the glow of the mountainous flowerage, the
>   high multitudinous bloom,
> Far down through the fathomless night of the water, the
>   gladness of silence and gloom.

Our idyllic mountain lunch also concluded poetically, and entertainingly, when Marc the ranger got up and sang us all a rather beautiful song. It was a hymn in praise of the former kingdom of Bigorre, which he sang in the ancient regional language of Bigourdain – a dialect of the southern French language of Occitan.

We said goodbye to M. Lebeau and Marc the ranger and began the walk up towards the apparently sheer wall of mountain at the end of the valley. The grass was soft and springy, cut through by unbelievably clear streams. By mid-afternoon we'd reached the mountain refuge of Oulettes. Here we stopped for a drink and to try to get in touch with the next refuge, the Refuge de Baysellance, which is where we'd planned to spend the night. The only means of contacting this refuge, the highest in the Pyrenees, is by radiotelephone, and through a lot of static we just about managed to understand that the places we'd reserved earlier would be kept for us, but only until seven o'clock. The mountain refuges in the Pyrenees are divided into those that are unstaffed, where you turn up and hope to find a place, and those that are staffed during the summer and run like hostels, providing meals and dormitory accommodation. Some of these, like the Refuge de Baysellance we were heading for, are extremely popular, so we were faced, not for the first time, with a race against the clock.

The terrain wasn't ideal for any kind of race. Beyond Oulettes, the walk that had previously been along soft valley grass had transformed itself into a steep rocky path. It zigzagged up the side of the mountain, towards the pass L'Horquette d'Ossoue, which at an altitude of 2,734m is the highest pass on the GR10. Just as we felt we were making good progress and our beds looked safe, we experienced an embarrassing setback. We'd reached a kind of crossroads where a left-turn sign (the Arsenal football rattle, remember?) indicated a well-trodden path, which seemed to lead uphill towards a notch, presumably the pass, in the mountain rampart. An hour later, after going round in a wide circle, we reappeared at exactly the same spot. This time, though, we came from a different direction and were able to work out that the red-and-white mark was actually supposed to be seen by people coming down the hill and therefore had quite the opposite message from the one we'd read into it. We cursed ourselves for being stupid and the signpost for being badly placed, and wished that M. Lebeau had been there to keep the waymarking under control.

The sun was dipping worryingly low, staining the rock golden-red, by the time the pass came into site. The last stretch, a hundred metres or so, was not so much a walk as a scramble up some loose scree, and for about half an hour it was impossible to stand up straight. Clinging to the slope more elegantly than us were the most beautiful flowers with five petals of the deepest blue: spring gentians. And then, we were over the ridge and astride the Horquette d'Ossoue. You always hope that the effort of getting up to a pass will be rewarded but often all you find is another, higher ridge, or else a cloud will have descended before you get to the top and blotted out the view. But this time there was no such disappointment, and completely bore out Charles Packe's observations from the mid-nineteenth century:

> The mountain passes over the lateral ridges called Cols, sometimes Horquettes, are also of extraordinary beauty and some difficulty. Those who cannot make the ascent of these lose the finest scenery.

Not only was there a chance to admire the view back down the valley we'd left, where the Lac de Gaube had added a silvery sheen to its blueish-green, but in front of us, as though we'd gone upstairs to a new landing, was a very different vista over a high grassy plateau, dominated by crags, cliffs and peaks, dotted and crowned with patches of snow. And much closer, on a slightly lower ridge, there was a bizarre sight. A low semicircular structure, which seemed to be made of some unlikely kind of silvery material, was gleaming in the sunshine, looking for all the world as if it had just landed after a journey from Mars. Far from being a spaceship, though, this was the Refuge de Baysellance.

The walk to the refuge from the pass was downhill, mercifully, and took only about twenty minutes, which was important in the light of our deadline. The last stretch was across a small snowfield, the first we'd encountered on this walk, and the snow crunched satisfyingly underfoot. Seen closer to, the building looked just as mad as it had done from a distance, though it was more in the Heath Robinson than the Space Age style: a wooden construction, which had been half-covered in a kind of silver foil. Outside, there were groups of people sitting on wooden benches, drinking and chatting in the last rays of the sun, looking as though they were at an English country pub, except that they were all drinking coffee. A few tents were dotted around and a young man was washing at a very public tap. We were less relaxed, as it was ten-past seven and our beds were at stake.

The entrance to the refuge was through a porch where rucksacks and boots were stored. The trouble we had trying to find any space for our own equipment suggested that the refuge was pretty full, and this was confirmed by the *gardien* who came out to meet and (kind of) greet us. 'You are *les Anglais*; you are late, but I have kept your beds for you,' he said. 'You will have to eat in the second shift at a quarter-to nine. Come, I will show you your beds.'

This was Monsieur Lacaze, a larger-than-life character, whose name for some years was synonymous with this refuge; for three and a half months every summer he would transfer himself from the plain to the high mountains where he organised proceedings with the flair and discipline of a top orchestral conductor. He showed us up a ladder, which was absolutely vertical as befits a mountain refuge, to the dormitory that was packed with bunk beds. 'We have fifty-five people tonight; we are completely full, and everyone must be in bed by ten-thirty.'

What fun we would all have.

Dinner was served at communal trestle tables and was pretty unmemorable, except for the copious availability of red wine labelled 'Réserve de Baysellance' and the fact that everything we'd eaten and drunk had been brought here by helicopter or on people's backs. Over the meal we made the acquaintance of a young French botanist called Romaric, who was intending to climb the nearest peak – Petit Vignemale – before breakfast the next morning. On discovering that all that we needed by way of equipment was a pair of boots, we agreed to go with him. Most of our fellow refugees, though, had more serious climbing in mind and were here to scale Mount Vignemale, which is a couple of hundred metres higher than its smaller sibling and involves crossing one of the few remaining glaciers in the Pyrenees.

Early to bed and early to rise is the rule of thumb in these parts and, while everyone else was making use of their climbing equipment to scale the stairs to the dormitory, we had more freedom to take in our surroundings and another bottle of the Réserve. The most unusual feature of the dining room, which took up most of the ground floor, was a high shelf that ran round the whole perimeter, on which were ranged a number of small empty baskets. Try as we might, we couldn't work out what these were for; nor could the only remaining diners, a young Italian couple who hadn't booked beds on M. Lacaze's spaceship and were putting off the evil moment of their return to a small, cold tent.

The framed photographs on the wood-clad walls were easier to decipher, as they all had labels. There were some striking images of the refuge in its early days, snow-covered. It was one of the first of the mountain refuges to be built by the CAF – the Club Alpin Français – a hundred years ago. The other notable subject, from pre-refuge and pre-Gore-Tex days, was a bearded figure, dressed in bulky protective clothing.

This was the legendary Count Henry Russell, a local but also an international kind of hero, whose relationship with Mount Vignemale was somewhere between a love affair and a certifiable obsession. He wasn't the first person to scale the peak but, once he started, he couldn't stop. The son of an Irish aristocrat and a Frenchwoman from Toulouse, Russell was brought up bilingually and wealthily; he made the most of his privileged background to travel and climb mountains. His early journeys were to the Americas, to Australia and New Zealand; he crossed Siberia, too. But it was the Pyrenees and in particular Vignemale that came to dominate the rest of his life, and became the subject of his writings.

His dream was not just to climb the mountain but to live in it, and during the 1880s he undertook the incredible task of excavating grottoes in the side of the mountain. The first of them, la Grotte du Paradis, was above the glacier at a height of 3,200m. Creating it involved two years of painstaking and dangerous work hauling explosive, wood, tools and provisions up from the valley below and across the deeply crevassed Ossoue glacier. It was completed in August 1882 and Russell spent his first night there at the relatively comfortable temperature of seven degrees Celsius. Other caves followed, in which Russell entertained his friends to lavish parties; by the light of candles, fine wines were drunk, the best Bayonne ham was eaten and cigars were smoked. Russell's possession of Mount Vignemale became complete when the French local authorities agreed to lend him the top thousand metres of the mountain at a token rent of one franc per year. In 1904, at the age of seventy, Russell climbed the mountain that had been such an inspiration for him for the last time. In his memoirs, *Souvenirs d'un Montagnard*, he reflected on his achievements:

> Excavating a cave at such an altitude might seem madness, since few tourists would sleep there for pleasure . . . But I have no regrets: I hope that my example will be followed on other Pyrenean peaks and that my Paradise of snows will not be a Paradise lost.

Before I'd spent a night in our refuge I would definitely have been numbered among those tourists who would not have chosen to sleep in a mountain cave. By five o'clock in the morning, when the early risers were up and preparing in stage whispers for their own conquest of Vignemale, I still hadn't had a wink of sleep and would have happily accepted a transfer to one of Russell's grottoes, with or without a sleeping bag. One of the many effects of high altitude on the human body is to turn up the snoring volume knob. Take 55 adults, crammed into a smallish and resonant space, 54 of whom are asleep and emitting the most extraordinary noises, at a range of pitches that would challenge a colony of marmots . . . you know, I think I'd have been happy with a patch of rock outside his cave.

The next morning, the sky was clear and blue and life seemed worth living again. Our friend Romaric, as good as his word, emerged from his tent at half-past seven and off we went to climb Petit Vignemale. I'd climbed one or two mountains before – maybe 'walked up' rather than climbed – but this was the first I'd managed before breakfast. It takes only about forty minutes from the refuge to the peak, and isn't arduous, particularly as we'd left our packs behind. Maybe the lack of sleep added to the sensation of triumph as we stood slightly unsteadily on the rather narrow double summit of the mountain. A number of crow-like birds with red beaks, Alpine choughs, wheeled around uttering echoing cries, and as far as the eye could see there were mountains, snow-covered peaks, in a whole palette of different-coloured rock. If you need to be convinced that the Pyrenees are not a single barrier, this is the place to come, as the overwhelming impression is of being surrounded by a dense forest of mountains.

The traditional French way to celebrate your first 3,000m conquest is with a bottle of Champagne, but we had to make do with water from the spring at Baysellance, which tasted nearly as good as the real thing. I was quite happy to have got to the top of any mountain at all, and the fact that I was probably about the 300,000th person to conquer Petit Vignemale didn't diminish the delight in any way. We watched a line of distant, tiny climbers crossing the glacier of Vignemale, roped and carrying ice axes, and well on their way to the top of the much more difficult summit of Vignemale. They must have been among last night's snorers. I tried hard but unsuccessfully to wish them well on their ascent.

On average, a hundred people a day now climb Vignemale during the summer months. The first 'tourist' as distinct from a mountaineer to reach the summit was a Yorkshirewoman, Ann Lister, and hers was an achievement not without drama. A woman of independent means, she was something of a local character, known as 'Gentleman Jack' for her masculine dress and ways. She had already made one previous visit to the Pyrenees when, in the summer of 1838 and at the age of 47, she returned to embark on this adventure. She employed as a guide a local man called Cazaux, who was the first known conqueror of the mountain, and they, along with three other guides, reached the top on 7 August 1838. She wrote the names of them all on a piece of paper and put it in a bottle, which they left at the summit to mark the achievement. But, unbeknown to Ann, she had a rival, the exotically titled Prince of the Moskova, who had inherited this honour from his father, who had been one of Napoleon's field marshals.

Dead set on being the first tourist to climb Vignemale, the prince also engaged the services of M. Cazaux and, when they reached the summit a few days later, on 11 August, there was no bottle to be found. It later transpired that the devious Cazaux had removed it, fearing that the prince wouldn't pay him if he found out that he'd been beaten to the top. Confronted later by an angry Ann Lister, the guide caved in and admitted his subterfuge and wrote out a certificate confirming that she was indeed the first tourist to climb Vignemale.

Back at the refuge, it was all go. M. Lacaze (who, sadly, has now retired from his post as warden) was already in full flow on the radiotelephone, loudly accepting bookings and giving instructions in French and Spanish. Meanwhile, his female (and very pretty) assistants were chopping vegetables for that day's *garbure*, the ubiquitous mountain soup, which can contain just about anything and is always welcome at the end of a day's walking or climbing. Before leaving we solved the mystery of the baskets on the shelves; they were now filled with the belongings of the serious climbers, to save them from carrying unnecessary weight on their day's expedition up Vignemale. We were looking forward to our day's walk, which would take us into the valley of Gavarnie, and should therefore be as much downhill as the previous day had been uphill.

A few minutes' walk from the Refuge de Baysellance, the GR10 (*variante*) passes right in front of the Grotte de Bellevue, which is the most accessible of Russell's caves. The *vue* was definitely *belle*, out over the high Spanish peaks towards the Cirque de Gavarnie, but the smell was certainly not; the grotto seemed to have been pressed into regular service as an emergency loo, leading me to revise that earlier thought about the desirability of sleeping in one of Russell's caves.

Our fellow mountaineer, Romaric, came with us for the first couple of miles and, being a botanist, was able to explain why it was that the tiny flowers that grow up here well above the tree line seemed to have such short stems and, in the case of some daisy-like plants, no stems at all; the flowers seemed to spring straight from the ground. Apparently, as there is a very short growing season due to the amount of snow that falls at this altitude, they take full advantage of the sun by growing flowers as soon as they see it, and can't be bothered wasting time and energy on long stalks.

Romaric's particular academic subject was carnivorous plants and he insisted on leading us, rather against our better judgement, across some marshy ground to examine a number of tiny plants growing beside a fast-flowing and perfectly clear stream. His normally lugubrious expression changed to one of radiant joy when he found one minute specimen, which, without my glasses, I was scarcely able to see at all. It was a replay of a scene from the nineteenth-century French writer Hyppolite Taine, who was commissioned to write a guide to the countryside around the spas of the Pyrenees and took great delight in the eccentric characters who are drawn to the mountains, including a botanist:

Ah what's that? 'The Aquilegia Pyrenaica!'
And my man leapt off like an izard, scaled a slope, dug carefully in the earth around the flower, lifted it up without damaging a single root and came back, with an air of triumph, eyes sparkling, holding it aloft like a flag.

The aquilegia, by the way, is just one of 160 species of flower which are indigenous to the Pyrenees, thanks to the wide range of climatic zones and ground conditions. Even at an altitude in excess of 2,500m, there were plenty of them to marvel at, though most of the natural colour was provided by the mosses and lichens which clung steadfastly to the rock, tinting it with greens, yellows and rusty reds.

For the first half of the day, the path plunged down a dramatic canyon, carved out by the river Ossoue, and at times was steep enough to require rock steps. We speculated on the difficulties of replenishing the supplies of Réserve de Baysellance via this particular route, and M. Lacaze gained a few more points on the estimation gauge. There was an entertaining moment when Simon almost trod on a marmot, which was neglecting personal safety in order to sunbathe on a rock. Presumably the mate who should have given the alarm had popped off for a quick drink; in any case we were close enough to admire the lustrous sheen of the marmot's coat.

After a couple of hours, the valley began to open up and the river had been dammed to create an unnatural lake, which wasn't a patch on the Lac de Gaube. There was now room for pastureland, and a large herd of cows were grazing lazily on our route. Some, presumably the team leaders, were wearing bells, which rang in strange rhythmic patterns as they bent down to eat or shook their heads to dislodge clouds of flies. We made our way, rather gingerly, through the middle of them and I recalled some vague piece of information about cows being responsible for more walkers' deaths in the UK than bulls. I expect the same misleading statistics can be applied to bears and cows in the Pyrenees. Anyway, we survived, and a little later a red rescue helicopter came throbbing up the valley on its way towards the Vignemale Massif, reminding us that mountain walking is not to be taken lightly. I hoped it wasn't one of the snorers. Honest.

As you get close to Gavarnie, the path crosses a mountain road and then proceeds steeply straight downwards, cutting off the hairpin bends in a satisfying but dangerous way, because just as you've lost control of your legs and are going unstoppably fast you find yourself having to cross the road again, at full tilt. Gavarnie itself is a modest tourist town, a village really; it can't boast the mineral springs which have brought fame and fortune to Cauterets, though its favoured location in a valley that penetrates deep into the mountains has made it a base camp for Pyrenean mountaineering. Many of its great early climbers are buried in the graveyard here.

But what has brought world renown and millions of tourists to Gavarnie is to be found just outside the village. This is the single most famous feature in the mountain chain, and high on the list of the world's great natural treasures: the *cirque* de Gavarnie. At the peak of its popularity in the late 1950s, the *cirque* attracted more than two million visitors a year. But, as the choice of holiday destinations has widened, the numbers have dropped and are now less than a million a year. The first thing we did after arriving in Gavarnie was to go and see the *cirque*. Actually it was the second thing we did, after booking into the Hôtel des Voyageurs.

If Gavarnie can be reasonably called the centre of Pyrenean exploration, its epicentre is the Hôtel des Voyageurs. The unassuming two-star establishment (with a stuffed izard in reception to welcome customers) has a visitors' book that is so filled with famous names that it has been transferred to the archives of the Town Hall for safekeeping. Victor Hugo, George Sand and Charles Packe stayed here (though not all on the same night), while Count Henry Russell lived here. He reputedly dealt with his morning post by the unusual method of reading the letters, ripping them up and scattering the pieces over the balcony, much to the surprise and entertainment of the local people.

And what about the *cirque*? It lives up to its hype, not least because of its size. Some very famous attractions, like the *Mona Lisa*, or lots of film actors, are much smaller in real life than you'd expect them to be, which is bound to cause a slight feeling of disappointment. The Cirque de Gavarnie has no such problem. The first impression, as you breast a rise in the trail, is that you've arrived at a huge amphitheatre. It looks as though it must have been designed and built – Victor Hugo called it 'nature's colosseum' and saw in it undoubted proof of the hand of God at work. Tumbling down the 1,700m wall of rock that faces you are shimmering ribbons of a dozen waterfalls, one of which measures a thousand metres from top to bottom. It was late in the day and we were quite alone on the broad, grassy stage beneath the massive cliffs. Alone, apart from a bird of prey, almost certainly an eagle, which glided high overhead.

How Victor Hugo would have enjoyed what happened next. As Simon and I were scanning the ramparts at the top of the Cirque in an attempt to spot the famous Brèche de Roland, which was supposed to have been hacked from the rock by Roland's sword (presumably during the battle of Roncesvalles), a brilliant flash of lightning ripped down the sky, paralleling the waterfalls. It was followed almost immediately by a crashing peal of thunder, which rolled and echoed round the mountains, and then the heavens opened. We ran for it – at least we weren't carrying backpacks – though long before we reached the nearest café on the edge of the village we were completely soaked. There, over a large warming cup of coffee, we remembered that the day's forecast had threatened *orages* for the late afternoon, and the *orage* had duly delivered. The rain redoubled in intensity and the tame rivulet that flowed beside the road soon became a foaming torrent.

While waiting for the rain to subside, we made a seamless transition from coffee to beer and had time to read the local paper, which added another chapter to the story of the brown bear. The main feature article was about one of the imported Slovenian bears, which had left its new home in the region of the Ariège, a couple of hundred kilometres east of here, and had set out on a journey which might eventually have brought him into contact with the indigenous female bears whose territory is around the western edge of the National Park. Unfortunately, before he'd met a nice local bear, he'd come across a number of local sheep and, in the carnage that followed, thirty of them were killed.

The response of the shepherds was predictable and ferocious and not mitigated by a government compensation scheme. The shepherds are a vocal lobby in the mountains and, as their sheep roam freely and virtually unprotected on the high grasslands in summer, they don't take kindly to attempts to increase the number of predators. At the beginning of 2004 sheep farmers set up roadblocks in the nearby valley of Luz, in protest against the behaviour of another predatory bear. We took a straw poll among other customers in the café and, being mostly involved in the tourism business, they felt that the bears were worth protecting for the interest they created. However, a dissenter asked what the point was of trying so hard to conserve a species when there were too few left to make a viable population: it's reckoned that about sixty would do the trick, though the current numbers have dwindled to ten, explaining why we never met anyone who had actually seen a live, wild, brown bear, which in the main are very peaceable animals.

Eventually the rain let up and, with raucous encouragement from fellow drinkers, we hurdled the muddy torrent outside the café and made our way back through the village to the hotel. There we met a Frenchman who turned out to be a teacher of English from Toulouse with a particular fascination for Henry Russell; he claimed that his wife, who was Scottish, was quite in love with the man. She denied this, but we spent an enjoyable time after dinner, looking at the sepia photos and admiring, in particular, the picture of Russell enveloped in an ancestor of the sleeping bag that he'd had made up from sheepskin.

The next morning we left Gavarnie under the watchful eye of the statue of Count Russell. I'm not sure he'd have approved of our direction, which was away from the mountains and back towards the main route of the GR10. This would have been easier if the whole landscape hadn't been completely blanked out by fog. The contrast with the day before couldn't have been more dramatic, and we thanked our lucky stars that we weren't in the high mountains today. Even the intrepid Russell was wary of the mountain fog and noted how good weather, like youth, makes us carefree and unable to plan for potential disasters, until, that is, we've had some serious and life-threatening brushes with them.

This wasn't quite our situation, as the first couple of miles out of Gavarnie were on a metalled road, which gave the sound of walking-boots an oddly muffled quality in the fog, and made you think you were suffering from a head cold and couldn't hear properly. We turned off down a very narrow farm lane and then entered a forest. The idea was to get back to the waymarked track, the GR10, which for some reason bypasses Gavarnie. A more detailed map, 1:25,000 scale, would have been helpful in this situation, but there's a limit to how many maps you can carry in a rucksack. Some very organised walkers post the maps back to their homes when they've used them, which lightens their load as they go along; we hadn't quite got round to that.

The map we did have showed a single dotted line crossing the forest; in reality there were any number of tracks, crossing each other and winding so much that the compass didn't help. When in doubt we opted for the higher path, on the grounds that if we got lost at least the undergrowth would be less dense. This worked well until we reached the top of a hill with a short but very sharp drop on the other side, at which point we were rescued by the sound of a car which emerged suddenly from the mist and disappeared almost immediately like an implausible sound effect in a radio play. But at least it told us there was a road nearby and, after a touch-and-go scramble through some barbed wire, we found it.

We also found two old men hoeing a field who pointed us in the right direction: at least, they told us which way *wouldn't* take us back to Gavarnie, which was helpful. Even better, Simon spotted a red-and-white mark on a fence post: we'd found the GR10, or rather we'd stumbled upon it, as it took one of its periodic trips along a proper lane. The lane passed a *gîte d'étape*, with a sign promising drinks, though only at weekends, apparently.

However, the French family who were staying there very kindly offered us a cup of coffee and, even more usefully, they had that 1:25,000 map so we could find out where on earth we were. In fact, we weren't doing too badly at all, and looked at on the map the lane gradually changed status, acquiring one dotted border, then two before it turned into a country path.

Walking in the mist can have its advantages. OK, you can get quite badly and dangerously lost. You also miss out on great views and the chance to spot rare and interesting wildlife. At the Col de Suberpeyre, an hour back, we'd been unable to enjoy an apparently wonderful panorama, which takes in not just one cirque but two: the Cirque de Gavarnie and the lesser-known but wilder Cirque de Troumouse. And the early part of the day's walk through the forest had passed beneath a line of cliffs, where we might on another day have caught sight of the lammergeier or bearded vulture. We'd been told that there was a nesting pair there but hadn't even been able to see the cliff, let alone these splendid birds, whose very specialised diet of bone marrow has given them their very satisfying Spanish name: *quebrantahuesos*, 'breaker of bones'.

What you are forced to do by the mist is concentrate on what's right in front of your nose, since it's all you can see. On this particular stretch of the walk, the 'it' in question was wild flowers. They were nearly all blue or mauve, and, in the case of the Blue Pyrenean Thistle, the blueness is total: blue flowers, blue leaves, blue stem – as though Picasso had been at them. We walked through a field of these thistles and it was like wading through a lake, albeit a rather spiky one. Equally striking, with even deeper-blue flowers were the Pyrenean Irises, which gathered in elegant groups on damp ground; and, prettiest of all, an occasional purple orchid.

Out of the mist loomed two shapes, which resolved rapidly into two middle-aged men in full running gear. We all four converged on a stile, which slowed them down enough for us to discover that they were actually *running* the mountainous stages of the GR10. Like us, they'd set out from Gavarnie that morning, but unlike us they'd already been to Luz-St-Sauveur, our destination, and were now on their way back. They were doing 50km a day and taking in a 3,000m peak for good measure. 'How many days can you keep this up for?' I began to ask, but they were gone, swallowed up by the mist.

As the fog began to clear, we came to another wood, which was a lot easier to cross now we were back on the waymarked path. It was a very steep wood, composed mainly of spruce trees, and scarred by mountain-bike trails. We went round it, just inside the perimeter, keeping to a fairly high contour line, until, after a few false alarms provided by the red-and-yellow markings of the bike tracks, the GR10 itself plunged down the slope. There followed a couple of miles of downhill path, softened by the previous autumn's fallen leaves – in short, a joy to walk on. It was such a joy that I ran down it, inspired by that encounter with the marathon runners, and arrived at the bottom, and civilisation in the form of a house and garden, about half an hour before Simon.

Like most other human activities, walking seems to involve a number of discrete subskills, which people are more or less good at. In our case, I was good at going downhill, whereas Simon was good at going uphill. Conversely, Simon was useless at going downhill and I was crap at any ascent with a gradient above about one in five. It didn't seem to make any difference whether either one of us was in good form or was tired, hungover or under the weather; if it was uphill either Simon would start out in front and get further and further ahead or, if I went first, I would gradually hear the metronomic plodding of his footfall, getting closer and closer and for some reason irritating me intensely; on the downward slopes like the descent through the Sapinière de Bué, exactly the reverse would occur and it would be his turn to be irritated by my hurtling ahead. On the rare patch of level ground we got on fine.

The GR10 reaches the bottom of the valley opposite a hydroelectric power station. The hillside above it is scarred by a vast pipeline. On the credit side of the environmental balance sheet, this marks the opening to the valley of Barrada, where the first colonies of marmots were reintroduced and where the National Park's activities to protect the izard have been particularly successful.

The path from here to Luz-St-Sauveur was pretty unremarkable, with nothing much of interest to report until you arrive at the Pont Napoléon on the edge of the town. It's a most elegant structure that bridges the Gave de Pau with a single span, and being high up the sides of the gorge it is an ideal place for a bit of bungee jumping. We stopped and watched for a while, which is the most sensible thing to do where bungee jumping is concerned, before going to have a look at Luz-St-Sauveur.

From a walker's point of view, this is a junction. The high-mountain loop of the GR10 that we'd been following comes back to the standard route, giving you a choice of closing the circle by going back to Cauterets or continuing east towards Barèges. The town of Luz itself is connected to Lourdes by bus and is well off for shops where you can replenish food supplies and buy any outdoor gear you've broken, lost or forgotten to bring with you. For those who've had a surfeit of natural splendours and want to enjoy some man-made achievements, there are also a couple of interesting Romanesque churches. We passed on the sightseeing and the shopping, but took the opportunity to call in on one of those grand old men of the mountains that the region seems to breed.

M. Richel grew up in the city of Tarbes, with the Pyrenees a tantalisingly distant view. After training as a vet he moved closer to the mountains and for fifty years he walked in them and climbed them. 'I love the mountains,' he said, 'and the mountains have loved me in return: they've kept me young.' He certainly looked remarkably spry and clear-eyed. A month previously he'd walked up the emblematic local mountain, the

Pic de Midi d'Ossau (2,800m), but, like many of these *Pyrénéistes*, he had his own favourite peak, one that he'd almost adopted. Le Mugna is one of the lesser-known high mountains (it is the loftiest part of the Cirque de Troumouse), and M. Richel had climbed its 3,125m sixty times. His last ascent, on his own, was at the age of eighty.

He was also one of the pioneers of the long-distance rambling movement and recalled how, forty years previously, he and a few like-minded people had got together to create the stretch of the GR10 that passed through the High Pyrenees. 'We looked for ways of bringing the ancient paths and byways back into use and linking them all up; we used drove-roads, animal tracks; we even made use of abandoned irrigation ditches.'

Their efforts hadn't been much appreciated by local shepherds and farmers, who were as keen on the idea of tourists in shorts tramping across their land or disturbing their flocks as they were on the reintroduction of bears. Nowadays, though, attitudes have changed, and rambling, walking or trekking is recognised as making an important contribution to the local economy. What's more, at their AGMs in May and June, the ramblers' associations can now expect a turnout of thirty or so willing volunteers. This is a significant advance on those early days when, as M. Richel said, 'We started with five of us, which was just enough to form a committee'. For our part, it was an uplifting end to an uplifting stretch of walk, though the next time we came to Luz-St-Sauveur, we were in a rather different mood.

6. TAKING THE WATERS:
THE LAKE DISTRICT

Simon Calder

Arriving in Luz-St-Sauveur by bus gives an entirely different picture to striding in across the Pont Napoléon. The SNCF bus takes a tour of the municipal car park in the centre of town, showing the very worst of the place, before tootling off towards Pierrefitte and Argelès. That was how we arrived on our second trip to Luz. But, given the two-day journey that had preceded it, we did not feel too slothful.

At this point, I should explain that among our compendious explorations of the Pyrenees we have never managed to complete a walk along the GR10. Plotting our exploits on the map, there are a few discontinuities, usually where we had taken a detour into Spain. By August 2004, the most notable gap was between the two spas of Barèges and Bagnères-de-Luchon. We decided to bridge the gap, and to tackle it in the 'wrong' direction – going against the usual west-east course by starting at Bagnères-de-Luchon and finishing at Barèges.To complicate matters, we had just two days to complete what was a four-day hike, according to the English and French guidebooks. At our attractively but mysteriously named Hôtel Panoramic – What was the view exactly? – we spent some time working out some cunning short-cuts but, as with many mountain plans, this one started to unravel before we'd even started.

The first of July is an illustrious day in Bagnères-de-Luchon. Not only is it St Thierry's Day, celebrating one of the lesser saints, after whom a leading Arsenal striker is named (or is it the other way around?); it is also the day the *télécabine* reopens for the summer.

When I finally discovered, while researching our trip, what *télécabine* actually meant, I was mortified. For many years, I had fondly imagined I had been asking for directions to the nearest payphone. It turned out that my request for a *télécabine près d'ici* was actually an enquiry as to the whereabouts of the nearest cable car of the type normally found in ski resorts. At last I could understand why, on a busy Parisian street or a small town in Brittany, I had been getting such strange looks and such little help. But now, I was in a position to use the phrase '*Est-ce qu'il y a une télécabine près d'ici?*' in its correct sense.

On a hot afternoon, on the last day of June, I was directed to the ski lift at Bagnères-de-Luchon, to enquire what time we could use it the following day. The trouble was, it was broken. A frowning man with a soldering iron explained there was a *problème electronique*. As a result, the 1 July opening had been postponed until the following day. Time to find a *cabine téléphonique*, as I now knew payphones to be, to organise a different solution.

Bagnères-de-Luchon is more or less the halfway mark along both the mountain chain and the GR10. It is commonly known simply as Luchon, to distinguish it from Bagnères-de-Baïgorry to the west, and is the most relaxing and elegant of the Pyrenean spas. For decades it prospered from the visits of *curistes* rather than tourists: until recently the French government permitted citizens with long-term health problems a three-week stint of treatment at an approved spa. These are located all over France, from Bercq on the Channel coast to Vichy in the Massif Central, but the Pyrenees has more than its fair share. Whatever your complaint, it seems, the minerals in the waters here will cure it. The Romans, who knew a good spring or *source* when they invaded it, began the industry when they established baths here.

Unfortunately for the hoteliers and medics at Luchon and elsewhere, the finance ministry in Paris has now decreed that *curistes* must take the time they spend at the spas out of their annual holiday entitlement. Employers were fed up with staff taking July or August off for their usual *vacances*, and neatly bolting on most of September for a cure.

As a result, these days, the emphasis in Luchon has gone back to tourism. Some visitors come for indulgent spa holidays; summer hikers are drawn by the excellent treks and climbs in the Spanish massifs of Maladeta and Posets (Luchon occupies a crook in the border, so has Spanish territory to the south and the east); and in winter, skiers can stay in this attractive French town at night, rather than the typical ghastly concrete mega-resort, and whizz up on the telephone kiosk, sorry cable car, during the day. When it is working.

The lure for us had been obvious: spending just under €5 each for the one-way ride in the small capsules that dangle their way to the ski resort of Superbagnères would save at least two hours compared with walking. Instead, we would have to take a cab. Those two hours of extra uphill walking would certainly scupper our already ambitious target of reaching another strange ski resort, two valleys across, by nightfall. So we asked the proprietor of the Hôtel Panoramic, where we were staying, to book us a taxi, and headed out to find something to eat.

On the eve of the official beginning of the summer season, Luchon had a curiously abandoned feeling. The handsome nineteenth-century villas and elaborate *thermes* – built in 1848 on the foundations laid two millennia ago by the Romans – look thoroughly anachronistic. Even the men repainting the zebra crossing in preparation for the pedestrian holidaymakers looked as though their hearts were not in it. There was at least some life at the northern end of the main street, Allés d'Etigny. We chose the most populated restaurant, a pizzeria, and psyched ourselves up for the following day's jaunt by looking at the map, and then rather wishing we hadn't.

The town is obsessed with football: the two leading bars are Le Extra Time and Le Pénalty. As it happened, there was a match on, and Mick wandered off to watch while I tried to view the panorama from the Hôtel Panoramic. If there was one, it wasn't available, because a thick, grey cloud clung low over the town, concealing the mountains and giving cause for concern about the next morning.

Luchon is one of the great junctions on the GR10, so it was no surprise to meet three fellow British hikers at breakfast. They were about to fly home; the trio, handsomely equipped, were doggedly crossing the Pyrenees in several stages. This morning they were heading home, having left a metaphorical marker in the breakfast room; the next summer, they would return and pick up the baton for another week or fortnight.

British tourists have acquired a shocking reputation in some parts of Europe for loutish behaviour, but can take some of the credit for bringing the Pyrenees to life, in summer and winter. The first visitors were officers from the Duke of Wellington's campaigns in the early nineteenth century who returned later as civilians to the Béarn – which has the distinction of being the location of the first golf course in Continental Europe.

In the 1960s, British European Airways flew from Heathrow into Biarritz, bringing high-class tourists; simultaneously, charter flights from Luton were carrying package-holiday-makers to Perpignan, at the other end of the Pyrenees. This soon came to a halt. The £50 spending limit was introduced in 1967 in response to a sterling crisis. The idea was to stop the British frittering away precious foreign exchange by limiting the amount that could be taken out of the country by holiday-makers each year. The law temporarily put paid to most excursions to the Pyrenees and other parts of Europe.

It was just as well that all such spending limits were abandoned by the incoming Thatcher government in 1979, because we were about to blow about three months' worth in a single cab ride. The assertion 'An hour's walking before noon is worth two after noon' has a corollary: a taxi ride after breakfast that saves two hours of misty, miserable walking is easily worth €35. But I still reckon the proprietor of the Panoramic should have been a tad more conspiratorial when he announced to the entire breakfast room, 'The taxi should arrive between eight-fifteen and eight-thirty.' Hitherto, we had tried to cultivate an impression of being serious walkers, but our cover was now blown. I went out to the *boulangerie* for the necessary baguettes, while Mick fiddled with boots and backpacks. Then we filled the water bottles and hopped into the waiting twelve-seater minibus.

Taxis in these parts tend to be big, because there can be plenty of hikers to move around. While we were lurching around the countless bends to Superbagnères, the driver's radio crackled out the next job: a party of six hikers to be picked up at the southern end of the Tunnel de Vielha, across the border in Spain. International journeys cost more; the fare for this ride was €80.

We drove past dishevelled farmhouses and dilapidated hotels, while learning useful winter-related phrases such as *chasse-neige*, meaning snowplough. The most impressive building was the Electricité de France mansion on the river, La Pique. Handsome EdF buildings can be found on almost every river in the French Pyrenees. They represent mid-twentieth-century attempts to harness water for hydroelectricity. Some still generate a few megawatts, but the current French appetite for amps is now largely met by nuclear power. We passed another minibus, belonging to the British travel firm Exodus, which runs summer hiking here as well as winter snow-shoeing – which it promotes with the predictable slogan 'Piste off with the piste?'

At the end of the half-hour, 24km ride (compared with a 15-minute, 6km trip in the *télécabine*), we were predictably piste off ourselves. The fog had gradually thickened on the way up, and at 1,800m (as the resort proudly proclaims) it was impossible to see further than a few metres. There was, we were told, a *table d'orientation*, but we were sadly unable to orient ourselves in order to find it. Locating the GR10 took a while, as well; had we not cheated we would have been on course, but we were obliged once again to cast around.

I would like to say that misty mountains transform the walking experience in a positive way, by obliging you to take a closer interest in your surroundings. I know that Mick espouses this view. Certainly there are advantages; on stretches where vertigo is a possibility, the phobia tends to be muffled by mist. I could not tell how worried I should have been by the way that the contours crowded together on the map, because the ground disappeared into the murk. And I guess a moist atmosphere is better for the skin than searing, dry heat from the midday sun. But the first two hours of the day comprised a gloomy squelch through a cloud that stayed glued to the hillside.

We gained nearly 500m in altitude, and contributed to the mist, and the general feeling of clamminess, by sweating profusely. There is a physiological rule about the amount of water that you should drink while exerting, but neither of us has ever been entirely clear what it is. One litre per hour, or per vertical kilometre, or per baguette? The 'drink when you are thirsty' rule may be medically suspect, but it has worked for us – always assuming that there is something to drink.

For anyone who has been brought up in towns or cities, the countryside is full of mysteries. My favourite is: where do rivers come from? The High Pyrenees are never short of precipitation, and some streams are clearly glacier fed. But most spring from holes in the ground. Mountains may look and feel inert, but beneath the surface much is going on: in particular, the filtration and circulation of water. Clear, fresh water emerges from thousands of springs across the Pyrenees. Many are at high altitude, making it possible for hikers to remain on the HRP across the crest of the mountains for days or weeks on end without descending. And, for those of us with more modest ambitions, they make life – and backpacks – slightly more bearable. 'There's a tiny spring just to the southeast of the col, in the middle of a pile of rocks,' reports the guidebook. When there is a chance for replenishing water supplies, even I can tell which way is southeast.

Most of the time, I err on the side of caution, usually carrying a couple of litres up an ascent only to find a spring at the top. By now we had encountered a surface that we had not bargained for: a drift of wet, slushy snow. Even in July, at an altitude only about two-thirds of the tallest mountain in the Pyrenees, we were having to scrabble up the hillside to try to make some progress past the sullen-coloured lake of snow. *Neige éternelle*, they call it poetically – snow that never melts is the prosaic English version.

This term, however, ascribes a degree of permanence that may not be warranted. Indeed, I was about to add 'avalanche' to the list of hazards to fret about, and was trying desperately to remember the rules from the refuge above Lescun. We were walking through boulders of snow that had been freshly hurled down the mountain – mobile water supplies for anyone who could be bothered to wait for them to melt. More worryingly still, you could *hear* the Pyrenees being worn away. From somewhere off to the north, there were low, angry creaks and roars that sounded like rocks being ground down. Water does not just carve valleys in the mountains; as snow is crushed to ice, it sculpts their shape in glacial valleys, and scours the mountaintops as it melts each year.

At the col, which I perceived as a knife-edge ridge and therefore had a brief statutory wobble, the transition between two valleys revealed, as it so often does, a change of weather and a change of mood. The cold, grey soup was left behind; the next valley was not exactly bathed in sunlight, but at least we were not to be walking through the cloud cover. Ten-thirty: our target for lunchtime was the Lac d'Oô, nearly 800m below, but before we could begin the descent we had another eighty minutes of undulations to the Hourquette des Hounts-Secs.

We met a couple of walkers who were leaving nothing transportational to chance. They had left cars at the two ends of the walk, Superbagnères and Germ. That allowed them to skip along with barely any weight, as opposed to my clumsy lumberings bearing an overloaded and unbalanced backpack. We also met Elsa Granratt, for whom, strangely, we had a message. 'I am expecting a German woman who is walking here from the west,' the hotelier at the Panoramic in Luchon had said.

'Please tell her that the *télécabine* is not working.' We duly did, and when she'd got over the shock of being addressed by name by two complete strangers, we briefly compared notes on vertiginous sections of the GR10; I was delighted to find that Elsa was a fellow sufferer.

'Oo' is the natural response when you look down from this pass at the lake below: partly because it shines like an emerald even on a dull day; partly because the perfect oval ring of hills around it, together with the edge of the lake, look like an 'O' with an 'o' inside it; and partly because it is not entirely clear how you are to reach it.

Walking is not as easy as it looks, especially when the mist has doused every surface with a slippery coating. Even if you thought you had mastered the technique some decades earlier, putting one foot in front of the other is a risky business if the foot bearing all your weight falls on a moss-covered rock, with your boot at a tricky angle. Before you know it you're lying like a helpless stag beetle, legs and arms flailing, your backpack anchoring you to the ground.

The variation in the surface of the GR10 is immense – a mix of mud, meadow, old cart tracks lined with ancient stones, and a fair amount of sharp gravel, but all of it is less pleasant when damp. Descents also play havoc with your toes; I have lost four big toenails in the course of our Pyrenean meanderings. But for Mick this morning it was worse; as he was not slow to point out.

Months earlier, Mick had taken a nasty twist while wearing trainers, not boots, and the tear had been slow to recover – not least because he had filled the intervening time with plenty of competitive football, which is at least as taxing on the ankles. The descent to the lake was on loam mixed with rough, loose stone, exactly the kind of surface calculated to punish even the fittest limbs. Furthermore, the GR10 is heavily disguised, and when searching for the right path your eye is obliged to shift focus from the more immediate concern of not putting a foot wrong. So I'm sure his curses and moans were justified.

Lac d'Oô is the last of a cascade of lakes descending north from the Spanish border. Lac du Portillon is almost at the frontier, and boasts a little Electricité de France barrage; it feeds the lakes of Saussat, Espingo and Oô – which by general agreement is the loveliest, not least because of the beautiful waterfall that feeds it from the south. When we finally limped down to the edge of the lake, the waterfall – at 275m, said to be one of the highest in Europe – was barely visible as the clouds had descended again. You could, though, hear the gentle roar echoing around the steep-sided valley, and the soothing rumble provided a suitable New Age soundtrack for lunch at a refuge that was big in crêpes.

The refuge was named Chez Tintin. Its main proposition was a plate of fourteen pancakes for €10, but we settled for a soup the colour of the lake, and a coffee. The presence of draught beer made it clear that we were within range of a road – hauling barrels of beer over the mountains would be even less fun than my backpack. Indeed, a notice in the refuge announced that three buses each day ran from Luchon to Granges d'Astau, just down the valley.

The refuge was crowded with day-trippers, for whom the journey from Toulouse or Tarbes was no further than a trip to Snowdonia from Liverpool or Manchester. A colour picture showed how the waterfall looked when it was not hidden by mist, while black-and-white photographs of early *Pyrénéistes* depicted mountain life in the days when everyone walked. I bet most of the men in the grainy images were British.

We resumed our trek steeply downhill through rain-stained woodland: The GR10 provides an excellent chance to see the power of water, as it follows the course of the stream from the Oô. It runs through a textbook glacier valley, its walls streaked with waterfalls, and the woodland that crowds around it feels as rich and moist as any rainforest.

I would, at this point, have liked to be able to describe the next stretch of the GR10 across the dramatic Couret d'Esquierry, which straddles the boundary between the Hautes-Pyrénées and the Haute-Garonne. At 2,131m it gives commanding views over some of the Pyrenees' highest peaks. But, instead, I'll have to tell you about our hitching trip across the mountains to the destination which we had no hope of reaching on foot before dusk.

The first stop was Granges d'Astau, where the GR10 emerges into an open valley, and which comprises a collection of semiderelict buildings, a confusing indication about what is supposed to be a sharp left-hand turn, and a half-full car park: in other words, the excuses we needed to turn our hike into a hitch. It was 3.15 p.m., and the next place at which we could reasonably hope to come down from the mountains was at least six hours away. Goodness knows what we were thinking when we had originally planned this day's journey; another reminder that talking about walking is sometimes preferable to the real thing.

We are supposed to be writing about hiking, but it is largely thanks to hitchhiking that we were able to cover enough ground during our visits to the Pyrenees. I have been hitching for 35 years, yet in 2004 alone had a couple of totally new experiences in the Pyrenees. Mick has already described how he deftly hopped into a car when I had thumbed a lift at Roncesvalles after our little excursion along the pilgrims' route to Santiago. Then to reach Luchon the day before, we had found ourselves on a road eleven kilometres short of the town and had flagged down a car, which stopped. It turned out that the two occupants were going only part of the way before turning off in the wrong direction, so they simply blocked the road and enquired of the car behind if they were prepared to take us down to Luchon. The surprisingly unexasperated driver agreed.

Hitching is not as good for you as hiking, and you may see time spent by the roadside as wasted hours. Certainly, we have suffered two humiliating episodes where we have waited so long that we have simply given up and taken taxis, which is the hitcher's final ignominy. But, most of the time, the wait has been just long enough to be entertained by the international language of gestures to explain why someone is not stopping. There's plenty of expressive pointing to left or right, signifying they're turning off just up the road, even from drivers busily talking on their phones. Some stand out: a wonderfully exaggerated circular movement that signifies 'I'm turning round in a minute', and a walking motion with two fingers that means 'Why don't you walk instead?' Best of all was an offering from a passenger seat – a driving instructor who took a moment from teaching his pupil to point at his head, enquiring presumably, 'Are you mad?'

There have been some tricky moments. Some years ago, I was diverted by the *Independent* at the end of a walk with Mick to go and cover the celebrated pig-imitating festival at a place called Trie-la-Baise, north of Tarbes. Yes, really, a pig-imitating festival. I hopped on a train to Toulouse, the nearest city, and – switching to professional journalist mode – walked into the car-rental offices to hire *une voiture*. The first available vehicle would be ready for collection in three days, I was told. I had four hours until the event finished. So I caught another train to Tarbes, hitched with reasonable dispatch to the fine old town, interviewed the remarkably urbane winner of a rural competition, and set off to hitch back to Toulouse to get the night train to Paris.

The driver of the second lift said, 'I'm afraid I'm turning off here, and there will be no more traffic tonight.' I smiled wanly and wondered how he could be so sure. Two hours later, in the pitch dark and with the temperature plummeting, I set up a makeshift camp in a field, just as Mick kindly phoned to ask how I was getting on. I reached London 24 hours late, and contemplated hanging up my thumb and giving up hitch-hiking, but only briefly.

Today, the gods of hitching were at work again. The second car, containing a couple from the Anjou, stopped and whisked us down the valley. We raced through Oô, the town that gives its name to the lake. In capitals and without the circumflex, as the name appears on the signposts, it looks like a pair of cartoon eyes.

Oô, like its equally perfunctory Picardy twin of Eu, is a pretty village strewn with flowers. Castillon, where we were dropped, is not, though it does have a striking medieval fresco in the village church. We took it in turns to hitch while the other went off to admire it. I saw what I thought might be a bus timetable by the town hall, but it was less than helpful. Our final destination, the village of Vielle-Aure, was in a separate *département*, Hautes-Pyrénées, and no self-respecting Haute-Garonne bus would dream of crossing the border.

A van stopped. The driver had room for one. By now, the script was set. Mick jumped in and waved goodbye.

Half-an-hour later, Aurélia went past my outstretched thumb at a terrifying speed, his Peugeot vibrating with the bass notes of some extremely loud rap music. He braked hard, reversed almost as fast and screeched to a second halt beside me. No, he yelled above the music, he was going nowhere near Vielle-Aure – it was in a very different valley. By a bizarre coincidence his name was the same as the hotel I was heading for, which didn't persuade him to go out of his way. But he was prepared to drive me up to the Col de Peyresourde, where I might have more luck.

This pass, standing at more than a mile high, is part of the ridge separating the Hautes-Pyrénées and the Haute-Garonne, and is blessed with a café. It offered crêpes, too, at a dozen for €4 – a pancake-per-euro rate more than twice as favourable as Chez Tintin. But I was feeling distinctly *pressé*, not to mention cold, and stood outside for half an hour seeking a lift from cars passing at about one every five minutes. The sixth vehicle (when you are despondent enough to keep count beyond three, things are getting desperate) contained a forester who had the great fortune to work in the mountains.

He bore a strong resemblance to popular images of Robin Hood, and waxed lyrical about the walk we were missing. No arrow pointed to Arreau, the town at the confluence of two valleys, where I needed to switch direction, but he dropped me off in a convenient place and I started heading south – which involved walking as short a distance as possible on the D929 out of Arreau until I could find somewhere to plant my backpack, and myself.

'*Très jolie*,' insisted the woman who picked me up. She was not describing her two-month-old baby girl in the back, even though the daughter was radiant, but Skegness. She had spent *quinze jours* there in the 1980s, and remembered her fortnight in the Lincolnshire resort fondly. Time does strange things to memory.

That was all I learned about her time in Britain, because about three kilometres along the road she pulled into the supermarket car park, my cue to get out. But, within a couple of minutes, and cars, another woman pulled up, and provided the ideal lift at the end of a difficult day. She ran the roast-chicken restaurant at St-Lary-Soulan, the ski resort that is contiguous with Vielle-Aure. Not only did she know the exact location where we were staying, the Hôtel Aurélia (no relation to my first benefactor of the day), but she also insisted on dropping me right outside.

'Yes, he's here already.' The news from the hotel *patron* did not surprise me. I climbed too many stairs, sat down on the bed and my mobile phone rang. It was Mick, calling to see how I was doing. His voice echoed through the ceiling, because he was in the room below. And, yes, we were in good time for dinner.

Starting the day's 'hike' with a €35 cab ride, and ending it by hitching a good 35km to the theoretical terminus of the walk, had not been an impressive performance. So, to try to mitigate our feebleness, we decided to make an heroic evening assault on St-Lary-Soulan, where a great deal more appeared to be happening than in Vielle-Aure.

If the gradient as we strode purposefully upstream beside the Aure was negligible, then our navigation was questionable (we got lost in the vicinity of the Hôtel Mercure), as was our timing;

the shutters appeared to be going up on every enterprise as we approached. Mick decided the only possible cure for his continuing ankle condition was to sit down and have a beer, and read a two-day-old copy of *France Soir*. The front-page headline read '*Le sexe, c'est bon pour les artères*' – 'Sex is good for the arteries'. Ah, maybe that was what we were missing. I wandered off – not in search of sex, but to explore a town that sees itself as a spa town as well as a base for skiing. I searched out the Maison de l'Ours, a celebration of the Pyrenean brown bear; the attraction proved extinct, at least for the night, as was the shop selling Spanish goods for anyone unable or unwilling to drive south across the frontier.

When I returned from my exploration, Mick was just finishing his beer, and we hurried back to the hotel for the prompt half-past seven summons to dinner, which we'd got quite used to, by now.

We spent most of the meal wolfing down the food (quantity combined with quality was the Aurélia's strength, which more than suited us) and discussing the following day's hike. The idea was to walk right through the closest the Pyrenees has to a Lake District: the Massif de Néouvielle, skirting around the northern side of the peak of that name – which means 'old snow'. It is one of a cluster of 3,000m mountains bunching up towards the Spanish frontier. No late-afternoon opt-outs, either: the few roads we would encounter led straight back to Vielle-Aure. As with pilots accelerating jets along the runway prior to takeoff, after the ripple of lakes there was a point of no return beyond which we were committed to finishing the walk, no matter how poor our shape or how late we were. It was to turn out to be the worst and best of days.

First, the challenge. Starting from our present altitude of 800m, we were to climb swiftly to twice that height. After three hours, according to the guidebook, we should be at a 2,200m col. Another couple of hours would drop us down for a lakeside lunch. Then the fun would really start: a col above 2,500m, followed by a long descent to half that altitude to meet a road at a location called Pont de la Gaubie. Here, it was said, there was a café where Mick would doubtless be faced with a quandary. Should he put his feet up with a beer while I wandered off to find a payphone (or possibly a ski lift) to phone for a taxi? To do so was to risk my poor French directing the cab to entirely the wrong valley, probably on the wrong day. But the rough plan was that we would be at our final destination, the town of Barèges, in time for dinner and a bed for the night.

On the clock of the guidebook – compiled, apparently, by an Olympian athlete carrying nothing heavier than a notebook – the walk was scheduled to take twelve and a half hours. So we vowed to start walking at 6 a.m., or as close as we could possibly manage.

There was some uncertainty about the other end of this walk, as well. Our focus was on someone I had spoken to a week earlier, who said that she indeed would have two single rooms for the night of 2 July. She was the proprietor of the Hotel Modern in Barèges. A couple of things worried me. The first was the price: €13 usually buys barely a simple dinner, let alone a single bedroom for the night. The second was our repeated experience that the tyranny of the French hotelier is even more oppressive than that of the average restaurateur. As with airline check-in staff: if you do not present yourself in good time, you lose your place.

I had found this out two years earlier when I turned up *sans reservation* in another mountain spa town, Vichy, where I arrived after midnight one Saturday. The rain had just begun falling when I emerged from the station. The lights were off, because everyone was home. The church, Notre-Dame des Malades, had nothing to offer those whose malaise was no roof over their head. Eventually I found a hotel where somebody appeared to be awake, at least judging from the racket emerging from a television.

'*Complet. Tout Vichy est plein.*' Just in case this message did not hit home, he added in English, 'Full up.'

What advice and encouragement, I wondered, would he give to someone who had been travelling since early morning and was keen on some sleep in a dry, warm bed?

'Chatelguyon,' he responded.

This was not the name of a hotel, but a town a good forty kilometres away. The only form of transport I had was a folding bike, and the idea of a long-distance pedal through the Massif Central on a dark and stormy night had limited appeal. I set off to look for alternatives. Outside the Hôtel Morland on *Rue de l'Intendance*, I encountered three guests returning after what constituted a seriously late night out in Vichy. They were evidently tapping the security code to open the door. In the manner of a sneak thief, I snuck in after them. The lobby was warm and dry, and had a reception desk with a call bell. My ding went unheard. Then I spied the residents' lounge. Guests at the Morland clearly enjoy a post-prandial nap, judging from the quantity of vast, womb-like armchairs that look designed to coax occupants into slumber. I picked one out of sight of reception, and snuggled down for the night. Just before I dozed off, I set the alarm for 5.50 a.m. In this sort of place, my argument ran, the morning shift is unlikely to start before six. Rather than have to explain myself, it would be easier all round to leg it. My calculation proved accurate. As I sorted out the complicated unlocking arrangement for getting out of the hotel, noises off suggested that the hotel was waking up for the day.

At six in the morning at the Hôtel Aurélia, I listened intently for noises off. While waiting for Mick, I hummed the French version of Blondie's 'Sunday Girl' and stared mindlessly at the books on offer to guests. *Le Goût de Malheur*, the taste of misfortune, was the title of one, with another next to it simply titled *Grief*.

There is nothing like a fast, purposeful first hour to get a long day's hike off to a good start. And we had nothing like a fast, purposeful first hour. For one thing, it was raining. This was certainly not part of the plan, and had not been forecast by

Mick's two-day-old *France Soir*. Rain in the mountains, from the hiker's narrow perspective (I was already too stressed by the deadline to care about the wider benefits), is always bad news. Whether you are heading uphill or down, every step is more difficult. The likelihood of slipping is magnified, which is a particular concern for anyone susceptible to anxiety about heights. And Pyrenean rain has the ability to infiltrate any kind of supposedly waterproof fabric and dampen backpacks, boots and – had we waited long enough for the *boulanger* to open – baguettes.

To compound our poor humour, we wasted twenty minutes and squandered energy trying to find the GR10. Rather than reading the results of a study by the unlikely sounding Department of Sexology at Marseille University, we should have been out the previous evening scouting the start of the following day's route, to be sure of hitting the ground running. But we had not. The guidebooks to the GR10 assume a west-to-east trajectory. Not unreasonably, the writers have concentrated on what the eastbound traveller will encounter. Although the path is the same the waymarking is not always even-handed. And the instruction at a junction 'you can go either way – the tracks meet up further down the hill' is not always helpful when you happen to be starting from the bottom of said hill.

We knew which bridge to take over the fast-flowing Aure, and that we had to walk straight through the baker-free zone that comprised the pretty village of Vielle-Aure. We even saw a red-and-white symbol to urge us on our way. But this embryonic trail ran cold, and we were reduced to casting around, in the rain and the gloom. We were looking for a path leading straight up the forbidding slope that blocked our escape to the west. I set off purposefully along a couple of residents' drives, and retraced my steps. We tried walking further along the road that curls around to start the long climb to the ski station. Eventually we concluded that a pathway that was marked with symbols representing just about every trail in the Bigorre *except* the GR10 was the only sensible choice. So it proved to be: about twenty metres up, we found the first waymark.

Soon we were rather wishing we hadn't. After a good start we encountered the worst possible walking conditions, a steep gradient on slippery stones and treacherous twigs, with thorny bushes waiting to strike at our arteries. Then we went through a forest of small very damp nut-trees, which slapped us about the face with their soggy leaves. The waymarker must have found it heavy going, too, because at some point he or she seems simply to have given up. That is our excuse, anyway, for getting hopelessly lost. We were in the region of the tracks that 'meet up again further down the hill', but both of them eluded us. Any parts of clothing that had somehow remained dry were soon doused in damp; our hands and knees were covered in mud, and we were lost. Terrific.

Eventually we found a track, which the guide had predicted. I set off the wrong way, but luckily Mick had looked in the opposite direction and spotted a GR10 waymark. Back on the trail. Soon the woodland abated, which was a good thing in terms of reducing our propensity to stray, and to be ripped to shreds by malevolent undergrowth. But there was nothing to attenuate the rain issuing from a cloud so dark that it almost matched our moods.

Human nature, like water, searches for the path of least resistance. In this regard the GR10 is usually quite humane: given that its purpose is to guide you across a ripple of valleys, it does so expeditiously, leading you up and across cols rather than *pics*. But for some reason, on this occasion, it leads straight over a minor peak called Cap de Pède ('minor' in this case meaning higher than Britain's tallest mountain, Ben Nevis). We reached the top two hours after we had begun the climb, at which point I would have been happy to call it a day.

In fact it was still quite early, given the time we'd set out, but the combination of the early start, the steepness of the climbs, the stress of getting lost and the prospect of the distance we had to cover were all, to put it bluntly, quite exhausting. On a clear day, without the time pressure, rather than cursing the multiple, eroded tracks in the turf that confused us greatly as we climbed the Col de Pède, we could have enjoyed the fact that this was a historic transhumance path, which shepherds had been driving their flocks along for centuries. The surface was pleasant enough to walk on; we weren't seriously short of water or food but I think the magnitude of the journey to come, without any of the previous day's opportunities to bail out, were niggling away at me. My sense of well-being in the mountains seems to be regulated by some kind of internal clock-cum-altimeter. If I haven't got to a certain height by a certain time, it starts to concern me. This doesn't matter so much on a normal GR10 day, when you'd one big climb and one big descent, sometimes two of them. But today we'd let ourselves in for about four of them, and they were going to get steeper as the day wore on, and we became increasingly worn out. The col de Madamète was lying in wait for us, with luck somewhere around tea-time, with a height of 2,500m and almost certainly some snow to get through. We'd already climbed the equivalent of the world's tallest building before breakfast, but we hadn't done it quickly enough. We trudged on though the mist, passing round the flank of la Serre, a mere 2,000m in height, but which could well have been the last straw if we'd had to go over the top of it.

We stopped for a swig of water to replenish the sweat that was mingling with rainwater. The good thing about walking through a district of lakes is that replenishing supplies is unlikely to be a problem. When Mick and I had found ourselves at a similar altitude in Panama's Darién Gap some years earlier, we came closer to death by dehydration than is wise. We had done a bit of skirting around to get that far, too – avoiding the guerrillas, narco-traffickers and right-wing paramilitaries who stalk the jungle border zone between Colombia and Panama. We travelled by cargo boat along the San Blás islands, a delightful trickle of tiny isles paralleling the Caribbean coast. At a point where we judged the terrain to be free of malevolent men with guns, we hired a launch to take us across to a river estuary. The plan was to walk across the Continental Divide to reach the Pan-American Highway, the closest thing to safety in those parts.

That fine day began with a wade through the estuary, collecting water in our 'hydration systems' – those plastic bladders with drinking tubes that some smartly attired Pyrenean trekkers use. We dissolved a couple of iodine tablets in the water to kill off some of the more life-threatening bugs, and started a long, hot walk up a track that appeared to have no end. In the tropics, the second-silliest thing you can do is hike through the middle of a day when the sun burns down unimpeded by the fluffiest cloud. The silliest thing of all that you can do is collapse for a rest by leaning against precisely the wrong part of your pack, triggering the release valve that empties the water.

Mick is nothing if not stoic, and took the news that I had imperilled our lives in his weary stride. We plodded on through the interminable uphill afternoon, and soon finished his supply of water. As the sun began finally to fade, so did we – reaching the stage where we were going to abandon our packs in a last-ditch bid to go in search of water. We were about to jettison them, when we rounded a corner and found the last ditch in the Darién: and, at its base, a tiny stream that could sustain us.

Ever since, we have gone for the plastic bottles designed for carrying mineral water, and filled them up with the purest H_2O we can find. The habit of selling water in sealed containers arose in the spas of western Europe in the eighteenth century. Gradually, suppliers realised that people were also interested in paying for water that did not taste of rust and bad eggs. Many of the proprietary brands still boast of the efficacious minerals they contain.

'Evian, Eau Minérale Naturelle, est reconnue "favorable á la santé" par l'Académie de Médecine', as the assertion goes on the bottle. Evian is good for you. Mountain water is also good for you, in my experience, as is the stuff that comes out of the tap in hotel bedrooms or high-altitude refuges in France and Spain.

Just as sex is good for the arteries, water is good for the muscles. It helps to rinse away lactic acid that is generated by (over-) activity and crystalises around joints, making the following day's hike even more of a pain.

One thing that this walk was so far lacking was human contact. Evidence that we were not the only people on the planet was provided by a sudden roar. Creeping up on our left, without our realising it, was a road from Vielle-Aure. Had we had a lie-in, taken a relaxed breakfast and wandered along to the roundabout in time to hitch the car that was growling up the hill, we would have been here in the same time and in rather better condition. But the mountains have too many 'what ifs' already.

The first leg-propelled human came along shortly afterwards, wisely following the direction prescribed by the guidebook. He was even less keen to stop and chat than were we. 'Can't see a lot,' was all he said as he vanished into the mist.

As we climbed, a cacophony of hollow bells, with cows attached, drew closer. They were steadier on their legs than we were: by now we had been walking, mostly uphill, for four hours. This was exactly an hour behind the demanding timings in our guidebook, though we had effectively completed a vertical mile in addition to our (not very fast) progress over the ground. The Col de Portet represented almost our last chance to make an escape by road – it has a car park for day-trippers – but we ploughed onwards, trying to make up time.

A relatively flat westbound section was haunted by ghostly ski lifts, possibly bearing telephone kiosks. Then we had to divert around one of the stranger sights in the mountains: a miniature bulldozer. It had presumably been helicoptered in to help repair a particularly eroded patch of the path. We speculated about whether we could drive it all the way to Barèges.

According to the guide, a sharp right turn would swing us north to parallel the first of the day's lakes (not counting the bodies of water that had formed in the bottom of my boots). But how sharply right, and how close to true north? We were not the only hikers to contemplate that question in the absence of reliable waymarking advice. As we took one possible path, a group of four hikers were coming the other way on a higher, parallel path. There ensued a confused conversation in rather poor French (in a very British way, neither party wished to be the first to default to English), in which it transpired that both of us were convinced we were on the right track when, in fact, probably neither of us were. But at least the three-dimensional reality could guide Mick and me to the lake in a bumbling, stumbling and occasionally swearing sort of way.

The intricate zigzag descent suggested by the map became a slither. We saw a *cabane* equipped with solar panels, which were harvesting few rays today. As the clock ticked towards our sixth hour of walking – which, for many people (especially us), would be quite enough hiking for one day – I was glad that the rain had finally drizzled itself out, and that the midday sun was concealed by cloud. As we had found in the Darién, hunger and thirst are not compatible with good walking. So we took a truncated lunch hour, just twenty minutes – a record by our normal standards of inertia after exertions. We had time for a brief conversation with another hiker, who thought he had misheard our intended destination. 'Are you going there *today*?' he asked with incredulity.

Still an hour off the pace, we embarked on the afternoon's entertainment. The first fifteen minutes took exactly a quarter-hour, consisting of nothing more stressful than walking around a quadrant of the Lac de l'Oule. When your legs are behaving adequately, as even ours were able to do when walking on a flat gravel track, the rewards of the GR10 are immense. On the map, the lake looks like a swelling in a brook that, unusually, flows from north to south (it performs the necessary U-turn a short way south, joining the Aure to flow north). In reality, it is a mirror for the mountains, drawing in all the shapes and shadows and even sounds, and reflecting them to the bystander in a ripple of tranquillity. How would it look beneath an azure sky? I did not stop to think. There was work to be done: we were having fun, I kept having to remind myself.

My notes, smudged with rain and sweat, show that we hauled ourselves up through the steep, heavily wooded 450m in 75 minutes – a respectable performance, given the altitude. By 2,000m, the rarefied air hampers the transmission of oxygen to the muscles, however robust one's arteries. It also does funny things to your water bottles. Usually I try to drink most of my supply at a col, before a long downhill stretch. This has two advantages: firstly, the stress on knees, ankles and toes is marginally reduced for the descent (mountaineers training for Everest sprint up hills carrying backpacks with filled water containers – they empty the water at the top, to avoid too much lower-leg damage); and secondly, I don't feel a fool for having carried water across the mountains without drinking it. Even so, between us Mick and I must have borne the equivalent of a keg of Kronenbourg to the top of Everest and back.

The beers that we had promised ourselves at the Pont de la Gaubie suddenly seemed nearer. At the Col d'Estoudou, which we had reached relatively nimbly, we had walked into a separate weather system, one where the sun shone benevolently (by now it was gone 2 p.m.) on a bejewelled valley containing the lakes of Aumar, Aubert and Oredon. They punctuate a delectably attractive vision of muscular mountainsides speckled with snow, yielding to grassy meadows at the foot of the valley. And the path was distinctly downhill, though with a gentle, wooded dip between us and the sapphire-blue Lac d'Aumar. We even spotted some tiny, golden orchids by the path down to the lake.

Our last chance. A road brings day-trippers to this beauty spot, and as though to emphasise the urgency of our go/no-go decision, a fifty-seater coach started up and headed towards us. Not a soul was on board, and we declined to keep the driver company in order to return to Vielle-Aure.

Happiness and hubris are often to be found together in the mountains. We calculated we had barely 300m more in height to ascend before claiming back all the potential energy with a continuous descent to Barèges. Knowing that we had achieved six metres a minute on the stretch from the Lac de l'Oule, a quick calculation meant we could expect to make the Col de Madamète in fifty minutes. So we indulged ourselves with a twenty-minute flop by the lake, where we watched birds catch more fish than the anglers were managing. A doze beneath the warm sun would be just the thing, but would also scupper our supper – and much else. A herd of goats intruding on our snacking finally drove us away.

You won't be surprised to learn that we took twice as long as predicted to climb to the final col. Our arterial trail passed a tiny lake in the shape of a heart. But the gradient sharpened, and what had been an occasional patch of snow expanded into large drifts that we had to crunch across or hobble around. We were approaching the Massif de Néouvielle, 'old snow', which was living up to its name.

Five minutes was all the time we could spend at the col. At the published rate, we would arrive at the café at 9 p.m. And looking down at the frozen lake just beneath the col, we realised that would require footwork as delicate as the Catalan dance, the *sardane*.

'If you encounter difficulties off the beaten track,' suggests a guidebook to Catalonia, 'a mobile phone can come in handy.' Sure, so long as it has a satellite dish attached. The usual day's hike in the Pyrenees is punctuated by a series of text messages. The signal is patchy, and every time you wander back into range of a transmitter, the mobile-phone firm assumes you have just arrived in France and sends a friendly message of greeting. Since leaving Vielle-Aure, neither of us had received one. Mick was the first to venture that the Hotel Modern had quite possibly given up on us and sold our rooms to less tardy hikers. We take it in turns to feel pessimistic, though we have specialist subjects;

Mick frets mostly about transport connections and finding meals, while I feel despondent about the chances of making the next col or, when not hiking, locating a payphone for radio interviews – though that process should in future be easier since my vocabulary was enhanced the day before. I shall henceforth ask for a *cabine téléphonique*, and passers-by will know what I mean.

No passers-by up here; most people had descended from the mountains. We tiptoed as quickly as we could around the ice and slalomed through the trio known as the Lacs de Madamète. 'Good fishing', remarked our guidebook. We did not stop to find out. The sun had now sunk beneath the artificial horizon created by the sharp valley in which we were failing to keep pace with a rushing stream. Then we did some passing by ourselves – specifically of a young couple outside a refuge. They must have seen us heading down from a long way off, and perhaps concluded that we were probably planning to share the refuge and possibly hamper any artery-enhancing activities. They smiled with relief as we scuttled past.

We had been on our feet almost continuously for twelve hours, and were desperate to stop. Our usual rigorous adherence to the GR10 (except, of course, when lost) was soon abandoned. The path leads due north and makes a meticulous right-angled turn to head west; we hurtled as best we could along the imaginary hypotenuse. 'Very pretty valley' – the guidebook speaking, not us. We were beyond, or below, aesthetics. We ate our last energy bars on the hoof, and bypassed what was asserted to be a botanical garden (Kew faces no competition from this barren display). We were only faintly impressed by the stream that had carved the valley disappearing into the ground and reappearing a few hundred metres later. Rounding a curve, we reached civilisation – as manifested by a beep indicating a mobile-phone signal.

'She says she doesn't usually go to sleep before midnight, so we can arrive any time before that.' Mick reported, as he spoke to Madame at the 'Modern Hotel'. That was a small mercy, at least, but the temperature was slipping as quickly as the light. If mistakes were to be made, they would come at the end of a ridiculously long day.

No moon rose to illuminate the lunar landscape strewn with rocks. When you are crossing difficult terrain under the burden of a pack that is still the wrong side of 20kg even when devoid of water, it is essential to blank out all the individual aches and pains. We could compare blisters over a beer at the café while waiting for the taxi on the last stretch into town. Well, that had been the plan, but when Mick had asked Madame to organise a cab for us she had declined to do so on the grounds that it would be a waste of money; certainly it would cost as much as a night in one of her fine single rooms.

The beginning of the end was signalled by a gate, on the far side of which was a track speckled with boulders but negotiable by vehicles in reasonable shape. Far down the valley, a pair of eyes shot through the dusk. The light traced out the course of the main road, and briefly illuminated the café. Nothing else did: when we reached the place, instead of welcoming us with beer and sympathy, it had evidently been boarded up for months. Fifteen hours had elapsed since I had stared at the bookshelves in the Hôtel Aurélia. The thought of a final hour plodding down the road, instead of swigging beers as we waited for our chauffeur, was the epitome of demoralisation. Another beacon on the far side of the valley indicated the chance of rescue, as it signalled a car was approaching. Five minutes later (the journey across the valley took a while), we were loading our backpacks into the car. The two mountain men were amused in a baffled sort of way, rather than impressed, when we told them where we had begun that morning. It was past 9 p.m., and we had spent a ridiculous fifteen hours walking.

'Barèges (4,068ft). This well-known spa is also a popular winter sports resort. It enjoys consistently good and lasting snow conditions.' Well, *Everybody's Travel Guide to France* had reckoned without changing tastes and climate. The woebegone town straggles down a narrow valley. We passed the tourist office – with a poster in the window showing a weary group of people with even more luggage than me walking across a Pyrenean pass. 'Les républicains espagnols dans les Hautes Pyrénées,' it explained, promoting an exhibition about some real heroes, the Republican fighters of the Spanish Civil War who had crossed the mountains as a matter of life and death, not for what might only tenuously be described as fun. To paraphrase the archbishop: these people were tourists because of their political beliefs.

Barèges has a series of places to stay that cannot hope to rival newer, larger and higher ski hotels. The lowest in every sense of the accommodation offerings was the Hôtel Modern. Madame was awake, as she had promised, and so was her Quebecoise assistant. I speculated that she was spending the summer working in France to enhance her accent; French-Canadian speech can be tricky to understand. Mick's ankle had performed miraculously during the day (and evening), but the extremely steep staircase in bare feet was an ascent too far; the young Canadian carried his pack to the third floor and he was in no state for macho protestations.

The adjacent rooms had not been held back for us; we were clearly the only guests. We did not pause to shower away the absurd amount of sweat from the day, because the only café in town was shortly to close. A couple of beers and toasted sandwiches was not exactly a celebration meal, but an early night was called for. I had an early-morning radio interview to attend to. Now what was that expression for payphone, again?

7. THE FURTHEST FRONTIERS: ARAN TO ANDORRA

Simon Calder

The world is full of preposterous frontiers. The random lines that carve up Africa ignore natural features and ethnic allegiances; and Portuguese-speaking Brazil is a linguistic aberration amid Hispanic South America because of an arbitrary division of the then-barely known New World. In comparison, the Pyrenean border is more logical than most: the 1659 treaty that prescribed the frontier began with the presumption that it should run along the highest ridge between the Iberian Peninsula and the rest of continental Europe. This division is not followed meticulously, and there are occasional geopolitical wrinkles – most visibly demonstrated on the section between Val d'Aran and Andorra. We chose not to walk between the two: partly because the terrain along the HRP, the high-level route, rarely drops below 2,200m on the whole stretch, and partly because there are two spectacular, but separate, hikes to make. The first lifts you out of the Val d'Aran, geographically in France but politically in Spain, into the Haute-Garonne, which is definitely in France; the second catapults you from the adjacent, and largely moribund, *département* of the Ariège into the economically hyperactive independent state of Andorra.

Many of the trails across the border were blazed by smugglers. To seal the high-altitude frontier between France and Spain has never been feasible, and in a region where legitimate jobs have traditionally been scarce and poorly paid, the contraband trade has flourished. It must have been tough, dangerous work. These days, we scale the same mountains for pleasure – and in particular for the thrill of finally reaching the *col* that marks the border. Mick may disagree, but I reckon our finest days walking in the Pyrenees were when we crossed the cusp between cultures, the barrier that divides the Iberian Peninsula from the rest of Europe. And one of the best base camps for such an expedition is the Val d'Aran.

About halfway along the frontier between Spain and France, where the mountains are at their highest, the border abruptly shifts north. This beautiful valley lies just on the Spanish side of the border, constrained by some mighty peaks. Its main geographical feature is the Garona, a river that has to suck in its cheeks to get through a narrow neck in the rock into France, whereupon it becomes the Garonne. The river follows a wayward course before emptying into the Atlantic at Bordeaux. Even though it is clearly on the French side of the Pyrenean watershed, the Val d'Aran has for centuries been Spanish. Yet for almost all this time, the valley has been only tenuously connected with Spain. It is officially part of Catalonia, but has its own distinct language: the deliciously soft tongue of Aranese.

Mick and I decided to test whether it was easier to reach the Val d'Aran via France or Spain. We both set off from our homes in south London to fly south with easyJet, but we caught separate planes: he from Gatwick to Toulouse, I from Luton to Barcelona. We were to see who made the fastest, easiest journey.

Barcelona rules a surprisingly large empire from its niche on the Mediterranean. If you're on public transport, the journey from the Catalan capital to its farthest-flung Pyrenean component starts by heading away from the Pyrenees. First, though, you have to find a train that is running. The CGT trade union had called *una huelga*, a strike, and many trains that day were cancelled. Luckily, by 1 p.m., I had identified and boarded a Catalunya Express that was probably being driven by some management lackey, and was speeding away from the Passeig de Gracia station in central Barcelona. The direction, though, was southwest, rather than north towards the Val d'Aran.

Approaching the station of Tarragona, the train crept past stretches of Roman wall – laid by the invaders who sailed across from present-day Italy, or marched around the coast. Lines of communication in Catalonia tend to run along the shore, or up the river valleys. Ninety minutes after leaving Barcelona, the train finally swerved around from Reus station to face the north. The journey inland was spectacular. The station of La Plana presides over a deep, narrow valley, where the riverbed is shared between old tracks and new roads. High above the valley, the futuristic high-speed line from Barcelona to Madrid drills through the mountains.

The train was bound for one of Spain's smallest cities: Lleida, a long, narrow urban strip in the Pyrenean foothills, with a forlorn air. But it does have the convenience of a lovely new railway station. I walked through it during the siesta, beneath the double oppression of a scalding afternoon sun and the usual overbearing backpack. At 5 p.m., when the bus to Val d'Aran was due to start, it didn't – but the ringing on my phone did. Mick was already in Vielha, capital of the valley, and I was delighted to learn that he was enjoying a large beer outside a café in the shadow of the town's handsome parish church.

At about twenty-past five, the driver of the 5 p.m. bus arrived, yawned, rearranged the contents of his bag, started the engine and made his drowsy way out of the bus station. I had grabbed a front seat – and, if the journey didn't wake him up, it certainly did me. The first part of the trip was arrow straight but soon we were into the mountains, taking a long, looping ascent up a road hacked out of bare rock, towards the final, forbidding crest.

For centuries, a trail of sorts has threaded up and over this barrier, one of the highest ridges in the Pyrenees. Yet the journey was so arduous and the snow so tenacious compared with the relatively gentle access from France that Val d'Aran was effectively cut off from the rest of Spain for half the year. Generalisimo Franco was the one who connected it – or, more accurately, forced thousands of his foes to do the dirty work.

At the end of the Spanish Civil War, the Val d'Aran provided a bolthole for many Republican fighters who feared (correctly) for their lives in the vicious retributions that followed the Fascists' victory. And many of the soldiers on the losing side whose lives were spared were turned into virtual slaves of the state, digging the tunnel to Val d'Aran.

The Tunnel de Vielha is long (5,240m) and dangerously narrow. Two trucks can barely pass each other; buses roar downhill. Like a lot of mountain transport it is an infrastructural anachronism. A second bore is now being tunnelled alongside, so that each tunnel will become one way – twice the capacity, one-hundredth as dangerous.

The bus swerved out of the end, and followed a steep, twisting descent for another seven kilometres. It was initially like dropping into a forgotten kingdom but this feeling soon faded. Val d'Aran has strong similarities with Pyrenean valleys in France – not least because of the depressing late-twentieth-century architecture we were passing on our long descent. Vielha's recently acquired range of large, angular ski hotels included the ugliest *parador* in the entire chain; I had always fondly imagined that these Spanish government-run hotels were supposed to occupy buildings of historical and/or cultural interest, rather than resembling genetically modified multistorey car parks.

These aesthetic affronts merely diluted, rather than spoiled, the appeal of the valley as a whole. The core of Vielha is a cluster of small hotels, modest houses and souvenir shops, but even the latter have steeply raked slate roofs that enhance the impression that this is some fictional and possibly Ruritanian enclave. And just beyond this coy core is a roundabout where each evening people cluster to welcome family and friends off the bus from Spain.

Even in the course of one sunny afternoon, Mick had caught some sun. He didn't quite greet me with a chilled bottle of San Miguel, but he did the next best thing: ushered me to his adopted bar, and let me buy him a rum and Coke. Then he unrolled his travelling tale: a minicab to Gatwick that had cost more than his flight; air-traffic-control delays that cost half an hour; a *manifestation* on the highway from Toulouse airport by trade unionists who drive their construction vehicles very slowly in protest against the privatisation of the electricity and gas industries. That caused a go-slow that cost another thirty minutes; a fast train and a slow bus south until French public transport ran out; then a quick couple of lifts that dropped him at the hotel. His total travelling time from home was eleven hours, a good ninety minutes better than mine (he had left earlier in the day). But neither of us had enjoyed a particularly easy ride; in the same time, we could have reached a decent bar in New York.

In terms of transportation, Val d'Aran may lean towards France, but in accommodation it has the very best Spanish practices. We could rarely be accused of overpaying for beds for the night, but the Hotel d'Aran must rate as the best value in the Pyrenees. The landlady was friendly and knowledgeable. She saved me the bother of figuring in which of four possible languages – Spanish, Catalan, Aranese or French – I should make myself misunderstood, because she had perfect English. 'Guests are welcome to use the Internet free of charge.' I filed a story to the *Independent* on the environmental harm caused by tourism that I had written on the bus, ironically while I was making a small but perceptible contribution to that damage.

Still, at least we were obeying one of the rules I had set out: stay in a small, family-run hotel. We were paying – or rather Mick was paying, because he was lagging behind in the euro-tally of our mutual spending – €50 each a night. This was a small amount for a clean, comfortable single room each, plus as much food as we could physically swallow. We did not realise this until we breezed in from the cooling evening air for dinner in the endearingly mock-rustic restaurant. A vat of soup was fetched, and served with a ladle possessing the size and curvature of a small Pyrenean *cirque*. This ensemble kept returning until we begged for mercy, and the next course. Meanwhile, the carafe of robust red wine was diminishing at a worrying rate, considering neither of us had done anything more strenuous than occupy seats on various forms of transport all day.

The main course was pork ribs. We devoured them in the manner of Pyrenean wolves, were they not extinct, and risked accelerating our own extinction by ordering another carafe of red. By the time the dessert and cheese arrived, we were feeling wildly optimistic about the next day's walking, even though our plans had somehow failed to achieve the coherence we had intended at the start of the meal.

When Mick appeared, he had already lost the colour in his cheeks acquired the previous evening. His pallor was the result of combining industrial quantities of beer, rum and wine. He settled the bill (the wine having added only a handful of euros to the total) while I went out to fail to get some bread. I am of the opinion that you can never have enough of the stuff, whether it's baguettes or, in this case, *pan*, that you're after. Mick seems to be more interested in what's beside it, but just as I never miss the opportunity to fill my water bottle, so I rarely pass up the chance to replenish the bread supplies. Mick considers this behaviour obsessional. There was, agreed the few townspeople who were out and about at 7.30 a.m., a *panderia* in Vielha. The trouble was, no one seemed too sure precisely where it was; I would get to the outskirts of the town and retrace my steps, only to be sent off by another well-meaning local on a different heading. On my third time past the hotel, Mick was waiting, looking cross as well as ill.

'Come on, let's go; we'll find some bread on the way.'

The way did not include any bakers' premises. The path we planned to follow – the cumbersomely named GR211-1 – plied a puzzling course, threading through some housing and the car park of an apartment block. We puffed and wheezed our way up to a narrow lane, which promptly led downhill. At least it provided a good chance to study the valley, where a film of morning mist was evaporating. Val d'Aran looked a contented, self-contained place, where enough livestock and tourists could be fattened up to make a decent living. At least half the numberplates of the cars in Vielha were French, showing where the valley's economic interests lay. Maybe Madrid is becoming an irrelevance once again, with Val d'Aran part of the 'Europe of a hundred flags' that some among the minorities from Scotland's Gaels to Slovenia's Ruthenians crave. The Pyrenees would account for a good percentage of these communities, and could even offer enclaves-within-enclaves, such as the Baztán Valley of the Basque Country.

At a gate above the village of Arros that was semi-detached from Vielha, about twenty minutes after our tardy start, I abandoned Mick and my backpack. Free of the burden of both, I set off on a quest for bread. After a couple of dead ends, the chimes for eight o'clock led me down to the church. A farmer in a pick-up saw my distress, asked in a language that appeared to be Spanish what I needed and pointed the way back to Vielha.

Terrific. We had a long, tough day ahead with only breakfast to sustain us. Mick had been in the valley for fifteen hours, me for a couple less, and we had so far covered about a mile. At this rate, we should reach France by Christmas. I had failed not once, but twice, to find the bread, and was therefore *le con du jour* twice over by 8 a.m. – a record. 'Contempt' barely does justice to Mick's expression.

Even if we were not blessed with bread, we were spoilt for sunshine. As the sun climbed, it gradually brought the valley cut by the Garona to life. One morning in 1931, the people of the Val d'Aran awoke to find the river running green. Its main tributary, the Joeu, was believed to rise within the valley. But the celebrated French speleologist, Norbert Casteret, was convinced that it entered the valley underground, and that its source lay on the far side of the Pyrenean watershed. To prove his point, M. Casteret poured green dye into the sinkhole below the Aneto glacier. He hurried across to the Val d'Aran, where – sure enough – the Garona had turned bright green and was on its way to alarm the French who lived beside the Garonne. But M. Casteret had proved his point, and solved another mystery of the mountains.

High above the river, which had returned to its usual grey, we were at last getting into our strides. After a testing climb beside a tumbledown dry stone wall, the gradient became easier and we could appreciate the arena of mountains. The peaks were daintily iced, while the terrain that draped from them was a deep green, rather more natural than the colour arising from M. Casteret's environmentally incorrect endeavours. At this altitude, even at the end of July, it felt like spring. The thin atmosphere was invigorating, and allowed the light greater clarity. Some of the flowers were dazzling yellow and electric blue; others were a more muted mauve, but all had the fragility and delicacy that comes with a high-altitude existence.

I stopped musing on the beauty abruptly when the cow chase began. As we approached a lake on our right, to the left a strange performance was under way. A stout man in a white vest and black shorts, brandishing a stout rope, yelled and cursed as he clambered up the hill. His objective was a stray cow that was munching contentedly beside a stream some way higher up. As he got close to it, the animal ran skittishly away, before stopping to feed again. The process was repeated. The man's wife joined in the hunt, to no avail. Perhaps we should have stopped to offer help. But by this time the three of them were almost out of sight at the top of the hill.

We were dependent, once again on the less-than-perfect 1;40,000 Spanish map. From a lake we were to head a touch north, but the track through the woods soon dissipated into a confusion of options. We stuck to what we thought was the right one, which wasn't – but which conveniently swung around eventually to re-join the correct path. It led us to the junction where we could join the awkwardly named PR-C 115-1, which was to take us across the crest into France. Streams hurried past, flowing down to the Garona. As the forest thinned, we passed a tree that resembled a totem: stripped of bark, with blunted limbs. Beyond it, the majestic mountains filled our frame of vision. In front of the beautiful view was what must rate as the world's silliest sign. It depicted a stylised box camera, with the message, I presume, that this would be quite a good location from which to take a snap.

The woodland gave way to meadows, which had an impressive population of dainty yellow flowers and ice-blue butterflies. We were still climbing, but the path was just on the right side of manageable and the views of mountains and valleys were straight out of a picturebook. Soon we found odd remnants of snow, lying in gullies that evaded the sun. At the *col*, some previous visitor who was, no doubt, pleased with themselves having got this high, had painted '2069m' on a concrete marker.

We were quite pleased with ourselves, too. The way into France was traced along a serenely beautiful valley. It was not without challenges; the way was at once point barred by an electric fence. The 'gate' through it was a narrow gap that was designed to impede stray cows, but also delayed us as we wrestled our backpacks through. rather sooner than we had expected, we found a track that led us past what appeared to be an early 20th-century customs house. Opposite was a monument to the men and women who had headed across the mountains into neutral Spain during the Second World War on a fraught and complicated journey to join the Allied forces. The pine trees thickened, the track became a road and we were soon seeing road signs placed for the benefit of those who prefer to remain within their vehicles – though the *Cascade du Parisien*, the modest waterfall to which motorists' attention was drawn, was not a patch on the wonders we had seen in the mountains. We were glad of the driving day-trippers, though, because we did not have to wait long for a couple of lifts down to Luchon and the start of another adventure.

Travelling with Mick is great fun, no, really it is. Honest. Occasionally, though, there are rewards to be had from venturing off alone.

Couples, whether mixed or same-sex, platonic or not, tend to be less open to the world when travelling, not least because they need to have energetic and ill-tempered debates about where precisely you think you're going to find a couple of loaves of bread in the mountains. 'Do you think they grow on trees?' Travelling alone, you are also more sensitised to the sights, sound and smells of the environment. And even if you have the linguistic abilities of the average British traveller, you can get more acquainted with the people. And, when on buses, you look out of the window more.

I mention this because Mick and I have done a fair amount of solitary travel in the Pyrenees. On one such journey, I found myself in Boussens, a village whose sole function is to act as a railway junction for a branch line that no longer exists. My destination was Foix, where I was hoping to rendezvous with Mick. But I was looking forward to the ride through the Arriège.

Somehow, I almost managed to send my backpack off without me. The train from Tarbes arrived on time, and the smart SNCF bus was waiting. We half-dozen connecting passengers loaded our luggage into the underbelly, and climbed aboard. Five minutes after the appointed departure time, there was still no sign of the driver. As far as bus punctuality goes, France and Spain match their national stereotypes, so this was unusual.

The train from Toulouse was late. Did that mean, I asked the ticket clerk in the station, that the bus would be held? Yes, he confirmed. So I went to the phone booth to call home, secure in the knowledge that the bus would not go until the westbound train had arrived. Hardly had I dialled before I was dashing out of the kiosk, yelling and waving at the bus that was now heading south without me. It grumbled to a halt, and I climbed aboard, wondering – fortunately academically – about the protocol for recovering possessions left on buses that are pretending to be trains.

A few kilometres into the journey, I was the only passenger

left on a 53-seater coach, and hence the sole spectator for another fine bus ride along the valley of the Salat. I can reveal exclusively that the town of Salies du Salat possesses an extraordinary gaudy neoclassical temple, and has a lazy, open feel to it – unlike the tightly packed, constricted towns higher up the valley. Fifteen kilometres from St-Girons, you enter the department of the Ariège, and the world seems to close in; the valley becomes narrower, the debris of the centuries more bizarre – an abandoned roadside chapel is all too common hereabouts. A sign points to the Château de Prat, forlorn on a hillside – which you can visit only at 4, 5 or 6 p.m. in July and August. Welcome to the Ariège – *les Pyrénées avec un capital A*, as the sign had pronounced. The evidence from the roadside was less triumphant; this looked like a district with a capital B for Bereft.

Access all areas has become a reality, at least once you get across the Channel from Britain. A united Europe has done much to enrich poorer areas of the Continent: plenty of projects on both sides of the mountains, from the shiny new station at Lleida to smartly designed tourism literature, acknowledge the generosity of the European taxpayer in funding the work through the EU. The free movement of people, goods and money has also helped – as any farmer who has sold a derelict outbuilding for a fortune to cash-rich Londoners will testify. Yet not everyone is happy with the invasion of wealth that has followed the erasure of frontiers. I found this out beyond St-Girons, where public transport ran out. It is, or was, a handsome town. A century ago, the tall warehouses that inhabit the place would have been well-stocked and busy, rather than boarded up, and the Grand Hotel would have lived up to its name; today, the original paintwork has faded, and the establishment calls itself the less ambitious Hotel Le Madrid.

The town of Foix lay a further 44km east, and in a succession of three quick lifts in decrepit vehicles, I was told the way the region is changing.

A local named Guy, sporting an impressive collection of

metalwork dangling from his ears, lips and nose, was alarmed by the way tourism is changing the area; new hotels and autoroutes are springing up to meet the needs of foreign visitors, he said. The four occupants of a battered Renault van expressed concern about the way British and Dutch people are buying up property as second homes. This lift was enlivened by a brief stop at a roadside hotel, where we loaded – with the owner's permission – an abandoned industrial-sized refrigeration cabinet in the van. One of the party wanted it for a new business enterprise, perhaps providing much-needed snacks for hikers. The final lift was with a woman named Clotilda who had a battered red Citroen AX, a large and friendly mongrel, and a dream. She had bought an old farm, high in the hills above the valley, where she hoped to start an organic farming collective and do a bit to reverse the depopulation of rural areas. Clotilda was raised in the Normandy port of Le Havre, but said she felt more at home in the southwest.

St-Girons played an important part in the limited success of the Chemin de la Liberté - 'Freedom Way'. This is a waymarked path with a difference. It marks the trail followed by escapees during the Second World War. The first wave comprised mostly Jewish people, in particular children. As Nazi Germany swept west across Europe, Jewish families sought sanctuary, mainly in North America. The obvious route from northern Europe was to travel via Britain, but, once the Germans had secured France's Channel ports, that route was blocked. Spain was the safest alternative.

Sanctuary depended upon crossing the dotted line across the Pyrenees. Once in Spain, escapees would typically be courteously arrested for technical infringements of immigration rules (until 1964, the Spanish authorities required every foreign national to buy a visa, price 50 pesetas). Initially, it was possible to leave without impediment at either end of the Pyrenees, or across one of the mountain passes. Southern and western France was ruled by the Vichy government of Marshall Pétain, and was under a less hardline regime than the Nazi-occupied portion of *la république*. But, in August 1942, the Milice – the paramilitary force run by the Vichy regime – was ordered to round up Jews and other minorities, such as Romanies and homosexuals, and deport them to concentration camps further east in Europe. Some went into hiding; others headed south with the help of the *passeurs*, local residents who acted as people-smugglers. On 11 November of that year, the anniversary of the ending of the First World War, German troops overran Vichy France, sweeping south and tightening the frontier with Spain.

A chain was established to usher Jewish children to the Pyrenees. Hundreds, perhaps thousands, were funnelled through St-Girons, the main railhead for the Ariège. Here, they were taken in vans or lorries to villages in the foothills, ready for the most dangerous stage of the operation: a hike across the Pyrenees.

The time when the border between France and Spain has been the most heavily policed was during the last three years of the Second World War. Hitler's commanders knew that the permeable membrane of the Pyrenees was being used by his enemies. Besides the people fleeing persecution, there were escaping Allied airmen who had crash-landed in, or baled out over France. If they were lucky, they were rescued by the Resistance before the authorities caught them, and were smuggled south. Spies, too, used the high mountain passes.

The occupiers needed neither maps nor waymarking to work out where the frontier was most frequently crossed: trails worn down for centuries predicted the tracks for the *passeurs* to follow. As elsewhere in France, some locals collaborated with the Nazis; at least a hundred *passeurs* died in ambushes arranged in advance, while others perished in chance encounters. But many of the evacuees survived, and hold regular reunions in the mountains.

These days, Ariège is a *département* that seems constantly on the edge of an economic breakdown. The limited agricultural potential in the upper reaches of the valley can sustain only tiny communities, and the realities of economic life are all too evident in the old mining district of Couserans, running southeast from St-Girons.

When the reserves of silver, manganese and tungsten began to run low towards the end of the nineteenth century, the local people began to supplement their meagre earnings from mining by trapping and training bears for circuses in Europe and North America – a few poor Pyrenean beasts were even exported to Barnum's Circus in the US. The rise of the motion picture depressed circus attendances. When this was combined with public opposition to the ill-treatment of animals, the *ours* industry went into decline. Parts of the valley look as though they have been ravaged by war; even the cigarette-paper factory has closed down, despite what you might imagine to be growing worldwide demand for marijuana and associated paraphernalia.

If you find yourself in a restaurant in New York City or Buenos Aires, you may find it run by a descendant of an Ariègeois. The biggest cities in the US and Argentina respectively were the main attractions when the fortunes of the region began to fade, and the catering industry provided the most accessible entry-level jobs for migrants who spoke neither English nor Spanish. There is even a meeting point in Manhattan's Central Park for Ariègeois, called the Roc d'Ercé after the village on the road ten kilometres northwest of Aulus-les-Bains, and five restaurants in the city are owned and operated by Ercéens.

The statistics of economic migration are telling: the winter population of Aulus-les-Bains has fallen from 2,000 to 60. In the 21st century, the town is trying to claw a living from tourism: specifically, by reviving the nineteenth-century spa concept, Aulus-les-Bains promises high-technology detox in historic surroundings, and promotes itself as an effective remedy for cholesterol. This is where we were to begin our walk across the mountains to Andorra. On his own journey through the Arriège, Mick had passed the Grottes de Gargas, a fascinating cave complex that answers some questions – such as, how long have the Pyrenees been occupied? – but poses many more, including the question of whether the early inhabitants deliberately mutilated their hands. On a previous trip, we had called in to see the Palaeolithic art to be found underground just at the point where the River Garonne changes direction.

The local legend about their discovery is worth repeating. In the late eighteenth century, a wild man was reputed to be stalking the area, catching unsuspecting milkmaids and other inoffensive locals, before hauling them off to his lair for dinner (he ate, they were eaten). He was eventually caught and revealed his lair to be these ancient caves. Whether or not this is true, the *grottes* tell their own enigmatic tales. They were inhabited at least 20,000 years ago, from time to time by bears instead of humans from the evidence of bones. They are modern by the standards of the more celebrated complex at Lascaux, but have an impressive gallery of art.

The minerals that are available locally, notably iron and manganese, produce red and black oxides respectively – a basic painting outfit for prehistoric man. The first painting in the cave is difficult to figure out – like a tyre track going up the wall. Sketches of izard and bison are easier to recognise. The most interesting images, though, are of human hands. Someone with more time to spare than us has counted them and decided there are 231, all depicted as 'negatives': the hand has been placed against the wall, and the pigment painted around it. The majority are left hands, suggesting these were self-applied by the (mostly) right-handed occupants of the caves. Most of the images are lacking at least part of one finger.

Some intriguing theories have been proposed. One is that an Ice Age caused rampant frostbite; another, that leprosy was widespread; a third, that ritual amputations were practised, perhaps after bereavement. According to a French expert on Palaeolithic art for considerably longer than Mick or me, André Leroi-Gourhan, there is an even better explanation: it is the original digital code. The hands were not damaged in any way; the owner simply lifted one or more joints away from the wall during the painting. The positions of the 'missing' digits, suggests M. Leroi-Gourhan, indicates where particular beasts can most effectively be hunted. I couldn't see it myself, but the echoing chambers resonate with antiquity. They also celebrate Norbert Casteret, one of the great twentieth-century figures of the Pyrenees. His speciality was exploring beneath them – discovering the secrets of the caves that riddle the range, such as locating the source of the Garona, outside the Val d'Aran. His writing on caving, in books such as *Ten Years Under the Earth*, is credited with inspiring generations of young French people to delve beneath the porous surface of the mountains.

The caves of the Pyrenean foothills were not entirely abandoned as dwellings when man moved into communities above ground; in more recent times, they were used by Huguenots to hide when the Catholic Church was persecuting French Protestants.

Mick and I met up again in Aulus-les-Bains on yet another stormy night, in the cheap and not altogether cheerful Hotel de Beauséjour. At least this rambling old residence, beyond its renovate-by date, had one advantage over the municipal Camping le Couledous: the roof proved sound during the rainstorm that began over dinner and continued through breakfast. It is generally true that the further east you go from the Bay of Biscay, the more likely you are to be blessed with blue skies. This morning, though, was to prove Basque-like in the belligerence of the rain. During *petit déjeuner* we consumed enough butter to send our cholesterol levels sky high, in a bid to make the previous day's bread palatable. Then we shuffled off to acquire some fresh *pain*.

From a hiker's perspective, Aulus-les-Bains resembles a town left isolated by a new motorway or TGV line that bypasses it. The GR10, the Pyrenean pedestrian superhighway, passes to the south of the town. About the only amusement of the morning was spotting the name of the waterfall that the official route passed: the Cascade d'Arse, according to the Michelin map.

The art of crossing moving water is something Mick and I had practised in Peru, where every trail is gouged by countless streams. We had not, though, made an exact science of it. Like a game of chess, you must plan a crossing several moves in advance, and know your strategy for coping with adversity when your boot slips on a slimy rock or gives way under your weight. When both happen at once, and momentum dissipates into the water, you know you will be spending the rest of the day with at least one soaking foot.

I was always happy for Mick to go first; we have similar builds, and when he crossed successfully I would emulate his choreography. If he failed to make it, I could cast around for a plan B. But because I had not been warned about the impending crossing, I found myself in pole position for the transit.

Peru's Río Urubamba in full flood had nothing on the Mérigue, the torrent that poured down from the mountains that morning. On days like this, Aulus-les-Bains could include white-water rafting in its touristic offering. The path led up the thickly wooded right bank until the football-rattle symbol ordered us to cross to the left bank, equally tangled with undergrowth.

I moved a little upstream where some overhanging branches offered the prospect of a little extra lift to hop between boulders. At least my Tarzan-like antics entertained Mick. He watched as the rotten bough snapped, sending me tumbling into the deluge. As I scrambled out, cursing him and the rest of humanity, he took advantage of the ridiculously light burden of his backpack to perform a manoeuvre that could earn him a place in a *corps de ballet*, were he not far too old and oddly shaped to wear tights. He was home, and dry.

I slogged back and forth up the 'easy climb' – as the guidebook described it - to the Port de Saleix, a mere 1,794m in altitude. The obvious direction from here was straight down the other side, but our path swerved south to head up the ridge towards Mont Garias to force a way into the next valley. Shortly before its 2,005m-summit, the track led down and my spirits went up as high as the dismal weather would allow. A strange sequence of lakes lay still and pallid in the valley: the Étangs de Bassiès. The path squeezed between them and a much smaller lake, perhaps the size of the Vatican City, but – to Mick's disappointment – further aquatic antics were not required.

The GR10, like a good walking companion, is always springing surprises. At the end of a steep, difficult descent, we started walking on water.

When the Centrale Electrique de Bassiès needed a reliable water supply, local builders were paid to install a long concrete duct high above the valley. In the intervening decades, the concept had been hatched of installing a guard wire to stop users falling to their deaths. Occasionally the overhang became extreme and clipped the top of my backpack, nudging me towards the drop, but mostly I relished the flattest, smoothest two kilometres on the length of the GR10. It was also briefly doubling as the HRP, the prodigal son of the Pyrenees. The high-level route pops up occasionally to spend some time with the GR10's more ambitious sections, then disappears off again when the GR10 descends.

Sometimes doing the opposite of what a guidebook suggests can be worthwhile. So it proved as we made our soggy way down into the village of Marc and headed for the *centre de la familiale*. Mick had done some research in advance and had discovered this holiday centre intended for groups of young people. He had also found out that there was no actual rule forbidding individuals from staying. Thanks to the munificence of the French taxpayer, it was extremely cheap. So he booked us a room.

The staff were amused when a couple of bedraggled men sloshed in and added a few years to the average age of the ensemble, but the kids thought it was hilarious. They were mostly around fourteen or fifteen, enjoying a subsidised break from life in the northern city of Nancy, and witnessing our arrival was the funniest thing that had happened all day. We squelched off to change out of our wet clothes into some marginally less wet clothes, and returned for dinner. We were served the same mountain of pasta and vegetables as the children, except in much larger portions – and with a carafe of wine that Mick somehow procured from the staff's supplies. The last drop of anger disappeared with the last drop of *rouge*, though outside the rain continued furiously. We retreated to our cavelike room, where the Ritual of the Socks began.

Mick's socks are a source of almost as much grief as his spectacles. I wear whatever cotton socks come out of the drawer and vaguely match. They are perfectly comfortable, except when inundated by much of the Mérigue stream, and when such calamities occur, have the advantage of drying rapidly. In contrast, Mick swears by (and often at), ludicrously expensive multifibre hiking socks that take about a year to dry. Still, there are less entertaining ways to start a day than observing his face as he painfully puts on a pair of damp, smelly objects that resemble drowned and flattened rats. The rain, though, had finally abated, and we set off up the valley at a purposeful pace to do a bit of country-hopping. We walked south on an easy track to the next village up, Monicou, where the GR10 turns abruptly east and stops being easy. So we ignored it and carried on south, on a track that led up to a dam.

Electricité de France had kindly provided the rough road, plus the utilitarian installations that detracted from what should have been a fine view of a narrowing valley. The track skirted the east side of the artificial *étang* (small lake), and climbed further up the valley before dissolving as the gradient increased. We followed the stream that was feeding the reservoir that was providing the electricity that was powering the radiators in the *centre de la familiale* that had failed to dry Mick's socks. We turned left, and up an unfinished road that was intended, one day, to connect the Ariège with Andorra. It remains unfinished, because of the difficulty of the terrain and mounting costs. It was the most testing of ascents on that most thankless of surfaces, loose shingle. The culmination – at the end of a long morning, at least – was a stupidly steep and precarious scree ridge that was negotiable only on hands and knees. The agony of every step and every breath suppressed any fear that might have been trying to well up. All of this was taking place above 2,500m, where the air is too thin to provide any comfort.

It is surprising how quickly humans can slip into a routine – a few steps up, then flatten against the mountain for respite while trying not to slip further back. I tried deviating from the path to try to reduce the angle of ascent, but succeeded only in sliding down. Towards the top, our progress was mocked by patches of snow that slowed us down even further. A jet flew overhead, its southbound passengers enjoying life at 10,000 metres considerably more than us at a quarter of the altitude. They were also, sensibly, planning to spend August by a Spanish beach rather than gasping for breath and clawing for some way out of France. This was, we have since agreed, the worst col in the entire Pyrenees, and it has an appropriate name: the Port du Rat.

Mick was first to scramble to the top of the ridge, where he stood up and left the country. When I finally reached the ridge, under a hail of badly aimed snowballs from Monsieur Multifibre, Andorra was not the alluring micro-republic I had hoped to see. As we lay on the frontier, gasping for a decent dose of oxygen, it looked awful. The best you could say for the ski resort of Ordino-Arcalis is that it was downhill from where we were, on a track that looked at least half-decent. But the valley had been denuded of its forest and scarred by uncivil engineering. I blame the President of France and the Bishop of Urgell – and there is method in my madness.

Until a semblance of self-determination was introduced in 1993, Andorra was a co-principality governed jointly by these two men. The local legend has it that the country was created by Charlemagne in 805 in recognition of help given by the people against the Saracens. Even so, it fell within the hegemony of the counts of Urgell, to the south. Ownership swapped from secular to sacred when the nobles did a deal with the local bishop to get their hands on lands in the Cerdanya, which were considered to be more valuable than the difficult-to-reach collection of valleys and mountains to the west. Yet Andorra remained a land to be fought and schemed over for centuries – with the rulers of Foix, to the north, taking a strong interest. Eventually, in 1278, the antecedents of Jacques Chirac and Joan Enric Vives Sicilia (the present co-princes) signed a 'Treaty of Joint Possession' granting Andorra independence in perpetuity. The French representative at the time was the Count of Foix, who later passed on the title to France's head of state. Andorra survives in a state of uneasy independence.

The country has traditionally had precious little relevance to either France or Spain. Until half a century ago, Andorra was on the way to nowhere; the only approach road was from the south, while the main route across the High Pyrenees, between Toulouse and Barcelona, passes to the east. Eventually the two were connected, and the easier access to duty-free goods meant Andorra began to change beyond recognition. The lowest point is around 1,500m above sea level, too high for much productive agriculture. So Andorra has long carved out a role as purveyor of cut-price tobacco and alcohol.

All frontiers leak. Even the Berlin Wall, the most tightly controlled border the world has ever seen, was not impenetrable, as the exhibits in the Checkpoint Charlie museum testify. Those who were prepared to hang-glide from East Berlin to the West, or curl themselves up into impossibly small spaces in west-bound cars, were the exceptions; plenty of smaller-scale smuggling went on, fuelling a thriving black market in the capital of the communist German Democratic Republic.

Capitalism thrives on discrepancies in prices, which are often the result of taxes. The duty-free status of the political oddity of Andorra has made it an exceedingly prosperous enclave. The average Andorran with a job in the high-turnover duty-free shops is probably greatly relieved not to have to haul brandy and cigarettes across the Port du Rat.

We hauled ourselves to our feet, and headed downhill. As we neared the ski station, the sun came out – and so did our thumbs. Yet another hitchhiking variation: the road zigzagged extravagantly downhill. Our path took us straight down the mountain, crossing the Tarmac repeatedly. The trick was to time the descent so that we happened to be on the road at a point when one of the rare cars was passing. Eventually we managed to hail a lift. The car slalomed down to Andorra La Vella – Europe's least attractive capital, not counting Minsk, and by far the busiest urban community in the Pyrenees. Our arrival coincided with the year's most important festival, in which huge papier-mâché figures are paraded around town to the accompaniment of marching bands and much duty-free drinking. We watched the festivities outside the Casa de la Vall, the sixteenth-century stone parliament building that doubles as the national law courts,

'In custom, language and geographical position, the inhabitants of Andorra are Spaniards,' was the view of the intrepid Pyrenean explorer and guidebook writer Charles Packe in 1862. In the 21st century, the bulk of the people are Catalan-speaking; Andorra is the only country in the world where it is the sole official language, though with Spanish and French minorities and also a significant Anglophone community involved in all sorts of business ventures.

The road from Andorra La Vella to the border town of Pas de la Casa on the French border traverses the highest pass in Europe that remains open all year; Lonely Planet compares it to the road from Kashmir to Ladakh in the Himalayas. Even in August, the temperature at the highest point drops to freezing, as we saw from the big digital thermometer in the bus that took us from the capital the day after the festival.

Legalised 21st-century smuggling is alive and well and thriving here, easily the most unpleasant blot on the Pyrenees. The profusion of vast, ugly shopping complexes is a direct result of a geopolitical anomaly. Even though Andorra is trapped in the jaws of two large European Union countries, it is outside the EU for the purposes of taxation. Alcohol and tobacco, the smugglers' staples, are priced well below even the generous rates of Spain, and are much cheaper than in France. Every motorist from Toulouse southwards can calculate how much liquor and cigarettes he or she will need to buy to cover the cost of fuel to the co-principality and back.

There are tight customs controls entering France, but none at all coming the other way. Before the abolition of duty-free allowances for trips within the European Union, all kinds of unnecessary journeys took place. My favourite was the *Butterfahrt* or 'butter voyage' between Germany and Denmark. You could sail across the Baltic free, because it was assumed your main purpose of travel was to buy up butter free of the punitive duty prevailing in both countries. Germans comprised the main customers, and the authorities did what they could to construct obstacles; it was obligatory to 'buy' a ticket with the price shown as DM0.00. As a hitchhiker, this was a very small price to pay for a ride to Scandinavia. I subverted the system by failing to buy any butter, though the salami I bought kept me going for days and – judging by its implausible scarlet colour – contained enough chemicals to corrode a butter boat.

At Pas de la Casa, we changed buses. Throughout the hour's wait for the next one, we obeyed the first rule of travel: in a border town, never take your eyes off your possessions for a moment. Mick declined my suggestion that he might want to repeat the rum-and-Coke experiment that he conducted in Val d'Aran. We spent the time drinking coffee and writing postcards; Andorra, like most tiny countries, has a profitable side industry in philately – with the added bonus of dual postboxes. You can choose whether you want your precious despatch to be handled by the Spanish postal service, in which case it would head south, or by La Poste of France. We wanted the cards to arrive home before we did, so chose the latter.

The bus dropped us in the middle of almost nowhere, where someone has planted a large, impressive railway station. La Tour de Carol is the Clapham Junction of the Pyrenees. Two of the most spectacular lines in Europe converge: the regular SNCF service up from Toulouse, and *le petit train jaune* – of which more later – down to Perpignan. A third line leads across the Spanish border and down to Barcelona. A tablet commemorates the Republicans fleeing Franco at the conclusion of the Spanish Civil War. The next stop down the line is a pair of border towns, Bourg-Madame and its Spanish counterpart, Puigcerda: 'A wretchedly dirty, half-Moorish, half-Spanish town', as Charles Packe unkindly described it. In the intervening 150 years it's obviously cleaned up its act.

We turned our backs on Spain, and headed north. To another and much lesser known part of Spain.

8. PLAINS AND TRAINS: THE CERDAGNE

Mick Webb

Llívia may look as though it's a brand of health food, but in reality it's a Spanish town that's entirely surrounded by France. This qualifies it as one the few truly urban curiosities in the Pyrenees, and is due to some seventeenth-century small print: a clause in the Treaty of the Pyrenees that sought to establish a sensible and mutually agreeable frontier between France and Spain.

At the time, Llívia was the principal town in a chunk of territory occupied by Spain and called the Cerdanya in Catalan. Under the terms of the treaty all the villages south of a certain latitude were to become Spanish and those to the north were to be French. But there was a catch. The treaty specifically referred to villages and, since Llívia was a town, the Spanish negotiators argued that it should remain Spanish, and it has remained so to this day. In fact, Llívia is more Catalan than Spanish and if you can find your way to it – it's resolutely ignored by French road signs – you'll discover yourself in a pleasant and quite affluent little place with a lively main street and many weekend houses belonging to the middle classes of Barcelona, to judge from the car numberplates. Simon and I arrived there on a very warm Sunday, and in a rush as usual. No one else was. They were enjoying a slow apéritif accompanied by the tantalising smell of garlic and olive oil that announces a Spanish lunch. We only had time for a hurried coffee, which, as a veteran of many Madrid breakfasts, I found reassuringly Spanish: strong, thick and vaguely sandy.

If Llívia is unusual, so are its immediate surroundings. It sits in the middle of a high plateau – the plateau of the Cerdagne – which, thanks to its protected position and its south-facing aspect, is far and away the sunniest part of the Pyrenees. It claims 3,000 hours of sun in an average year and promotes itself as something of a paradise for health and leisure activities: skiing, paragliding, walking, riding, rock-climbing, river rafting, even the unexpected mountain sport of golf. In fact, seen from a mountaintop the whole of the Cerdagne looks like a very large football pitch, 50km long by 20km wide, with one half in Spain and the other in France, its grandstands provided by the 3,000m peaks of the Pyrenees, which surround it on all sides. There are hills in the Cerdagne, but they're gentle English-style ones that agriculture has robbed of most of their trees, giving it a flavour of Wiltshire.

The villages that dot this high plain still have a charming jumble of stone houses with slate roofs and hay barns; they also have curious, clipped Catalan names, ideal for a crossword-compiler's lexicon or an international Scrabble game where proper nouns are allowed: Llo, Hix, Err, there's even an Ur, and close to Llívia is a railway station called Ro, where we were hoping to catch a train.

I know this is a chronicle of walks and walking but we're not talking about any old train here, rather one of the main tourist attractions at this end of the Pyrenees. *Le petit train jaune* links the high plateau of the Cerdagne with the coastal plain surrounding Perpignan, and it also connects France with Spain; the steepness of the gradients and the difficulties of the terrain that were overcome during its construction at the beginning of the twentieth century have made it something of an engineering miracle. Our intention was to cross the Cerdagne on the *train jaune*, joining up with the GR10 after a pause to visit the other local technological attraction, *le four solaire* – the solar oven – which is conveniently on the railway route.

With its narrow gauge, single track and its bright yellow-and-red livery, *le petit train jaune* (also known affectionately as *le canari des montagnes*) may look like a toy railway but it's a serious part of the SNCF, France's rail network, and this means that it tends to be punctual. So there we were, under the toasting midday sun, running out of the Spanish enclave of Llívia towards Ro, the nearest station in France – the little train doesn't deign to stop on Spanish territory. Running was putting it a bit strongly, given the weight of our packs and the fact that the strap of Simon's right flip-flop had snapped, which left him, flip-flop in hand, hopping quickly and increasingly desperately, like a contestant in a particularly sadistic game-show. Luckily, most of the residents of the enclave were well into their Sunday lunch and had more important things to occupy their attention than our bizarre antics. Still, I'd like to think we've added another leisure pursuit to the long list of those already practised up here in the Cerdagne and that the next print-run of tourist brochures will include a reference to high-altitude hopping, with optional heavy backpack.

It goes without saying that as we arrived exhausted and, in Simon's case, footsore at Ro station, *le petit train jaune* was pulling away, with a jaunty toot just to rub it in. We agreed that this was suitable retribution for cheating – we also decided that the sensible alternative was to carry on cheating and hitchhike. This didn't go very well either: it was a Sunday and the few cars that passed were full to bursting with families and/or duty-free shopping from the supermarkets of nearby Andorra. It was also very hot and there was no shade, so to save a microscopic amount of energy we stopped bothering to wave our thumbs at the less likely lifts.

Eventually, by the reverse of Sod's Law, which states that good things happen when you least expect them, the fullest car of all came to a screeching halt. It was an estate and the two teenage children were decanted into the rear compartment, alongside a large and smelly dog, while we sat comfortably in the back seats. Our benefactors offered to take us to Font Romeu, the site of the solar oven, which was a fair bit further than they'd intended to go, as we discovered a few minutes later when we passed their home outside the village of Saillagouse. It was no ordinary *maison* but *une maison de jeunes*, a residential home for children with emotional and learning difficulties.

After some linguistic and cultural confusion we worked out that the father was the director of the establishment; he and his family lived above, well actually beside, the shop in a pleasant, modern house with sloping lawns that connected it to the less pleasing-looking institutional quarters. They were from northern France and were unanimous in their praise for the quality of life in the Cerdagne: it's a very outdoor kind of place, with much sport and a healthy climate; there's a high-altitude training camp for athletes and a number of clinics which treat asthma. There's even the story of a successful racehorse being brought to the Cerdagne to have its allergy cured. As the English version of the tourist brochure charmingly summarises it:

> The sunny climate and altitude are propitious to tonic stays. Added to the spring hot waters that gush out in many places, you can enjoy the pleasure of an outdoor spa even in the coldest periods. The sulphurous emanations are an advantage to people with breathing problems.

I privately wondered whether being in such a healthy and generally uplifting place would be beneficial for the residents of the children's home, but I couldn't work out how to put it in French without seeming a complete wally, so embarked on the much safer topic of food. Cerdagne's cuisine is filling and healthy rather than subtle. Highlights, we were told, are the *charcuterie* (ham, black pudding, etc.) and a typical mountain soup, more of a meal really, called *ouillade*: it's based on cabbage, potatoes, carrots and beans, with bits of bacon, black pudding and pork added according to taste or what happens to be available. *L'ouillade* is a winter treat, and not all that different from the omnipresent Pyrenean *garbure*, which we'd sampled in the central and western mountains. A truly local speciality is 'duck with turnips', the turnips being a wild variety which have much the same taste as the cultivated kind, apparently, but a very different shape: long and thin, like carrots. Our friends also recommended the wild autumnal mushrooms, and a tiny mountain dandelion called *xicoia*, which I've never seen or tasted but sounds a lot like the very fashionable rocket.

We were dropped off on the outskirts of the mountain resort of Font Romeu, the largest French town in the Cerdagne. Here at Odeillo is the site of one of the most visited buildings in the Pyrenees, and one of its most spectacular man-made structures: the solar oven. The building itself is a tower block, completely out of place on the edge of a grassy hillside. And, more bizarrely, the hillside is dotted with large reflecting mirrors, a hundred or more of them. Their job is to reflect the sunshine, so prevalent around here, onto a huge concave mirror on the side of the building; this concentrates the sun's rays and creates temperatures of up to a thousand degrees Celsius. Even more interesting for those of us who aren't research physicists is that the mirrored surface of the building provides an accidental artistic installation: a weird, distorted cloudscape, which changes constantly. We walked round the exhibition (see, we hadn't completely given up on walking) which had a very French emphasis on serious education, with vast quantities of data and impressive models, some of which you could play – I should say interact – with.

There was a film theatre where you could watch a video introduction to the oven. It opened with a scene from the Stone Age: two chilly Neanderthals are trying to light a fire using a boy-scout-approved method involving a couple of rocks. A voice-over announced: 'Since the dawn of time man has relied on heat, and progress has required higher and higher temperatures . . .' Sometime later I awoke to hear: '. . . the technology now available to us at Odeillo can increase the power of sunlight sixteen thousand times'.

This means that, even during a bad sunshine year like 2000, the solar oven can emulate the temperatures experienced by a space shuttle during re-entry into the earth's atmosphere. It's also played a part in testing nuclear-power programmes. What it hasn't done is produce any domestic power itself. A few kilometres away is the derelict 'Termis' solar power station, which closed in 1986 through lack of economic viability, when France decided to put most of its electric eggs in the nuclear basket. Apparently it's now sitting around in a state of abandonment, waiting for a bid from the Japanese and giving London's Millennium Dome a run for its money in the Eurovision White Elephant contest.

Like all great ventures, the solar oven has an engagingly unlikely story to explain its origins. In 1944, the Germans retreated from the fortified town of Mont Louis, a few miles away, leaving behind a powerful anti-aircraft searchlight. A few years later a French physics teacher on holiday saw the light, as it were, and wondered what would happen if you used it during the day rather than at night, and then, instead of using a bulb to create light, you reversed the process and exploited the light from the sun to create energy. Thus he created the first *four solaire*, which might or might not have been called a petit four.

It wasn't sun but snow that first put Font Romeu and the Cerdagne on the international map. If we'd come here a hundred years ago there would only have been a few farmsteads and Romanesque churches, but then came the Grand Hotel, which was at the heart of Font Romeu's development as one of Europe's earliest and most upmarket ski resorts, attracting royal families and other notables to come and stay at the imposing but rather hideous building. The heyday of the Grand Hotel was in the 1920s and 30s, but the seeds were sown for the growth of a more inclusive tourism in the second half of the century, providing jobs for younger people of the Cerdagne who otherwise would almost certainly have fled to the cities, following the pattern that's repeated itself across the Pyrenees.

As with other outdoor activities, there's no shortage of opportunities for walking in the Cerdagne. We could, for instance, have walked from Err along the gorges of the river Segre or up the Eyne Valley through a nature reserve to the Col d'Eyne, which is second only to the Basque pass of Orgambidexca as a crossing point for migrating birds. We might also have taken a few days out and trekked through the Carlit Massif, but our old friend the GR10, which doesn't have much to do with the Cerdagne, was waiting for us just over the mountains to the north of Font Romeu. We let it wait a bit longer and decided to make good our earlier omission and let the little yellow train take the strain.

This railway is as much a symbol of this part of the Pyrenees as the formidable Mount Canigou; the red-and-yellow livery is no accident, but echoes the colours of the Catalan flag, while its playful exterior hides the wealth of challenges that confronted its pioneering engineers. It took seven years to construct the switchback narrow-gauge line that climbs over 1,000m on its 40km journey. Among its incredible 650 *ouvrages d'art*, as the French quite rightly describe their classier feats of civil engineering, the most visibly spectacular are the Séjourné viaduct and the Gisclard suspension bridge over the Têt river. The gradient of the railway was so steep that no conventional steam train of the early twentieth century had the oomph or the puff to get up, so *le petit train jaune* was powered by electric motors through power passed on by an extra rail; the electricity was generated locally by damming the Marais de Bouillouses to form a huge reservoir, which was a Herculean task in its own right.

At Odeillo's ticket office we discovered that our destination, Planès, in common with some of the other small stations on this line is a request stop (*un arrêt facultatif*), which means you have to let the driver know where you want to alight. The train arrived, with a clatter of machinery and a chorus of good-humoured cheers from the hundred or so passengers waiting for, or already filling, the open carriages affectionately known as *baignoires* (bath tubs). It was all very *Thomas the Tank Engine* and extremely yellow. I ran to the business end of the train and endeavoured to catch the attention of the driver, who was in the middle of an enthralling phone conversation with the Fat Controller, or maybe it was his girlfriend. I shouted 'Planès' and he nodded vaguely either in response to my request or something said on the other end of the phone, and, seeing as there was now a bit of an evening chill in the air, we took our places in one of the less-crowded closed carriages.

Our journey, though short, was extremely sweet and amply made up for the earlier grief that missing the train had caused us. We followed a ridge through the valley, with spectacular views in all directions, including a stop at la Bolquère, the highest railway station in Europe (1,560m, since you ask). It was late afternoon, and the sun, which hadn't faltered all day, was now low in the sky, projecting the shadow of the train onto the golden cornfields that bordered the track. The harvest was in full swing and, though, in this high, isolated, beautiful landscape, there should really have been lines of happy peasants gathering in the sheaves and loading them onto horse-drawn carts, in fact this is 21st-century Europe and the work was being done by state-of-the-art combine harvesters and tractors with the unmistakeable stamp of the Common Agricultural Policy on them.

As the little yellow train rattled and rolled through the Cerdagne, it was followed by a number of kestrels. Maybe the noise disturbed the mice and voles, or maybe the harvest had something to do with it. But, whatever the reason, should the enigmatic and flawed football genius Eric Cantona ever feel the need to replace his gnomic utterance about seagulls following trawlers, which bemused a generation of sports journalists, I'd like to offer him a mountain version: 'Ze kestrels follow ze train.'

The driver didn't disappoint us and stopped at Planès, where we were the only people to get off. If we'd stayed, the next stretch of line would have taken us past the site of the worst event in the little train's history. *Le catastrophe du Paillat*, as it came to be known, occurred on 31 October 1909, during a test run to monitor the strength of the Gisclard suspension bridge across the river Têt. As the train took one of the tight bends at the bottom of the descent, there was a brake failure and the train came off the rails, killing six people.

Among the casualties was the brilliant engineer and creator of the bridge that bears his name, Albert Gisclard, who died beside his masterwork. He was a mathematician by training, from the southern city of Nîmes, and his revolutionary design used cables fixed into the mountains to solve the problems of carrying the huge loads that the railway exerted. The elegance and lightness of Gisclard's solution for the 150m-long bridge were much admired and copied in the years following his death. After the accident, which led to the man behind the railway project, Jules Lax, being branded *un assassin*, another backup brake system was added to the train, and, if you're thinking of travelling on it, you'll be pleased to know there are now three of these in operation and there hasn't been a serious accident since it came into public service in 1910.

A short walk from Planès station took us back to the GR10 along a grassy cart track bordered by blackberry bushes, but there was soon an excuse to stop walking again at the village of Planès. Temptation to go no further that day was provided by the attractive Gîte de Malaza with its little restaurant. But we resolutely turned our back on the '*plat du jour: côte de porc avec ratatouille*' and bought sandwiches and a bottle of wine for the supper we were hoping to eat at the unattended mountain refuge where we planned to spend that night.

Planès is also host to one of those architectural mountain gems that I would include on the list of Pyrenean buildings not to miss. A counterpoint to the solar oven in every conceivable way, it's a tiny Romanesque church, called Notre-Dame de la Merci. Apart from its minuscule size – a capacity congregation would be 25 people at most – the striking thing about the church is its triangular shape, which, combined with its bulging apses, makes it look for all the world like a tiny paddle steamer. There's debate about whether its unusual architecture is evidence of Moorish influence, but I personally would have suspected the hand of Le Corbusier, if he'd been born eight hundred years earlier. The most important thing, though, is to know what Notre Dame will do for you, and according to the notice outside she had a pretty wide remit: providing remedies for fever, antidotes to infertility as well as protecting your crops against disease. In short, a good person to have on your side.

It was six in the evening when we walked out of Planès, and as usual we'd left ourselves with a tight schedule and a looming deadline. We really had to get to the Refuge de L' Orry before sunset, since, apart from the potential difficulty of finding the place in the dark, we would almost certainly have to collect wood to make a fire. The path began with a serious uphill gradient which would have taxed *le petit train jaune* but fortunately levelled out after an hour, and there followed an enchanting stretch along a path carpeted with soft needles from the surrounding pine forest with ceps, fly agarics like toffee-apples and wild pansies. The surroundings lent wings to our boots, but even so the sun was almost gone when we reached the end of the forest and spotted the refuge, a rustic shack beside a stream.

Our new home was a single-storey building with a roof of corrugated iron that actually turned out to be a semidetached shack; a faded sign planted in the turf pointed out that one half was for ramblers (*refuge randonneur*), while the other was reserved for shepherds and cowherds (*refuge pastorale/vacher*) – and also, unfortunately, for their dogs. Four extremely unwelcoming hounds came hurtling towards us, obviously hungry and almost certainly rabid. We scrabbled around for stones to throw and as we did so became even better targets; it was only when we remembered our SAS tactics, one person moving, the other providing covering fire, that we managed to reach the door to our half of the building. We pushed it open and tumbled noisily through it only to discover that we weren't alone. A couple were crouched beside a fire, half-turned towards us and illuminated by its glow as though in some nineteenth-century painting of life in a peasant dwelling.

When you reach a certain age you feel you've come across most social situations, but this was a new one on Simon and me. What were the unspoken rules about sharing an intimate space with two complete strangers, particularly as they'd arrived first and were, technically, in the position of landlords? Of course, it turned out not to be a problem because we were all on our very best behaviour. They offered us a cup of tea, which we gratefully accepted, and we offered them some red wine, then they offered us some of their chocolate . . . and so it went on until they drew the line at a bite of our sandwiches. Our fellow travellers were a French couple in their late thirties or early forties, and, as they had sensibly arrived a couple of hours earlier, there was a very fine fire crackling away in the grate. They had bagged the best beds, it's true, but this was no big deal as the choice was between top or bottom shelf on a kind of industrial bunk bed, which was supposed to hold six sleepers on each level, but on this occasion would only have two – unless, of course, anyone arrived even later than us.

Pierre and Claire were from Paris, where she was an opera singer (the only one I've ever spent the night with) and he was an audio technician – I don't know if they met during a production of *Carmen* but she was striking enough to have played the lead role in it. They were rather better equipped than we were for this kind of jaunt, with a little stove and saucepan and supplies of powdered soup and coffee. In what you could call a mélange of French and English we asked them whether roughing it like this was popular among the arty classes of Paris, and they told us that their friends were more than happy to talk about walking in the Pyrenees, but doing it was another matter entirely. As for their three teenage children, they'd never be seen dead in a pair of walking boots, said Pierre, though he thought they might virtually walk the GR10 if it was part of an interactive game, with plenty of things to be shot en route. I couldn't help but think that Pierre and Claire were probably slightly less delighted to see us than we were to see them, but if so they were very gracious about it; they said without any prompting that what they liked about walking was that, though you didn't come across too many people, those you did meet you could spend a bit of quality time with. I seem to remember it sounded much more elegant in French.

We chatted and played cards – rummy seemed to be the game that best bridged the Channel – carrying on until all drink was gone and the fire was reduced to a few embers. None of us felt much like braving the *chiens des vachers/pasteurs* in the dark, though we did wonder who our next-door neighbours were and whether they were at this minute drinking rotgut liquor and themselves playing some incomprehensible local game of cards. As bedtime approached I began to hope that Pierre and Claire would not feel the urges of *l'amour*, but luckily it got so cold when the fire went out that we all slept with every stitch of clothing on. And even that wasn't enough to keep warm. For hours I was tormented by the chill-induced need to get up and have a wee and the equal and opposite desire not to go outside in the cold and meet the dogs. It was one of those nights when you pray for the morning so you can get up, get out and get going, never mind how tired you feel.

The next morning we crept from the refuge at about six in the morning and packed outside to avoid waking Pierre and Claire, who still seemed to be sleeping soundly. Maybe Pierre's herbal tobacco roll-ups had contained a few extra herbs. The GR10 continued east towards Mount Canigou, a couple of days away, and then gradually downhill to the Mediterranean, but we decided to head upwards and southwards towards Spain on what was probably an old smugglers' trail.

The sun was shining brightly already, looking keen to maintain the local sunshine record. After half an hour we caught sight of our mystery neighbours of the previous night and their dogs. This resolved the question of whether they were *vachers* or *bergers*, as they were dealing with a herd of reddish-brown cows; these were gathered around a chilly-looking tarn and showing no inclination to move any further despite the curious whoops and calls of the herders and the close attention of the dogs, which were too busy to resume the previous evening's hostilities.

The next encounter was quite bizarre and provided a salutary reminder that the mountains should always be taken seriously, particularly at night. A young woman came running down a steep hillside, looking surprisingly pleased to see us, and shouting in French, 'Excuse me, is this France or Spain?' We were able to clear that up and offer her some water, which she gratefully accepted, before explaining what had happened to her in a rush of rapid French that we eventually managed to slow down to manageable speed.

Her name was Nadia, and it transpired that she was from St-Nazaire (on the Atlantic coast) and was on her way to climb the Spanish mountain of Pic d'Estats with her boyfriend and a tent. The previous evening they'd been walking on the high ridge that forms the frontier between France and Spain when the weather had taken a couple of turns for the worse. They'd become totally enveloped in freezing fog and completely lost; they'd met another couple who were equipped sensibly with a GPS, but rather less sensibly didn't have the right map to make use of it. Night had fallen and they'd been unable to put up the tent as the ground was too hard, but had found a shelter where they'd huddled together until morning. It was '*très, très, très froid*', said Nadia, whose only protective clothing was a thinnish fleece; it put my own cold, bad night into perspective. Her boyfriend, Laurent, now came down the same slope, but a lot more slowly than she had, as he was limping after a fall during the events of the previous day. Neither of them seemed particularly dispirited, however, and Laurent was very keen to talk about the flock of twenty izards they'd spotted at seven o'clock that morning, and which they certainly wouldn't have seen if they'd been more prudent.

With the help of our map and our compass, we pointed them in the right direction for the *gîte d'étape* at Planès, feeling vaguely envious of the hot breakfast they'd undoubtedly find there, but decidedly superior as navigators and explorers. We continued up the mountainside towards a V-shaped notch on the skyline that just had to be the Col de les Nou Fonts (2,652m) where we would join the HRP, the high-level path.

Pride was soon followed by the inevitable comeuppance, however, as we followed the track down the other side of the pass and into what we fondly imagined was Spain. But was it? Why had the path petered away just before an almost impassable slope of scree? A suspicion that we hadn't actually crossed the Col de les Nou Fonts began to worry away at me. 'Are you sure this is the right way?' I asked Simon, who was in the lead.

He consulted his compass in an expert manner – 'Yes, due south.'

As there's no arguing with the compass we scrambled painfully across the rockfall. On the other side, after a careful look at the position of the sun, I had a more serious crisis of confidence. 'Let *me* see that compass?'

And this brought the reply: 'Well, if you must, oh ... eh, you're not going to believe this . . . I think I might have got south and north muddled up.'

We crossed the almost impassable rockfall again, and an hour later we were back where we'd started at the col, which wasn't the Col de les Nou Fonts. It didn't take long to find a serious-looking path heading away in the opposite direction to the sheep track we'd taken earlier. I was angry for a bit and then irritated for a bit longer and then amused at the thought of the travel editor who couldn't tell his north from his south.

There is a serious point here, which the great sage of Pyrenean walking Hilaire Belloc might have summarised as: 'Don't trust gut feelings in the mountains.' Of course, he would not have used a phase like 'gut feelings', but he did make the point that one's intuitions are often guided by misleading emotions: the wish to have arrived somewhere can convince you that you have got there, while in actual fact you're still a distance away; equally, you can be absolutely certain that it's the incorrect downhill path you want rather than the correct one which goes uphill, for the simple reason that you're tired and don't fancy any more climbing. Also, as we'd already discovered on a number of other occasions, one col can look a lot like another, so it pays to check the map and the compass, whether or not you're in doubt . . . but it helps if you do it properly, Simon.

It was midday when we eventually found our col, one of those odd Pyrenean crossroads where walkers can be seen converging from four different directions, either trudging and scrambling up from Spain or France, or as rows of matchstick figures getting even tinier with distance as they followed the ridge going east and west.

The reason for this relative crowd was that the path down into Spain leads to the sanctuary of Núria, one of Catalonia's most popular religious shrines. It commemorates the miraculous discovery there of an image of the Virgin in the eleventh century; female pilgrims to the sanctuary were believed to be blessed with the gift of fertility and this may or may not be linked to the popularity of the name Núria in Catalonia. Even without this motivation, the journey up the Freser Valley to Núria is worth it for the views alone, particularly if you take La Cremallera, a rack-and-pinion railway, which is a smaller and even steeper counterpart of the yellow train. From Núria, you can get up onto the frontier ridge for a day's exhilarating walk, before heading back down the next valley, the valley of the river Ter. This was also what we were intending to do, although we'd started from the French side.

The walk along the top of this ridge was the highest and, ironically, the most frequented stretch of path we'd come across so far: every couple of minutes there was someone else to say good morning to, and since we were walking along the precise line of the frontier there was the inevitable question of should it be '*Bonjour*' or should it be '*Hola*'?

The contrast between the two countries was striking: on the French side clumps of trees, meadows, enticing blue lakes, a generally softer look, whereas Spain was all rock and scree: greys, silvers, harsh pinks, dried-up water courses. But the weather was an entirely different story: from the French side came a bitter northerly wind while Spain was sunny and, in the lee of the highest rocks, extremely warm.

We were sheltering from the wind and eating an early lunch, when something unusual came into view: a small figure moving at great pace, almost running along the ridge, hurdling boulders and overtaking the line of trudging walkers like Michael Schumacher amid the Sunday drivers. As it grew closer the figure became familiar and, when he waved, it all clicked into place: this was Yannick the photographer, who we'd met three weeks earlier in a *gîte d'étape* in the Basque Country, the young man who bore a striking resemblance to football's *enfant terrible* Dennis Wise.

Since that encounter Simon and I had returned to London, done some work and then returned to the Pyrenees, and all the while Yannick had been walking the HRP. Well, not exactly walking . . . he was on day 33 of the trek and was on course for a very fast time, if not the HRP record, as he was expecting to be in Banyuls-sur-Mer in four days' time. Why the rush? Well, he had to be back at work on 1 September at a photography shop in Bordeaux. And how had it been? In a mixture of English and French he described the challenge of following the path which was often no path at all, the five days of permanent snow, which had been no problem, in fact, '*génial*' was how he put it; he'd even managed to stop off in Andorra to replace his boots (which had fallen to pieces) with a very stylish pair of boots-cum-trainers for half the usual French price, as well as to buy a duty-free bottle of Baileys to help him get to sleep on the cold nights. I made a note of that for my next stay in a refuge.

Yannick was carrying one very cool piece of kit: a wristwatch plus altimeter plus compass. It told us that we were now at 2,700m and that the highest point he'd reached on the HRP had been 3,005m. There was also a way of adding all the ascents together, which would have revealed how far he had actually climbed since he'd set out from Hendaye on the Atlantic shore. But we weren't able to complete the calculation because looking at his watch reminded Yannick that he'd been standing still for long enough, so with a combined 'aurevoirgoodbye' he exploded into action and within a few minutes was quite out of sight.

We followed at a more sedate pace and as the path dropped back onto the French side of the frontier we came upon a scene more in keeping with the African savannah than a European mountainside. An animal, almost certainly an izard, was lying at the foot of a high cliff, having presumably fallen from the top to its doom. Gathered around it was a knot, a skein, a riot of griffon vultures, who were making the most of the unexpected lunch. They fought and screamed and waved their wings frenziedly, while colleagues who'd only just heard about the party kept arriving, swooping in with a great whooshing of air just above our heads, before they piled in as well. These birds are supposed to adhere to a strict pecking order, with the junior members having to wait their turn, but it looked about as orderly as a London pub at closing time on a Friday evening.

When the path had skirted a couple of highish peaks, and crossed back into Spain out of the wind, we were at last able to add a live izard to our previous sightings of dead and stuffed ones. In fact, there were two of them, mother and child, posed just as they should have been, proudly on a jutting platform of rock. They were medium-sized deer with the most beautiful dark-golden coats, and when she saw us the mother gave a snort of the most evident disgust, shook her head with its characteristic backward-curving antlers and away they bounded, leaving us fumbling unsuccessfully for a camera.

It was getting on for six in the evening, after almost twelve hours of walking, when we reached the first solid sign of civilisation since we'd left the Refuge de L'Orry. It was another refuge, the Refuge de Ter, where sensible walkers were easing off their boots, drying their socks and enjoying a leisurely drink in the fast-sinking sun. For some odd reason we'd booked ourselves beds in the village of Setcases, which was a dispiriting if appropriate seven kilometres away down a mountain road, newly built for the winter skiing traffic.

As with the earlier experience near Llívia (had it really been only the day before?), fortune favoured the daft, and a sporty but battered Renault hurtled past, screamed to a halt and reversed back towards us as fast as I normally drive when going forwards.

The driver was, of course, in his mid-twenties with long dark hair and super-cool shades, and the ensuing journey to Setcases was terrifying but mercifully short. We had a beer with him at the hotel and he turned out to be no poseur but a real mountain man and an aficionado of extreme sports in the best Spanish tradition. His favourite winter sport was ice-climbing, up frozen waterfalls, which I'm told ranks alongside Russian roulette in the canon of dangerous pastimes. He was also a member of the local ski patrol and over a second beer told us about the problems posed by off-piste skiers from Barcelona and of his most difficult rescue, which had involved an izard with a broken leg that he'd carried back on his shoulders for three hours. On skis, into the bargain.

He roared away down the mountainside and we were able to give some attention to our surroundings. This was the village of Setcases, which translates as seven houses, and to discover the origins of its name you need to go back to the year 965 when a shepherd and his family of seven sons were caught here in a blizzard and decided to stay and build themselves houses. Come to think of it, there should've been eight houses in that case, but presumably two of them agreed to share. Anyway, that's the legend and now there are quite a lot more than seven houses and a few small hotels, one of which was our new base. It was pleasant enough with huge stone fireplaces and cosy wood-panelling that suggested its main trade was during the winter skiing season, and that summer was just a bit on the side. We went up to our room and had some difficulty getting in, as a spare folding bed had been leaned eccentrically and dangerously against the door. It was good to be back in Spain.

The next morning we shared a breakfast table with José and Carmen, a couple from Barcelona. They'd chosen to come to Setcases for a quiet break, though they were used to seeing it during the skiing season and thought the landscape looked a bit odd without any snow.

The breakfast was a spectacular spread that included delicate pastries, an array of hams and sausages and of course the Catalan speciality *pan tomaquet*: toasted bread topped with tomato and oil. José, who was an international businessman, said that he'd recently been with some colleagues at a conference in Singapore, where the hosts had made a generous attempt to welcome the Catalans by providing *pan tomaquet* for their first breakfast. Unfortunately they'd been unable to find the rough country bread that's a key ingredient; it just didn't taste the same, according to José, on floppy white processed slices. Unlike his wife, he wasn't a real Catalan but had been brought up on the opposite side of Spain in Extremadura. He was not a fan of Catalan nationalism, but, when we asked about the relative differences between the Catalan culture in Spain and in France, they were both equally dismissive of the French version, claiming that it was mostly window-dressing, and didn't extend much beyond folksy dances and red-and-yellow flags.

We were intending to make our way back into Catalan France, but didn't have time to walk there. We had missed the morning bus to nearby Camprodon, which is the chief town of the Ripollès region, and is on the main road that crosses the frontier. So there was nothing for it but to stick the thumbs out again. At first it went well and we got a quick lift from the edge of the village, opposite two flagpoles: one flying the Catalan flag, the other rather pointedly flag-free, I thought. We were soon in Camprodon, where we stayed, and stayed and stayed. It reminded me why I'd given up serious hitchhiking when I'd left university. It also reminded me that two hours of standing still is a great deal more tiring than two hours of walking.

There was ample time, then, to become familiar with our immediate environment. We were outside a factory devoted to the making of *embutits* – sausages. The sign with the company name also featured a colourful and sinister scene: a large man in butcher's garb with a big grin on his face and an even larger cleaver in his hand was pursuing a very pink pig through a very green landscape. From time to time unmarked white vans entered the factory, suggesting that the pig had not escaped. A little further down the road another sign indicated the presence of what must count as one of the world's more unlikely museums: the museum of washing machines. Honestly. After a while we decided that a look at some early top-loaders might be more interesting than standing around and looking stupid beside the C151. The fact that Prats de Mollò was our immediate destination should have been a warning.

The washing-machine museum was closed because it was Tuesday. Traffic and time passed. I read the tourist brochure we'd got from Setcases tourist office. It told me:

> We all know that the finest landscapes are those which, like memories, are traced in the heart with the brushstrokes of experience. Rather than a holiday spot, Setcases is a state of mind, with its narrow streets, steep-pitched slate roofs, the babbling of the river's cold waters, trees, fairy-tale woods . . .

. . . and so it went on in similar vein. I wondered if we'd missed something in Setcases and read out the paragraph to Simon, who suggested we add 'the cacophonous early-morning racket of the refuse lorry'. Even he was beginning to lose his good humour. But the brochure did help jolt us out of our torpor with the advice: 'Though it might seem that time stands still, you don't have to.'

'Let's get a taxi,' said Simon. We did; then a bus and two hours later we were in Arles-sur-Tech ready for the last three days on the GR10 before it reaches the Mediterranean, the description of which must wait until our final chapter.

It should have become quite clear by this time that, when it comes to walking, Simon and I could not be considered purists. Walking is enjoyable, but so are lots of other things; quite often it's worth getting a bus or train, hitchhiking or even taking a taxi in order to get to some better walking. Sometimes you don't have any option but to do this. And it *can* be great fun, and of course it's another way of getting to know the Pyrenees.

Three years after the wasted morning outside the sausage factory, Simon and I returned to the Cerdagne and the Catalan Pyrenees through a sequence of accidents rather than through any process of planning. It was a mid-May expedition in which we'd hoped to enjoy what the Setcases tourist brochure had called 'the joyous bursting forth of spring' in the central mountains. Unfortunately, a late snowfall had delayed the bursting forth, and also made it quite impossible to walk anywhere except at the two ends of the mountain chain or in the foothills. After a few days in the Basque Country, we decided to try out a lower-level route: *le sentier des Cathares,* the path of the Cathars.

We travelled, mostly by rail, along the length of the Pyrenees, which was an adventure in itself; it began with an advanced examination in the interpretation of French railway timetables, which we failed comprehensively. So when we turned up at five to ten at the Basque station of St-Jean-Pied-de-Port, expecting to catch the train to Bayonne in ten minutes, we found we actually had three days to wait. The mistake we'd made was to think that the abbreviations 'Lu' and 'Sa' meant that the train would run each day from *Lundi* to *Samedi*, i.e. Monday to Saturday, when in fact it means Monday *and* Saturday. You may think this is an odd pattern of timetabling and I suggested as much to the man in the ticket office. 'In July, it runs every day,' he said.

We managed to control ourselves and thank him for his help before going off to try our luck at hitchhiking. It was not a lucky day at all and we finished up with an expensive taxi fare to a town called Orthez, which in 1814 was where the Duke of Wellington's forces defeated the French during the countdown to Waterloo. Our taxi driver was actually a builder on downtime, but he was a charming fellow with an encyclopaedic knowledge of football in the English Division One – we discussed Crystal Palace's chances in the impending play-offs. He also had a builder's appreciation of the transition from the Basque Country to the ancient region of the Béarn; the most obvious difference is in the roofs of the houses: the red tiles give way to slates when you get to the town of St-Palais in the Béarn.

The eventual rail journey east included a change of trains at a station called St-Agne on the edge of Toulouse: shoddy tower blocks, graffiti everywhere, people who wouldn't meet your eyes – a reminder, in short, what life is like beyond the mountains. Posters on the station were promoting a campaign to befriend old-age pensioners, a lot of whom had died during the lethal summer of 2003, perishing in a heat wave while the younger generations were on holiday by the sea, or in the mountains. We carried on to Foix, the chief town of France's most remote and depopulated department, the Ariège, for a walk with a difference through countryside where, in the Middle Ages, the persecution of a religious minority became a national obsession. *Le sentier des Cathares* leads you through hilly, wooded countryside and takes in the ruined castles on remote, high crags where the heretical Christian sect of Cathars tried to defend themselves against their powerful establishment enemies, a reminder that life in the mountains has also had its periods of social and political crisis.

In Foix it was pouring with rain, which might have explained the low turnout at a recruitment fair being held by gendarmes in the town centre. We gave it a miss as well and caught a school bus to a village called Roquefixade. In rural France quite a few school buses take other passengers as well, which is fine unless you're trying to get somewhere during the school holidays, when the school buses don't run. Anyway, this was Wednesday afternoon and a school half-day, so the bus was crowded with talkative but very well-behaved children who were going home early; it was also covered with warning signs, jocularly headed with the picture of a bomb, which might explain why the young passengers were so good.

We got off after half an hour at a remote road junction and walked up and across the fields to the village of Roquefixade. In the damp mist, it was grim and very medieval: no sign of life in the main square apart from one badly parked car. There were supposed to have been Cathars living here in the thirteenth century, including a man who was involved in the affair of Avignonet, when eleven inquisitors were assassinated by a group of the previously peaceable Cathars. Towering over the village was a high crag, topped by the castle of Roquefixade, which was owned by vassals of the count of Toulouse and Foix until the King of France bought it in 1278, so an informative sign told us, and assured it of a garrison comprising 'the Lord of the manor, a look-out, a porter, twelve sergeants-at-arms and some guard dogs'.

Nowadays there are only the ruins, which are a brisk, steep climb from the village ('*site vertigineux*' you are warned) and I can't imagine it would have been much fun trying to take the castle under fire from those sergeants. There might, on the other hand, have been a great view from the top, but not today.

We took the path of the Cathars out of the village; actually we failed to find it for quite some time as the guidebooks were unhelpful and there was no one around to ask the way, just a few descendants of those guard dogs to hurry us on our way. As a result of the mistake we had to walk for half an hour or more down a busy main road with no pavement, which was doubly unpleasant as I'd sustained some weird injury to the ankle that meant every five minutes or so it seized up in a convulsion of pain, which then gradually wore off, until it returned. Simon helpfully suggested that I might like to hitchhike, but I decided on the kill-or-cure approach.

Don't get me wrong. I love walking in the mountains but there are some days when it's better not to have pulled your boots on: apart from the ankle injury, I seemed to have become allergic to the dried apricots that were our regular source of in-walk sustenance, so a feeling of nausea now accompanied the limp. The track, when we eventually found it, didn't help matters; the rain had turned the steep forest path into a mudslide and the stream that we had to cross periodically became a demanding obstacle.

We came to a village called Montferrier and, as our mobile phones wouldn't work, we tried to use the public phone-box to book a hotel room for the night; it had been vandalised. This meant that the stopwatch was ticking (again) as we set out up the next hill towards our goal of Montségur. A thunderstorm with rain accompanied us through the wood and after an hour or so of river-hopping and mud-sliding we reached a road through a pass and spotted the castle of Montségur perched even higher than the one we'd left at Roquefixade. It was seven o'clock and the path had another surprise in store: instead of descending gently from the col to the village it crossed the road, entered a wood and climbed very steeply for another twenty minutes before finally allowing us a chance to go downwards towards Montségur. There was another icy downpour just to complete the misery, so we arrived chilled, soaked and without a booking, outside the inn at the bottom of the village.

The inn was at right angles to the narrow street; it was a long, stone building, maybe two or three houses that had been knocked together many years previously. The front door was open but it revealed a dark hallway, with no sign of a light switch. There was no sign of any person either, but after several shouts of '*Il y a quelqu'un?*' there was the sound of movement from upstairs; then there was light and we stumbled up a narrow staircase to find, to our great relief, that there were also rooms available. The proprietor was a woman well into her sixties, who took our sopping wet clothes to a drying room, and even stuck our boots on iron contraptions specially made for drying footwear, beside the glowing log fire. There was a hot shower and then an evening meal comprising four very solid courses: soup, salad, pork with lentils, plum pie and a small jug of wine that required frequent refilling and received it. All of which led to a very good night's sleep.

The next day I opened the shutters to see Montségur Castle perched dramatically on top of its hill. This was as close as I got to it, although Simon had already clambered up the demanding slope to the top before we sat down to breakfast. My excuse was that I was (a) injured and (b) had already done it, many years previously when on holiday in the area. It is hard to say what's more extraordinary, the setting of the castle or the historical events surrounding it: as retaliation for the assassination of the inquisitors at Avignonet, a force of around 10,000 soldiers laid siege to the castle of Montségur in 1243, and its tiny community of 500 managed to hold out for a year. When it finally surrendered, the 225 surviving Cathars refused to renounce their beliefs and were burned at the stake *en masse*.

Our walk that day continued on the path of the Cathars to the tiny village of Comus, where we'd arranged to drop in on an Englishman who lives there all the year round. It was to be a brisk four-hour walk. As I seemed to have packed my glasses at the bottom of my rucksack, I was prepared to accept Simon's assessment of the walk at face value. 'We'll be doing a lot of contour-hugging,' he said, peering expertly at the map. This phrase was to come back to haunt him, as the path made no attempt at all to stick to any particular contour line but cut straight through them at right angles.

First we went up very steeply through a beech forest, then down very steeply on a slippery track of red clay. At one moment both feet went from under me and, as the Pilgrim's Prayer had forecast, the ground came up to meet me with a solid thump. 'About that contour . . .' became a refrain. Still, we survived intact and the second half of the walk was much more enjoyable: through the Gorges de la Frau. France is very good at gorges and this one was suitably dramatic, dark and chilly, and there were notices warning about the risk of *éboulements* (landslips) and unexpected *crevasses*, which added a certain sense of excitement.

Comus is an airy village in a wide valley beyond the gorge, with views of high hills and serious mountains to the south and west. We called in on a man who, after a career in the Royal Marines, has become one of the thirty-odd permanent residents of the village. As we arrived, Guy was putting his lawnmower away, as this was the first day of the year when grass cutting had been possible. Along with his wife Molly, a painter, he takes a full part in village activities and is delighted that their arrival has reduced the average age of the place. What he loves most of all is the winters, being a great cross-country skier; for three months of the year – sometimes more – he can ski across virgin snow as far as Spain. As a sixtieth birthday present to himself, Guy walked the GR10, taking a tent and setting himself a demanding schedule of dawn-to-dusk walking that left Simon and me exhausted just hearing about it. As we talked, a beautifully marked feral cat stalked across the steep lawn. In a field behind his house lurked rare spider orchids and in the local forest he'd seen the very uncommon and threatened bird, the capercaillie.

On the southern edge of the valley and an hour's walk from Comus is the best-known medieval village in France – Montaillou. It was the subject of a book by Laroy Ladurie, which shed light on the daily life of the period in a way fiction could never have equalled. Montaillou was the last village in France to actively support the heretical belief of Catharism, in which the Devil was given an equal billing with God, while the simple and abstinent life of the Cathar elite, called *parfaits*, threw into sharp relief the corruption of the Catholic clergy. When the last Cathars of Montaillou were sniffed out and snuffed out in the early 1320s by a relentless local bishop – a very devil of an Inquisitor – that was the end of Catharism in France.

After Comus we could have continued on the Route des Bonshommes – another Cathar path, which claims to take you on the route followed by the Cathars as they fled the increasing persecution into Spain. Instead, with only one day of holiday left, we decided to try and get up to the snowline of the most famous mountain at this end of the Pyrenees: Mount Canigou. Above 2,000m, where the fresh snow was lying, it would be difficult, and most definitely dangerous, but that still left plenty of mountainside to walk up. To get to Canigou required a complicated journey through valleys and round mountains.

Guy dropped us off at a pass on the road to Ax-les-Thermes, the nearest town of any size, and we soon got a lift in a large and ramshackle white van, belonging to a bearded hippy. The side doors were held on with string and the back seat had become a bed; curiosities of all sorts dangled and jangled around inside. Hippies are very prevalent in these parts and maybe they have a touch of modern-day Cathars about them. But they don't operate entirely outside the social rules and norms: our friend was going on his monthly trip to Andorra to stock up on cheap tobacco.

He left us in Ax-les-Thermes, which would have been OK normally, but not today as there was a train strike – which was described euphemistically on the official notices at the station as *une mouvemente sociale*. So we walked back up through Ax to find the road out and hitchhike. It's a twee town, where everyone seemed to own a poodle and the dogs' toilets were better signed than the railway station, and a lot busier on this particular day. After an hour waiting on the bridge across the river Ariège, we got a lift with an air steward, who was also going to Andorra for cheap cigarettes but otherwise was on a different planet from our hippy. Apart from the contrast in personal grooming, he was driving a brand-new car, rented expressly for this trip!

He left us on a high pass where two main roads diverge at a kind of motorway junction – and just before the tunnel of Puymorens. This was not an ideal spot for hitchhiking; it suddenly got very cold and then it started to snow. The situation cried out for my waterproof trousers, and while searching through my bag I found that I had managed to lose not only them, but my glasses as well.

But then, as the snow turned to freezing rain, salvation arrived in the shape of two chaps from Barcelona, in matching checked shirts, who were on their way back from a gig in Toulouse where they'd seen one of the members of a band from another age, Supertramp. We squeezed in to the back with our packs on our laps, crushed and relieved in equal measure. It had occurred to me before to ask myself why anyone in their right minds would wish to share their car with two ageing hikers; in this case it became quite clear that it was because they thought that we were another gay couple. And I suspect that we did seem just that – answering questions at the same time and finishing each other's sentences. After the tunnel we crossed the Cerdagne – confirming the impression we'd got of it three years previously, that it was very flat – although this time its sunshine record seemed likely to be compromised.

Our saviours asked us if we'd like to go with them to Barcelona, which was sweet of them, but might have been taking things a bit far; so, at seven o'clock, there we were standing on the frontier with Spain and still seventy kilometres from our destination of Villefranche in the foothills of Mount Canigou.

Amazingly, one hour later we were there. A young woman in a very smart four-wheel drive took us along the winding roads following the railway line belonging to the yellow train which we would have taken, but for the *mouvemente sociale*; there was a dramatic view of the suspension bridge where Gisclard met his end, and then tantalising glimpses of the massive Mount Canigou's snowy top glowing pink in the setting sun. Our latest benefactor worked for a company that arranged extreme corporate leisure activities where managers are scared into team-working via dangerous sports. She'd been researching an off-road 4×4 experience in Spain, with stops at very good hotels an essential ingredient. The next day she had to oversee a group who would be jet-skiing. Also very popular with her clients was quad-biking. We suggested walking in the mountains but she said it might be considered too dull – and too much like hard work no doubt.

We spent the night in a Fawlty Towersish hotel outside the pink-walled and beautiful village of Villefranche, but where the torrent of the river Têt provided the most soothing of lullabies. We also found that there was a bus up to Vernet-les-Bains, a spa village at the foot of Canigou, scheduled to leave from a stop outside the hotel at the very convenient time of eight-thirty in the morning.

But there's many a slip twixt cup and lip where Pyrenean transport is concerned: we were expecting to see a bus arrive, so failed to flag down the minibus which hurtled up the road and past us, without even slowing down. So it was hitchhiking again, this time with a woman who had an apple orchard and made organic apple juice; then, on the kind of stunningly clear and sunny morning that always blesses the last day of a holiday, we walked from Vernet up to a tiny village called Casteil and then on to the abbey of St-Martin du Canigou.

It's another wonder of Romanesque and pre-Romanesque architecture whose cloister has decorated capitals with profane scenes, in a similar vein to the church of Ste Engrâce in the Basque Country. Above all, it's the crags and ravines of the savage mountain setting that makes it a thrilling place to visit, though you have to sign up for a guided tour before you are allowed inside.

We were now too close to Canigou to see its towering snowy ramparts, and I'm sorry to say that, despite our best efforts, we didn't have time to get to the snow. Instead we walked back down to Vernet the pretty way. According to the photocopied route map we'd got from the very helpful man in the tourist office it was an easy walk, one which rated only one walking boot on their scale of difficulty. In fact, the path had been washed away in places; there were ropes to dangle from at a couple of points and it took rather longer than we had at our disposal. I remember noticing an edelweiss, white and beautiful beside the path, but we ended up having to run the last twenty minutes back to Vernet – at least we'd left our packs at the hotel.

We caught the bus by the skin of our teeth, but there was still room for a sting in the tail as the road had been washed away by all the melting snow, so the bus went off on a lengthy diversion up another valley. I became increasingly tense at the thought of missing the train to Perpignan and the flight back to London. Simon remained unruffled, made notes and took photos, and of course we caught both train and plane with time to spare.

9. LAST GASPS: TO THE MEDITERRANEAN

Mick Webb

After the medley of different paths, routes and even modes of transport that we'd used to zigzag from the Atlantic end of the Pyrenees, it seemed only right and proper that for the last stage to Arles-sur-Tech to Banyuls-sur-Mer we should stick to Shanks' pony. We'd also decided to stick to the GR10 for the three-day hike. Well, we intended to follow the GR10, but you won't be surprised that it didn't quite work like that.

Arles-sur-Tech is a hilly town with a medieval quarter built around its abbey. It's one of those places where the long-distance walker *should* take a well-earned rest, but is unable to do so because of the enjoyment to be had from walking up and down the extremely narrow streets with their evocative names like Carrer de l'Ovella (Sheep Street), their splendid wooden doors and the wrought-iron balconies, which were made with the iron that was mined from the flanks of nearby Mount Canigou and worked in the forges of Arles.

The most attractive feature of the abbey is its elegant cloister surrounding a pleasant little garden; but what brings most visitors here is the miraculous tomb, which provides an endless supply of spring water without an obvious connection to any external source of water. The tomb, which originally contained the bones of two Christian martyrs, Abdon and Sennen, produces hundreds of litres of water a year, some of which is handed out to the faithful every 30 July, the feast day of the two saints. How the supply of water renews itself has been a source of great interest and puzzlement for hundreds of years. According to recent scientific investigations, the most likely reason for the miracle is, prosaically, condensation.

If you're in Arles-sur-Tech in February, there's the opportunity to enjoy their *Fête de l'Ours* – Festival of the Bear. It's a throwback to pagan times and traditionally featured a village girl whose job was to attract a bear, which was then caught, tied up and shaved. These days the part of the bear is taken by a young man clad in a bear's outfit, who is captured and stripped of his costume, but not shaved.

An equally bizarre event occurred one midsummer evening on the edge of Arles-sur-Tech. In a small square surrounded by sweet-smelling plane trees, Simon and I danced the *sardane*. Arles has a reputation for its folk-dancing, which we did nothing to enhance as we joined the circle of twenty or so local people of varying ages, who elegantly stepped in and out, raising and lowering their arms in time to the changing rhythms of music from a portable CD player. A very patient woman of about eighty took me under her wing and gave me special remedial coaching, but after half an hour I had to retire, tired, not much better at the *sardane* but looking forward to the simpler physical require-ments of walking.

The GR10 leaves Arles rather apologetically, by the back door as it were, across a car park, but soon begins to climb though the forest of Arles and up into the Albères mountains. At least it did when we walked this way in the year 2000. Since then, there have been readjustments of the route following complaints from landowners, which is an unusual occurrence on the GR10.

We were aiming for the Col de Paracolls, which at 900m can hardly be called high, nor is the ascent particularly steep. It just seemed so, because we were now inside the Mediterranean climate zone and the weather had become appreciably hotter. The vegetation had changed as well: olive trees, different varieties of oak, some of them evergreen, and scrubby thorny bushes that manage to survive on unpredictable supplies of water, because the rainfall is much less than it is at the Atlantic end of the Pyrenees.

This is the Mediterranean stretch of the GR10, through the

department of the Pyrénées-Orientales, and though there are some similarities with the other end of the mountain range (both have a vibrant minority culture, more roads and more signs of human activity than in the high mountains) it's also quite distinctive: in fact, as different as ocean and sea. It's only three days from here to the Mediterranean itself but, though the mountains are lower, the path retains its challenge to the end and you can't give in to the euphoria of completing the traverse until you feel the hard pavements of Banyuls-sur-Mer beneath your boots.

At the Col de Paracolls we celebrated by unwisely finishing the day's water supplies. And that wasn't our only schoolboy error. We would have done well to heed the following advice from Hilaire Belloc: 'It is absolutely necessary to cross the col or port on the route one has traced out for the day, before that day is far advanced,' and more specifically, 'If you break the back of the day by ten or eleven, before the first meal, you are safe for the end of it, and breaking the back of the day usually means getting over a port.'

As someone who didn't suffer fools gladly, Belloc would certainly have frowned on our lazy start to the day, dallying as we had done over breakfast on the wisteria-clad terrace of the Hotel des Glycines back in Arles (well, who wouldn't have?). And what Belloc would have thought about our cavalier attitude to the water supplies, I hate to think. By now, the day was certainly far advanced and the sun was well and truly up. The heat was crackling, literally, with the bursting of seed pods on dusty bushes providing a random percussion to accompany the cicadas' melody, while the smell of sage and thyme, bruised underfoot, gave an inappropriate reminder of Sunday roasts.

Thankfully the path now went downhill, eventually passing a new chalet with a water sprinkler in full flow, which unfortunately was being guarded by a muscular Doberman. Faced with the options, we chose thirsty over savaged. According to the guidebooks, there are no fountains, springs or accessible streams on this stretch of the route, but even in the Pyrenees time does not stand still and as we reached a narrow, Tarmacked road there was a brand-new hand-painted sign advertising a *gîte d'étape* – it was off our route, but only by ten minutes or so and we were lured there, like ancient Greek sailors towards the sirens.

The Moulin de la Palette was so new it was hardly even open for business, but the fridge was filled with cool drinks and the owner, Pierre, was on hand to dispense them and to show off the gîte's two immaculate new bedrooms, where bunks, handcrafted from chestnut wood, were eagerly awaiting their first weary walkers. Fifteen years ago, Pierre gave up his job with a Parisian firm of accountants for the good life in the Albères mountains. Here, surrounded by chestnut forests, he acquired the traditional Catalan skill of basketry. 'It's very simple, really,' he said, cutting strips of wood with amazing dexterity from green branches, using a viciously curved knife. 'Have a try'.

We did. It isn't. Grainy old photos on the walls of his workshop showed quarry workers with baskets like Pierre's, filled with huge quantities of rock, which they were carrying on their heads, testifying to the strength and durability of both baskets and workers.

The conversation with Pierre had been accompanied by a muffled buzzing, like the onset of tinnitus, but luckily there was another explanation. The room next door, which should have been a lounge, turned out to be a honey factory. And that strange artefact in the middle of the room wasn't a wood-burning stove but a kind of indoor hive, which was connected to the outside world by a plastic pipe, along which bees came and went. These particular ones were bringing pollen from the flowers of the surrounding chestnut trees, but Pierre had hives in other locations for the production of acacia, lavender or more chestnut-flower honey, depending on the season. We tasted some of the different varieties, with Pierre enthusing over the different qualities and flavours like a master wine-maker extolling his grape varieties and vintages. For the record, I preferred the sweet-chestnut honey, which was sweet and faintly nutty.

Energised by the honey tasting, we took the pretty route back towards the GR10 through the forest and happened upon an even more extreme example of getting away from it all. At least Pierre and family had the support of a road of sorts, but at the top of a precipitous track, which most mules would have balked at, we came upon a farm complex. It was the kind of property that an estate agent would call 'perfect for development' and a normal person would call 'ruined'. It was certainly far from deserted, though: a man of Scandinavian appearance was roofing a barn; in the shelter of a plastic lean-to a group of weather-beaten young people were lunching on bread, cheese, salad and wine; and an extremely pretty barefoot girl was leading a sheeplike animal on a string. It looked for all the world like a hippy remake of *Manon des Sources*, which is more or less what it turned out to be.

A Parisian family had become dissatisfied with their life in the suburb of Clichy, and, over one of their regular meals with their friends, the conversation had moved on from the usual complaints about traffic jams, parking problems and the stresses of daily commuter life to what they might do to change matters. A plan was hatched, involving goats and healthy self-sufficiency, and for a couple of years their holidays were spent prospecting the more isolated reaches of the Pyrenees for land and buildings suitable for a fresh start, far from the madding crowd and just about everything else to do with modern life. In Amélie-les-Bains their enquiries had finally borne fruit with an isolated and abandoned farm which had been on the market for some years, and whose farmhouse had recently suffered serious damage in a mysterious fire. There'd been rumours of a local vendetta and suggestions that a neighbour had indulged in a spot of arson in the hope of getting the land more cheaply. Undeterred, the two families had taken the plunge and here they were, a year later, looking out over their own expanse of hillside, with views in the other direction down across the valley to the nearest centre of any kind, Amélie-les-Bains, which was tiny in the distance.

Compared with this project, the typical Brits-abroad undertakings that have provided such fun and entertainment for TV audiences and production teams alike are very small beer indeed. It had been complicated enough for us to get to the place on foot, but to transport building materials of any size up here was a logistical challenge on a military scale, and had required a number of enormously expensive helicopter charters. So expensive, in fact, that one of the owners had needed to go back to Paris and return to his trade as a draughtsman to earn enough money for essential roofing materials to be flown in.

Not that a roof seemed a priority that sun-drenched lunchtime. Apart from the owners and their daughter Sophie, there was a full complement of young European students who'd answered Internet adverts and come to work here for the summer in return for board and lodging. Slave labour?

'Not at all,' said Robert, who was studying French at Norwich University and was thoroughly enjoying his open-air work as a goatherd, as well as the chance to extend his linguistic skills through some demanding encounters with the local dialect. 'It was a bit of a shock at first,' he admitted. 'Although most people understood what I was saying, I could only get about ten per cent of what they were saying to me. It took a while before I realised they weren't speaking French at all, but Catalan.' Which made him feel relieved that his previous years of study had not been entirely wasted.

Sophie, the young Emmanuelle Béart in the film, seemed to be having no difficulty adjusting to life in the wilderness. She'd exchanged toys and dolls for real animals and introduced us to her particular friend – Romule – the sheeplike animal we'd seen earlier. He was in fact a mouflon, a wild ancestor of the sheep, which you can still see running wild in Corsica and Sardinia and which were imported into the Pyrenees by a Belgian entrepreneur after the Second World War. Though his business had failed, the mouflon adapted quite happily to Pyrenean life. So much so that further west, in the high mountains around Gavarnie, there's a flock which have been given the great French food-industry accolade of AOC – Appellation d'Origine Contrôlée. Romulus didn't come from such classy stock, but had been rescued from premature death by one of the well-trained farm dogs, which had found him abandoned in a spring snowdrift and had brought him home, unharmed, in its jaws. Sophie's mother, a former teacher with a firm grounding in the classics, had named the animal Romule, and now he was a pet, along with a baby wild boar who lived with the domestic pigs and was called, of course, Rémus.

The founding of ancient Rome seemed an appropriate image for their undertaking. Like the eternal city, it was going to take a lot more than a day to rebuild the farmhouse. They reckoned that they'd have to spend another winter in makeshift accommodation, and weren't expecting the farm to be self-sufficient for another couple of years. What was likely to take even longer was building bridges with the local community. The inbuilt distrust of anyone arriving from Paris seemed to have been exacerbated by suspicion about the families' domestic arrangements – who was sleeping with who, exactly? And then there was the dodgy business of the fire that had helped to bring them here. At least, unlike Gérard Depardieu and family, they had their own water supply.

We wished them well and set out again to try and rejoin the GR10. The best route seemed to be by way of the Roc de Fraussia/Roc de France – which is the highest summit hereabouts. It was one of those routes that looked simple enough from a distance but, though there were plenty of paths, they were mostly animal tracks that disappeared either into impenetrable thorny thickets or over the edge of sheer drops. We eventually found a likely one that matched a dotted line on the map and which stretched upwards through woods and gorse towards the Roc de Fraussia. The bad news was that every time we reached a clearing the path disappeared among the sparse grass and white stones, so to try and find where it resumed on the other side we had recourse to the method that Hilaire Belloc calls 'casting about'. He noted that:

> The native knows where to pick up the track again upon the further side; the foreigner has no chance but to guess, from the last direction it took, where he is likely to find it again. He will almost invariably be wrong, and then he must cast about in circles until he finds it upon the further side of the pasture, entering a wood or picking its way between gaps of rock.

So cast about we did, frequently and irritatingly, though it was good to bring some joy to the brown Pyrenean cows who left off from their depressing lunchtime menu (it's the sparse grass and thorny bushes again today) to watch us doing something equally silly.

Having eventually conquered the Roc de Fraussia we reached a ridge, which seemed to mark the border with Spain, and for an hour or so we walked due east along it, ploughing through the soft, high grass. After so much time spent following other people's paths or looking for traces of them, we experienced the new and entirely unexpected thrill of making our own way. What a liberation it was to be able to look up, around, downwards into green France on one side or arid Spain on the other, without running the risk of missing the red-and-white splodges of paint or a precarious cairn. It was a very different excitement to Belloc's, whose journeys took place many years before waymarking and signposts and even the advent of serviceable walking maps. For him:

> A Pyrenean path is the vaguest of things: it is a patch of trodden soils here and there; a few worn surfaces of rock, then perhaps a long stretch with no indication whatsoever.

Yet upon this chain of faint indications with only occasional lengths marked, your life depends; and the finding and picking it up has the same sort of interest and excitement as the following of a scent or a spoor.

But if there's one thing more exciting than finding your path it has to be the joy of making your own one. Even so, it was a relief to meet up with our old friend the GR10 at the pass of Salines, which by our standards was something of a major crossroads involving the GR10, the HRP and a spectacularly bendy mountain road that crosses the border and unites the Spanish parish of Massanet de Cabrenys with Reynes. On the last Sunday in January each year, these two communities meet for the joint celebration of St Paul's day, which rather confusingly is known either as Saint Pau dels Embistadors (St Paul of the Betrothed) or San Pau de las Botifarras (St Paul of the Sausages). Maybe there's a connection, maybe there isn't, but the day is certainly celebrated with much feasting on *botifarras* and the dancing of *sardanes*, and may well end up with some new *embistadors*. The current twinning is a recent arrangement dating from 1988, but less formal relations between Reynes and Massanet include centuries of smuggling and the assistance given on both sides of the frontier to people fleeing the Nazis during the Second World War.

The last stretch of a long day's walk is downhill towards the village of Las Illas through a forest on a leaf-softened, peaty surface, which renews all your confidence in the makers of paths. We met a family of French people ambling along in the same direction. It had been unusual enough to meet anyone else at all on the GR10, and those we had met tended to be Australian, British, Scandinavian, Austrian, Swiss, but very rarely French. This may seem odd, given their wonderful network of paths, but rambling doesn't seem to suit the French temperament. I expect they find the classic outfits of the rambler unappealing, or perhaps it's just the lack of a clear practical outcome; I mean, if there are mushrooms or wild strawberries to be picked, mussels to be gathered or the chance of shooting something, you won't have any trouble at all getting the French out of doors and into the woods.

Our own family had a very good French reason for being on this stretch of the GR10. They were on their way back from a restaurant just over the border in Spain, which was inaccessible to cars. This explained their rather impractical attire – high-heels for the ladies, sports jackets for the men. And, as if to remind us of the real purpose of their expedition, the father offered us cigars. We walked with them for a while, discussing the respective merits of French and Spanish food, with a brief nod in the direction of English cuisine – 'You cook things for a long time, don't you?' After a while the track widened a little and became just about accessible for a vehicle, and this is where two four-wheel-drive land-cruisers, belonging to our new companions, were parked. They kindly offered us a lift to Las Illas and managed not to look too surprised when we said thanks, but we'd like to walk. *Bouff, les Anglais!*

Buffoons or not, we completed our walk to Las Illas, which had a handful of houses, a *gîte d'étape* and a restful hotel with a turbulent past. It's called 'Les Trabucayres' – the highwaymen – after a notorious band of robbers who operated in the area during the nineteenth century and escaped detection by hiding in local caves. A plaque on the hotel wall commemorated the night in 1939 when two Republican generals had sheltered here on their way out of Spain – a reminder that the mountains between here and the sea were the crossing point for the tens of thousands of Spaniards escaping from Spain after Franco's victory in the Spanish Civil War. Dinner had a Mediterranean flavour with fish and a kind of ratatouille; not long to go now.

Swish, swish, swish: the sound of a broom slowly but conscientiously removing the night's accumulation of dust from a terrace. It's a good way to wake up, a gentle but insistent alarm call, with the gradual and enjoyable realisation that someone else is already up, about and working. Over breakfast on the newly swept terrace we decided to conduct an experiment with that day's stretch of the GR10. Instead of consulting the guidebooks before we set out, we'd keep them firmly shut, make our own notes and then see how they compared at the end of the day. This was partly out of curiosity, but also from a desire to turn the tables on those we'd become overdependent on during previous weeks. We got out new notebooks and pencils and set off.

It was easy enough to begin with as the GR10 followed a white, dusty track out of Las Illas and then, rather unusually, stayed on it. From time to time we were sprayed with dirt by a passing four-wheel drive or half-heartedly attacked by scrawny brown-and-white dogs. The track was bordered by semi-derelict farmhouses and on the roof of one of them half a dozen goats were hanging out. 'Goats on roof' was the only thing I had to show in my notebook for the first two hours of the walk. This was followed by 'cork oaks', as the path was now cutting through a forest of these strange trees, some of them indecently free of bark from the waist down, showing the pinkish wood underneath the thickly ridged bark.

Cork production, mainly for the champagne industry, was the economic mainstay of this area at the beginning of the twentieth century and this forest was once the world's largest. Indeed, the nearby village of Reynes claims to have the world's most ancient cork tree. It's on the Mas Santol farm and is twenty metres high, two metres in diameter and is reckoned to be three hundred years old. Over time, the bark has twisted into patterns that Bridget Reilly might have been proud of – among them one which bears a rather troubling similarity to a human eye. The golden age of cork was followed by a decline, brought about by competition from cheaper Portuguese imports, but recently there's been a revival in the industry's fortunes because the trees are much more resistant to the increasing ravages of forest fires than other types of cultivation, thus proving that cork will always bob to the surface.

'Lost!' was my third entry of the morning. How could we have achieved such a feat without even straying from the path? Ashamedly, we scrabbled around in the bottom of rucksacks and consulted the maligned guidebooks. Streatfeild-James supplied the answer:

> At a sharp left-hand bend, the GR10 departs to the right on a footpath. Many walkers lose their way here, owing to the haphazard route marking: although the last 1¾ hours along the rough road have been adequately marked, the one unexpected turning during the morning is not indicated in any way.

Couldn't have put it better myself. This is just the sort of thing you need from your guidebook and it's what makes a good one an ideal travelling companion. But, like any intimate relationship, when truth is found wanting, trust is shattered. If your book says, 'The path between here and the village is downhill,' when in actual fact there is a sharp uphill stretch, you will be doubly disappointed, not just by the ascent but also because you weren't expecting it. It's like catching your lover in another's embrace, or your walking companion craftily swigging the last of your water on a very hot afternoon.

The other thing you need from your guidebook is the right amount of historical information about buildings, sites and sights that you will be passing and on the whole will be too tired, hungry, thirsty or in too much of a rush to visit. Mind you, even if you're not any of the above, the key to the fascinating chapel or castle will almost certainly be in the keeping of some ancient custodian who will live in a 'nearby' village, and may or may not be at home when you make the effort to seek him out.

In fact, the next stretch of the GR10 becomes something of a historical pageant, the interesting sights contrasting sharply with the walk itself, which is boring and tiring and leads into the traffic-clogged town of Le Perthus. On the outskirts of Le Perthus, there's the opportunity to take a brief Roman stroll along a fragment of the Via Dolmitia, the road that joined Rome with Cadiz and was the route taken by legions bound for Africa, and, coming the other way, Hannibal with his army and his elephants on his ill-fated expedition against Rome. A small military cemetery is the resting place for seventeenth-century French conscripts sent here to keep the Spanish out.

Next there's a Vauban fort, which is bit less of a surprise as there seem to be very few towns in France without one of the maestro's forbidding constructions, and Vauban's military architecture was a defensive cornerstone of Louis XIV's empire. The Fort de Bellegarde lives up to its name, with commanding views over the plains of French Rousillon in one direction and Spanish Ampurdán, in the other. It could hold a garrison of a thousand soldiers and construction began in 1769, a mere twenty years after the signing of the treaty of the Pyrenees, which suggests that the treaty didn't precipitate an outbreak of Franco–Spanish trust. The fort has seen plenty of action, particularly in the war that followed the French Revolution, but has never fallen to a military assault, though on three occasions sieges forced its garrisons to surrender due to lack of food, proving that an army doesn't just march on its stomach, but also needs to sit around on it.

None of our guidebooks had a kind word to say for modern Le Perthus, though, if you're a collector of frontier towns, it does have a curious kind of charm. One side of the road is French and the other side is Spanish, and, while the Spanish part is devoted to the sale of cheap booze and cigarettes, the French side of things is more concerned with nice *boulangeries*, *charcuteries* and *patisseries*. Shopping was more fun here before the advent of the euro, as you could wander into shops without being at all certain whether you needed francs or pesetas, let alone which language you were supposed to be speaking or whether you were getting a good deal.

This broad valley is the main gap in the mountains at the Mediterranean end of the Pyrenees. Le Perthus calls itself, rather charmingly, *le trait d'union Catalan*, the Catalan hyphen. In the summer, there is a constant stream of cars crawling through the town, while on the motorway outside there's an even greater flow of holiday-makers crossing into Spain.

At the frontier itself, there's a poignant monument to another great exodus – a pyramid created by Ricard Bofill. On one night alone, 5 February 1939, 20,000 soldiers of the Spanish Republican Army entered France in search of sanctuary, following the fall of Catalonia to Franco's nationalist troops. They were part of a much greater number of Spanish troops and civilians, who more than doubled the population of the Pyrénées-Orientales department. Their arrival sparked a hysterical reaction in sections of the French press, with headlines such as, 'Will the army of riot reorganise itself in France?' and the welcome was not exactly warm: the new arrivals were escorted to detention camps on the beaches of Argelès, Barcarès and St Cyprien, and those identified as communists, radicals and criminals were committed to more secure prison camps at Vernet and Collioure under a regime of hard labour.

After this heady historical brew, mixed with the pollution and noise of Le Perthus, which is in its own way a living monument – to twentieth-century commerce – it's a relief to be climbing away up the other side of the valley, to the village of St-Martin de l'Albère.

The path continues upwards to the Col des Trois Termes and the Pic de Neulos, which is the last peak over 1,000m before you reach the Mediterranean. It's also the easiest to climb, as there's a Tarmac road leading right up to the transmitter station on top. There's also a sign with the very welcome information: BANYULS 7 hrs 20 minutes. Looking back, the very exactness of this timing should have aroused some suspicions, but in fact it gave us new energy and so, as the path went downhill along some particularly springy turf, we decided to carry on walking till dark and, for the first time on the journey, sleep out under the stars.

Now, according to Hilaire Belloc, spending the night out in most parts of the Pyrenees is not something to lose sleep over, as there is nearly always a 'convenient overhang' where you can huddle up in your cloak and keep warm and dry. Maybe, Hilaire, but I'd prefer to keep this treat for a beautiful warm midsummer evening, towards the Mediterranean end of the mountain chain. In the event, there weren't any appropriate overhangs and it was quite difficult even to find a patch of flat ground. When we did, it was covered with tiny, hard pine cones, which we had painstakingly to sweep away. But any doubts about the enterprise disappeared when we'd managed to light a fire – thanks to those pine cones – our sleeping bags were stretched out and our staple supper of tuna, bread and wine arrayed on a rock.

Our campsite was on a thin, sparsely wooded ridge on the border between France and Spain. Away in the distance were the lights of Banyuls, to the north the nearest French valley was completely filled with cloud, like a brimming soup bowl, while above the sky was so packed with stars your eye was drawn to the dark spots in between. But best of all was the view into Spain, where, thrusting up from the mist in a deep and isolated valley were the towers and turrets of a castle, straight from Transylvania. Around us, owls of different varieties hooted and screeched.

About four in the morning I woke from a particularly vivid nightmare in which a band of soldiers dressed in blue uniforms were marauding through our camp. The stars had been blotted out by cloud; it was extremely cold; the soft grass had turned into knobbly concrete and I'd gained a whole new respect for Hilaire Belloc.

Luckily the sun rose spectacularly and warmingly – almost compensating for the lack of coffee. Picked out by the sharp rays, the Spanish castle looked even more dramatic than it had done the evening before. I discovered later that it's the Castillo de Requesens and was built during the eleventh century, when wars were more local affairs, by a certain Gausfred the Second, Count of Rousillon, on the borders between his territory and that of Ampuries. In 1148, during the War of Requesens, it fell into the hands of the Rocabertis and it was a member of this family, the splendidly monikered count of Perelada Rocaberti de Dameto, who much later had the castle refurbished in a way that matched the exotic flourishes of his name. Following the romantic fashion made popular by Viollet le Duc's Versailles, he had towers added to the original structure, which was inaugurated with a great fiesta on 24 June 1899.

You can get to Requesens from within Spain, by car or on foot, following in the footsteps of the townsfolk of Figueres, who used to make a pilgrimage here to pray for the Tramontane wind to bring its purifying air down from the mountains to the humid coast. The castle, surrounded by huge cedars of Lebanon, is in the middle of a natural wood where you might come across wild boar or the small wild cows of the Albères, which roam free in these mountains, and whose horns are razor sharp. It's possible to visit the castle, but the key is held at a local farm, so don't hold out too much hope of gaining entrance!

A great advantage of sleeping out under the stars is that you can be up and on your way in no time at all. No tent to pack, no drawers to search in, no bills to pay; it was all downhill from here to Banyuls. Well, it was and it wasn't. What should have been a pleasant early-morning stroll to the Mediterranean, culminating in a triumphant swim at midday or thereabouts, went badly wrong at the Pic de Sailfort. This is the last proper gasp of the Pyrenees before they tumble away into the sea, and it's not so much a peak as a long grassy ridge, covered in huge pieces of shattered rock. From the top there's a marvellous view to the sea, over wooded hills, some of them crowned with circular watchtowers.

Finding the right route down on the other side, though, was by no means obvious, and required the help of the waymarkers as never before. This was the moment, of course, when their supplies of red and white paint had apparently run out, so we, lacking a 1:25,000 map to fill in the gap, were left to our own devices. After a brief debate in which Simon was in favour of going down one of the rocky buttresses and I was convinced that the right route was down the other, we split the difference and opted for the direct route, straight down from the centre of this rather odd 'pic'. The attempt ended ignominiously and painfully an hour later in an impenetrable forest of brambles.

And there was more to come, entirely our fault this time, when we were too busy fantasising about our celebratory drink in Banyuls to notice a fork in the path: the GR10 had taken the right-hand route round a forbidding granite bluff, while we'd taken the left-hand option, and only discovered our mistake after another lost hour.

If this had happened in the higher Pyrenees, it would have led to arguments and might have proved dangerous. On this occasion, though, the sudden, ridge-top view of the Mediterranean, just a few miles away, banished all irritation and fatigue. We ran, stumbled and slid through the woods and vineyards towards Banyuls, passing a severely overcrowded-looking campsite with hardly a square centimetre of shrivelled grass showing between the tents and reaching sea level and flat ground at last beside one of France's least appealing railway bridges. Then it was under the arch, along a street lined with caves, containing the wine that's synonymous with the town of Banyuls, and finally we reached our goal.

On the wall of the town hall is a fine plaque announcing the end, or conversely the beginning, of the GR10. Then it was across the traffic-filled esplanade to the beach, hot, crowded, but who cared? Off with the boots, on with the swimming costume and into the water. Splash! Bliss.

My first real impression of Banyuls was from an unconventional angle: floating on my back in the sea. It was set in a bay, and squeezed into a narrow ribbon of flat land before the start of the mountains, which ringed it protectively, or maybe menacingly. Along the seafront ran the main road, to Spain in one direction, and towards Collioure, Banyuls' more up-market neighbour, in the other.

On the landward side were rows of restaurants and hotels, then away behind the resort, raised on a commanding hill, was a cluster of houses that had formed the original Banyuls. Called Puig del Mas, when seen from closer up it's a very appealing mixture of steep narrow streets and tiny squares built on the site of a Roman hill-village. Fishing and viticulture were the mainstays of the small population, which was bolstered by a lively interest in smuggling. In its heyday, there were eight *sociétés officielles* dedicated to different branches of contraband, including salt, oil, rice, tobacco and paper.

This century, fishing and smuggling have been displaced by tourism and wine as the key economic activities. The speciality of Banyuls is the *vin doux naturel*, the sweet wine which is drunk both as an *apéritif* and a *digestif*. The vineyards are as distinctive as the wine: planted on steep terracing, separated by dry-stone walls, they have a system of drainage ditches that are arranged in a weird bird's-foot pattern up the hillsides. The wine trade now goes hand in hand with tourism as Banyuls' money-earners and, though not as pretty as Collioure or as cheap as nearby Spanish resorts, Banyuls has three nice enough beaches, quite a lively nightlife and, it goes without saying, some good walking in the neighbouring hills.

Our night of celebration started with a meal at one of the many fish and seafood restaurants that line the seafront road. We started and finished with Banyuls wine: they are actually fortified wines like port, whose sweetness is achieved by adding alcohol at a critical moment in the fermentation process. There are a few whites, but they are mostly red or tawny, and when you hold the latter up to the light, they are a true amber nectar, and one of the few wines that can provide a successful accompaniment to chocolate. The main dishes were bouillabaisse, the Mediterranean fish dish *par excellence*, or zarzuela, which is the Spanish version. The English translation – fish-stew – does no justice at all to this dish, which is a kaleidoscope of tastes and textures. The most local delicacy is the anchovy, the speciality of neighbouring Collioure, and don't be put off by any previous experience of those small, briny, spiny things we find in tins; these are succulent and delicious.

The excellence of the food and drink was completely unmatched by the live(ish) musical accompaniment. A man with a toupee and a guitar treated us to 'La Cucaracha' and a particularly soul- and ear-rending version of '*Ay ay aya ay canta, no llores*'. Luckily there was more authentic entertainment in the main square – a *sardane* competition, pitting teams from towns on the French side of the border against their Spanish neighbours. It was surprisingly entertaining and pleasantly raucous.

It was interesting to see how many perfectly normal-looking young people were involved; the sort who ought to be staring at a Play Station game, hanging around a phone-box or texting each other on mobile phones, which in the UK is exactly what they would be doing. The scoring system was as mysterious to us as that of a cricket match would be for Mediterranean people, but no one seemed put out when one of the visiting teams, from Figueres, carried off the prize. Being the majority stakeholders in Catalan culture, I suppose you'd expect the Spanish representatives to be better.

As we sat at our table, drinking in the atmosphere and the draught lager, we met a group of fellow trekkers from a previous stage of the GR10. They seemed like old friends, though I don't suppose we'd spent more than ten minutes in their company. It was comforting to find they'd had as much difficulty as we had in negotiating the last stretch of the journey. We swapped moans about the waymarking and discussed what reward we'd all been dreaming of at the end of the path. The clear favourites were the prospect of a swim or a cold beer, but one girl had been accompanied and tantalised by the vision of a huge juicy peach.

You'd have thought the urge to walk would have left us by now, but like most intoxicants it takes a while to wean yourself off it.

The next day we walked up to the Col de Banyuls, which was on the border with Spain and has seen much action. In 1793, the local populace put up a spirited resistance to the Spanish troops commanded by General Ricardos when they invaded French Rousillon. The people of Banyuls, unlike other villagers, fought ferociously before being overcome and were at first fêted as great patriots, though recent historians have suggested that they were less committed to defending France than their smugglers' way of life. Then, during and after the Spanish Civil War, this was a conduit for both the Republicans and the Nationalists, plus visitors such as George Orwell – who was injured during his time fighting against Franco's fascists, and chose this route home:

> My wife and I got off the train at Banyuls, the first station up the line, feeling that we would like a rest. We were not too well received in Banyuls when they discovered that we had come from Barcelona. Quite a number of times I was involved in the same conversation: 'You come from Spain? Which side were you fighting on? The Government? Oh!' – and then a marked coolness.

From the top of the Col de Banyuls, for as far as the eye could see on the Spanish side, the vegetation was blackened; the earth was scorched and small plumes of smoke eddied around, the results of a recent vast forest fire. It was as though the war had only just finished. On the path up, there's a sight as curious as the island that changes nationality at the Basque end of the mountain chain. It's the Château Carrotx, a manor house that is, uniquely, divided in two by the frontier. In today's united Europe this is no big deal, but it's entertaining to speculate on what might have happened in less enlightened times and whether you might, for instance, have been searched or arrested on your way from the bedroom to the bathroom.

Another pleasant walk – for the hardened ramblers a mere stroll – is the three kilometres through the mimosas, olives and

Barbary figs to the Musée Maillol, former home of Banyuls' most famous son, the sculptor Aristide Maillol. Born in 1861, he was a significant influence on Henry Moore and much admired by Picasso. Two of his best-known works are still in Banyuls – *Le Monument aux Morts* in the town hall's garden, and then on the seafront there's a more characteristic piece, *La Femme Allongée*, by an artist who found in the young female form a constant source of inspiration. Another nude, the bronze *Méditeranée*, was hailed by André Gide as the most perfect manifestation of beauty when it was exhibited at the Parisian Salon d'Automne in 1905. You can judge for yourself if you're passing through Perpignan, as it's in the courtyard of the town hall.

Maillol was in many ways a Mediterranean symbol – his name means 'vine-shoot' in Catalan, and it's in the Mediterranean that there's a final path for the indefatigable rambler. It's made to be swum, not walked, and it's just off the beach of Pierrefitte, a couple of miles south of Banyuls. You don mask, snorkel and flipper and for a lazy 45 minutes you can follow a submarine nature trail, and read about the flora and fauna on underwater panels.

The path is part of the Marine Reserve of Banyuls–Cerbère, France's first protected underwater environment. The rocky depths mirror the relief of the coastal mountains and create ideal conditions for sponges, algae and rare seaweeds. You can see red coral seahorses, and maybe a harmless basking shark or dolphin. Above all you can feel you're enjoying the final stretch of the trans-Pyrenean walk; and, even if the mountains technically plunge down to the seabed a bit further south at Cap de Creus, I reckon it's near enough.

RECOMMENDED READING

The Rough Guide to the Pyrenees, Marc Dubin (fifth edition, 2004, Rough Guides). The best general guide to the region, packing in an immense amount of information – and particularly strong on the Spanish side of the Pyrenees.

Trekking in the Pyrenees, Douglas Streatfeild-James, (second edition, 2001, Trailblazer). The definitive guide to walking in the region. The author sets a cracking pace, judging by his timings for the GR10, but it is a good companion for the trans-Pyrenean path – and for anyone keen to explore some other great walks in the mountains.

Topo-Guides (ref. 1086, 1090, 1091 and 1092) published by the FFRP, *Fédération Française de la Randonnée Pédestre.* These four guides in French, cover the GR10, and include detailed maps.

Through the Spanish Pyrenees: GR11, a Long Distance Footpath, Paul Lucia (Cicerone Guides). This guide makes sense of the sometimes confusing meanderings of the Spanish trans-Pyrenean path.

Pyrenean Haute Route: A High-level Trail, Ton Joosten (Cicerone Guides). A very detailed guide in English to the challenging mountain trek

Haute Route Pyrénéenne, Georges Véron (twelfth edition 2004, Rando Editions, France). The definitive guide to the HRP in French, by the man who invented the path.

Walks and Climbs in the Pyrenees, Kev Reynolds (Cicerone Guides). This guide suggests many different mountain walks and moderate ascents of Pyrenean summits.

The Enchanted Mountains: A Quest in the Pyrenees, Robin Fedden (John Murray Travel Classics). An enchanting and poetic description of visits made by the author to a little known corner of the Spanish Pyrenees.

The Basque History of the World, Mark Kurlansky (Jonathan Cape). A very readable and informative introduction to this fascinating culture.

Montaillou, Emmanuel Le Roy Ladurie (Penguin Books). A gripping account of daily life in a French medieval village at the time of the Cathars.

The Pyrenees, Hilaire Belloc (Methuen and Co., London, 1910). Out of print but worth getting hold of for the author's trenchant views on all aspects of mountain walking

A Guide to the Pyrenees, Charles Packe (Longman, 1862). Out of print but a classic and incredibly detailed early guide to the mountains.

INDEX

New adventures in travel literature from Virgin Books

Published in January 05

BARBED WIRE AND BABUSHKAS
A River Odyssey Across Siberia
Paul Grogan
£7.99

The Siberian Amur River: 4,400 kilometres from source to sea of fast waters, flash floods, roaring canyons and quicksand. Glacial currents and weather hot enough to melt sand pale in comparison, however, to the stormy political climate along this geographical frontier.

   Paul Grogan, a young journalist with a passion for his paddle, undertakes an epic journey from the river's source in Mongolia to its mouth on the coast of the pacific, taking his canoe and his mate Rich for companionship. The river, which forms part of the Russian/Chinese border has long been a no go area, off limits even to the Russians for decades. Facing armed guards with AK47s, and suffering arrest on several occasions, the pair treads sensitive political ground. As they canoe their way into the record books, they experience the suspicion and the hospitality of the locals in equal measure, enjoying a champagne beach picnic, falling prey to a nasty pork 'n' vodka hangover, and sharing the company of prostitutes, pimps and the poaching police. What they find to be most common to the Siberian people, recovering from decades of neglect throughout communist rule, is warm-hearted generosity and seemingly endless optimism. Their trip is the stuff of young men's adventures of old in a world where backpacking and remote travel have become commonplace.